Relationship Building in Public Relations

This book aims to provide an interdisciplinary approach to highlight the importance of relationships in public relations, delving not only into the organization-public relationships but also into interpersonal relationships within the industry to offer new, empirical insights into the impact and formation of such relationships. Theunissen and Sissons theorize that public relations cannot exist without interpersonal relationships and the ability to create and maintain such relationships. Taking a critical stance, the book will move beyond mere rhetoric and conjecture by providing solid evidence-based research results to inform their theories about the impact of relationships and dialogue on public relations thinking. Rather than following contemporary thinking, it aims to embrace current changes, look ahead and prepare a new generation for the challenges of 21st-century public relations practice.

Petra Theunissen is Senior Lecturer and Curriculum Leader for Public Relations at Auckland University of Technology, New Zealand.

Helen Sissons is Senior Lecturer in Journalism and Media Relations at Auckland University of Technology, New Zealand.

Routledge Research in Public Relations

Relationship Building
in Public Relations

Petra Theunissen and Helen Sissons

Routledge
Taylor & Francis Group

LONDON AND NEW YORK

First published 2018
by Routledge

2 Park Square, Milton Park, Abingdon, Oxfordshire OX14 4RN
52 Vanderbilt Avenue, New York, NY 10017

Routledge is an imprint of the Taylor & Francis Group, an informa business

First issued in paperback 2019

Library of Congress Cataloging-in-Publication Data
Names: Theunissen, Petra, author. | Sissons, Helen, author.
Title: Relationship building in public relations /
by Petra Theunissen, Helen Sissons.
Description: New York, NY: Routledge, 2017. |
Series: Routledge research in public relations; 9 | Includes bibliographical references and index.
Identifiers: LCCN 2017018906
Subjects: LCSH: Public relations. | Interpersonal relations. | Customer relations.
Classification: LCC HD59 .T4748 2017 | DDC 659.2–dc23
LC record available at https://lccn.loc.gov/2017018906

ISBN: 978-1-138-18323-0 (hbk)
ISBN: 978-0-367-87623-4 (pbk)

Typeset in Sabon
by codeMantra

This book is dedicated to our respective families who have patiently supported us through this endeavor.

From Petra:

This book is dedicated to my husband of more than 25 years, Christopher, for his love and unwavering support, and to our daughter, Catherine, for being the young woman she has become. I love you both.

From Helen:

For my husband, Paul, for his unstinting support and very practical help during the writing of this book, and to Anna and Oliver for their encouragement and cups of tea.

Contents

List of Figures

Acknowledgments

We would like to acknowledge the practitioners in this research for their willingness to be filmed during their everyday practice and their openness in their responses. Without their participation, this book would not have been possible.

We would also like to thank the reviewers of the original proposal and the commissioning editor who not only saw value in producing this book but were enthusiastic about what it might bring to the public relations discipline and scholarship.

We would also be amiss not to thank our colleague and friend, Dr. Gudrun Frommherz, for her review of Chapter 3.

1 Setting the Scene

We are like islands in the sea, separate on the surface but connected in the deep.

—William James (1842–1910), American philosopher

Relationships as a Focus for Study

At the core of all public relations activities are interpersonal relationships and consequently interpersonal communication. Indeed, it is impossible to conduct any public relations work without the ability to build, maintain, and—at times—end relationships. It is conceivable to argue, as Zaharna (2015) did, that "relations" and thus "relationships" are half of the concept "public relations," indicating that relationships are embedded in public relations, and yet we appear to gloss over this when theorizing about the discipline.

In 1999, Hutton expressed concern that the field of public relations had not "articulated in any depth even its most basic premises, such as the nature of 'relations' or 'relationships'" (p. 200), leaving the void to be filled by other scholars outside the field. Most definitions, he argued, did not even identify public relations' core concepts: communication and relationships, stating that other disciplines were far more advanced in their research "in developing, what should be the central, organizing theme of public relations theory and practice—relationships" (Hutton, 1999, p. 209). Fourteen years later, Heath (2013) pointed towards a similar lack of progress in our understanding of relationships, and particularly, organization-public relationships, arguing that these relationships were significantly more complex than we had acknowledged thus far. As he rightly identified, at best, the organization–public relationship is "multidimensional and multilayered," but is hardly reducible to "some*thing* between the organization and its public(s)" (Heath, 2013, p. 427, emphasis added).

While there are a multitude of relationship types that can be formed in the context of public relations work, ultimately, public relations is about *people.* Our fundamental argument is that *relationships* are the key to effective public relations, whether it is publicizing the organization, advocating on behalf of a client, or maneuvering through complicated minefields of power play. In our view, effective relationships are more important than, for example, having a "seat at the table," which has traditionally been associated with power and influence in public relations, or *hierarchical power* (Ihlen & Verhoeven, 2012).

Research by Moreno, Verhoeven, Tench, and Zerfaß (2014) showed that more communication managers are now "part of the dominant coalition" and have "a seat at the table where decisions are made" (p. 83) with nearly 60% of communication managers in Europe reporting directly to the CEO. But not all practitioners are necessarily in a position where they can enact hierarchical power, and therefore they rely on other types of power, such as relational power embedded in, for example, *personal influence*, which we discuss in the next chapter. Indeed, one needs to consider that in countries such as New Zealand, there are a disproportionate number of small public relations consultancies whose representatives are unlikely to be sitting on a company's board and who may not have the hierarchical influence that appears to be a requirement for "excellent" public relations.

The question then arises whether not having a seat at the table makes these practitioners less effective? Our research suggests it is not the case. Having a seat at the table is only one indicator of power and specifically, hierarchical power. Practitioners who do not have access to such power may need to rely more on *rhetorical* and *social power* than has been acknowledged in current scholarship. Rhetorical power lies in the skills required to use language and symbols effectively, and social power allows practitioners to act *through* and *with* other people (Ihlen & Verhoeven, 2012).

In his visual approach to leadership, Lewis (1999) made an interesting, but perhaps simplistic, distinction between various countries' leadership and listening styles, stating that the United States (where incidentally much of the current public relations theory originates) "symbolizes the vitality and audacity in the land of free enterprise" (p. 68). In the United States, he proposed, senior managers drive and inspire people lower on the pyramidal structure; they are not averse to using hard sell in presentations or employing catchphrases. Overall, he said, they value *individual* freedom. The latter is a point of interest when considering relationships and the effects of relationships in practice. In her article explicating the underlying cultural assumptions of relationships, Zaharna (2015) addressed the perception of individualism that underpins much of United States-based scholarship: that as individuals Americans seek to connect and build relationships, which is in stark contrast to other cultures where existing connections are assumed.

While Lewis (1999) made no mention of New Zealand per se, we believe that the research presented here can provide interesting and unique insights into the practice of public relations as a cultural endeavor. Besides it being predominantly an English-speaking country, it is also a postcolonial one where Kaupapa Māori, an epistemological framework grounded in Māori history and culture, has been used to reassert the values of Māori into society (Love & Tilley, 2014).

New Zealand is a country of immigrants, with a quarter of all New Zealanders having been born overseas (Statistics New Zealand, 2014). In Auckland alone, where much of this research was conducted, nearly 40% of the city's population was born overseas (Statistics New Zealand, 2014). Many of these overseas-born Aucklanders were born in Asia (mainly China), the Pacific Islands, the United Kingdom, and Ireland. Of those who have been in the country for 20 years or more—and presumably had some effect on the local culture—more than half (53.1%) were born in the United Kingdom and Ireland. More recent immigrants, that is, those who arrived in the last decade or so have come primarily from these countries, as well as Australia and the Pacific Islands.

Given the large number of immigrants, it is reasonable to assume that they have had a significant influence on interaction and communication in New Zealand's workplaces. For example, a casual management style is quite common in the United Kingdom, where the manager is not necessarily a team member "but is in close contact with them and well able to conduct effective supervision without interfering unduly with their daily routine" (Lewis, 1999, p. 62). Lewis also noted the British people's debating tradition, where polite listening is mandatory and where speakers remain understated. About Australians' listening habits, he said, "It is fatal to talk posh or be in any way pompous in front of Australians, who have a healthy and enduring disrespect for anyone in a superior position or who seeks to promote oneself" (Lewis, 1999, p. 38).

While not all scholars agree (see, e.g., Skilling, 2013), New Zealand is generally regarded as an egalitarian country where there is, like the Australians, a healthy disrespect for authority. Because of its low power distance in comparison to the United States, for example, managers and employees expect to be consulted on important issues and information is shared freely (Countries – Geert Hofstede, 2016). These expectations shift the nature of relationships, and may also mean that instead of power being enacted formally and explicitly, it is enacted under the surface, as Holmes and Stubbe (2015) suggested.

Thus, rhetorical power and social power are significant forms of power to investigate in a New Zealand context, specifically in the context of interpersonal behavior and communication within the practice of public relations. As such, workplace interactions as sites of research become increasingly important. By analyzing the verbal and non-verbal communication between and with people, we can start exploring what *really* happens in practice and what meaning is constructed about public relations work. By doing so we aim to present public relations work as it *is*, rather than as it *should be*.

Origins of This Study

The research presented in this book has its origins in a doctoral study exploring the relationship between journalists and public relations practitioners (PRPs), asking who is really controlling the news (Sissons, 2015a). As the research progressed, it became increasingly evident that public relations work relied heavily on relationships and that even strategic thinking involved considerations of a relational nature. In most cases, interactions were aimed at preserving the longevity of relationships between, for example, the PRP and the client or journalist while constructing and framing messages that would achieve the desired outcomes. At times this process became a delicate balancing act that required skill and expertise—skills we felt were undervalued in public relations scholarship. We found that although many of these relationships were evidently *functional* (Heath, 2013) and often *non-voluntary* (Waymer, 2013), they were also highly interpersonal.

Consequently, the collected and unused thesis data provided rich and fascinating material for the deeper exploration of relationships in public relations and what these mean for public relations theorizing and practice. Typically, public relations scholarship tends to align itself with corporate rather than societal need (L'Etang, 2013), and it is therefore not unusual to find significant emphasis on management-related theories and the management of communication, rather than the interpersonal nature of communication. In fact, the *excellence* and *systems theories* remain the two most discussed theories (Macnamara, 2012). Macnamara (2012), for instance, found that of 8,547 public relations textbook pages analyzed, only 19.3 (0.002%) pages were dedicated to theories of interpersonal communication. The reason may lie in the fact that interpersonal communication appears "softer" than management and system theories, and that the notion of "two-way symmetry has a 'feel good factor' for students and scholars alike" (L'Etang, 2013, p. 805). Heath (2013) questioned, however, whether a commitment to symmetry resolves relational tensions in, for example, organization-public relations or operationalizes the idea of mutual benefit—two key concepts often discussed in public relations. Still, as we will see in Chapter 7, the excellence and systems theories remain among the top four theories for thinking about organization-public relationships (Ki & Shin, 2015).

One of the challenges facing public relations scholarship is that the practice and discipline remain contested, and definitions can include, even merge, "the functional, the idealistic and the critical" (L'Etang, 2013, p. 799). Unsurprisingly, scholars often conflate *normative ideals* with *actual practice*, resulting in a gap between descriptive and normative studies (Ihlen & Verhoeven, 2012). By interrogating the relationship concept and by presenting critical incidents selected from real interactions involving PRPs at the *micro level of the interpersonal*, we attempt to address the existent gap between the normative and the actual practice of public relations.

Following a Qualitative Approach

Because the research presented here is concerned with people's reasoning, their practices, their interpretations, and their descriptions of events, it relies on a qualitative research design. It places emphasis on (interpersonal) communication theory (Ihlen & Verhoeven, 2012) rather than management theory and, by acknowledging that the practice of public relations is context-dependent, it moves beyond early scholarship which, according to L'Etang (2013), sought to "develop generalizable theory about practice and to apply such theory to all cultures" (p. 804).

Researchers using a qualitative, and in this context, a *social theory perspective*, believe that human beings and the social world cannot be studied and judged as if they were forever constant and unchanging. Social theory is, "necessary to describe, understand and explain what happens to whom in the realm of public relations and with what consequences" (Ihlen & Verhoeven, 2012, p. 168). In any interaction, all participants have a purpose, a reason for taking part (Heracleous, 2004), and bearing that in mind, within the tradition of qualitative research, we accept research is conducted with a purpose and is context-dependent.

As qualitative researchers, our goal is therefore to *understand the participants' lived experience* instead of constructing abstract generalizations, and our objective is to build an understanding of culture (see Geertz, 1973)—in this case, *professional culture*. We are particularly interested in the processes of meaning-making by PRPs. This understanding involves gaining insights into their intentions, their situations, and their practices, as well as the context of their actions and interactions. While we draw from published critical theory, it is important to note that this work does not situate itself within the scholarship of critical theory. Rather, it follows a *pragmatic, interpretivist*, and *constructivist* approach to public relations, thereby being more closely related to the co-creational approach and social theory.

Within this interpretivist tradition, the research relied on a practice-based approach. That is, we as researchers draw on our experience of practice to inform our analyses (Cotter, 2001). As Gumperz (2001) argued, participants in interactions always rely on background knowledge to understand the communicative intent of those involved. This could include constructing possible scenarios or intertextually remembering other uses of an expression to make sense of what was being said. Gumperz said the aim is to find a plausible solution to how the interaction may be interpreted, and the more the analyst appreciates the *situated context* of the practitioners, the more understanding he or she can bring to what has transpired in an encounter.

Making Generalizations and Drawing Comparisons

As the research aims to relate to public relations practices beyond New Zealand, we argue that while we accept we cannot make broad generalizations, we can make some. Williams (2000) distinguished between *total generalizations*, which he defined as deterministic laws or axioms; *statistical generalizations*, where the probability of a situation or feature occurring can be calculated from its instances within a sample representative of the population; and *moderatum generalizations*, where aspects of a situation are seen as illustrative of more widely occurring situations or characteristics. He suggested that interpretive research does not aim to make total or statistical generalizations, but can make moderatum generalizations, and he concluded that one can generalize from a small number of cases to unknown cases provided there was *categorical equivalence* and where the cases operate in a similar sociocultural context. Any generalizations that go beyond the moderate, or any generalizations within one category of experience or domain that are applied to other categories, are unjustified. In other words, while one cannot make total generalizations from a critical incident, one can generalize based on the aspects of a situation being illustrative of a broader set of features rather than being axioms or deterministic laws. Furthermore, moderatum generalizations can only be made after considering that every public relations researcher has his or her own "deontological background and disciplinary roots" (Ihlen & Van Ruler, 2007, p. 244), which provide specific (ideological) perspectives, and therefore, public relations is not an "ideologically neutral management technocracy" (L'Etang, 2013, p. 803).

Thus, while this study is situated in New Zealand, an island off the coast of Australia with a population of just over 4.7 million people (Population Clock, 2016), some moderatum generalizations are possible where there is categorical equivalence such as similar interactions in similar-sized public relations departments in organizations engaged in similar activities in countries with similar political arrangements.

In the first instance, comparisons can be drawn with English-speaking Western countries within a liberal democratic framework, for example, Australia, Canada, the United Kingdom, and the United States. Indeed, professionalization of public relations in New Zealand has been strongly influenced by practitioners from the United Kingdom and the United States (Macnamara, 2012; Trenwith, 2010). However, it would be overly simplistic to suggest that language (English) and political frameworks are the only variables that might enable comparisons across countries. Various cultures—national, professional, and organizational—develop in specific ecologies (Triandis, 2006), and are therefore dependent on the context and temporality in which they are used (Hong, 2014). In a contemporary and global world, similarities can be drawn across nations. Triandis (2006), for instance, discussed the role of *expressed values* in globalization, namely survival (emphasis on food, shelter, money, and hard work), self-expression (friends, leisure, and concern for the environment), traditional (God, obedience), and secular-rational (emphasis on permissive attitudes towards sex, abortion, and other issues). Comparing nations on the Inglehart-Welzel Cultural map (World Values Survey, 2016), New Zealand's expressed values place the country amidst English- and non-English-speaking countries such as Switzerland, Iceland, Australia, the United Kingdom, and Belgium. Furthermore, research by Frey and Powell (2005) found similarities between New Zealand and Jamaica, which have very different ecologies and histories. While there was a greater left-right ideological polarization in the New Zealand sample (Frey & Powell, 2005), there were patterns in the cluster of attributes that emerged in both nations (Triandis, 2006).

Love and Tilley (2014) also suggested that as a post-colonial country, New Zealand has developed unique and constructive practices that may be of significance to developing public relations theory and understanding on a more global scale. Here they referred specifically to Kaupapa Māori, as mentioned earlier in this chapter. It is, therefore, appropriate, we argue, to draw comparisons across various cultures that go beyond the obvious variables such as language. Indeed, "culture" is an amorphous concept, and any discussion needs to acknowledge that it is temporally situated, reflecting "evolving discourse as well as societal changes" (Hong, 2014, p. 102).

Designing the Research

Critical Discourse Analysis

The research employed a critical discourse analysis (CDA) approach (Fairclough, 1995a,b, 2016; Van Dijk, 1988, 2001; Wodak & Meyer, 2001). From a theoretical perspective, CDA sets out to ask questions about the way discourses are harnessed in the production and replication of social dominance. Specifically, how particular social groups, institutions, or organizations enact their power through discourse and social interaction. It uses the analysis of talk and/or texts (including linguistic analysis and analysis of other relevant semiotic forms) to illustrate how power is normalized, often hiding agency and invisibly supporting the interests of dominant groups. Analysis of critical incidents (Flanagan, 1954; Keatinge, 2002; Tripp, 1993) collected through video ethnographic research allowed us to explore empirically, and in detail, how current PRPs enact power and build relationships with others in their professional lives. These critical incidents highlight the complexity of the relationships practitioners must navigate, how they are conducted and, perhaps, used to benefit the PRP. Consequently, these relationships become *functional* (cf. Heath, 2013), and it is, therefore, fair to say that the research is concerned with functional relationships.

In the CDA framework, language is always used for a purpose and is seen as an instrument of control as well as communication (Tracy, Martinez-Guillem, Robles, & Casteline, 2011). The more a group has access to information and elements of the public sphere such as the media, the more successful it will be at influencing discourse and thus, enact to some extent, rhetorical power. From that perspective, access to the media (traditional and social) becomes a site for a struggle for power. Hardly ever does this struggle for power play itself out in the public sphere. It happens behind closed doors, and it starts with people, their interactions, their communications, and therefore their *relationships*.

Following Fairclough (1989), we view *language-in-use*, written or spoken, as a *social practice*. Our analysis explores not only the text produced by the language-in-use or discourse, but also the processes of its production and its interpretation within a larger social context. As Titscher, Meyer, Wodak, Vetter, and Jenner (2000) wrote, discourses occur not only in the macro-context of organizations and institutions, but also in the micro-context of "a particular place with particular participants" (p. 27). They argued that for us to understand the meaning of a discourse in the micro-context, it must be seen in the rightful macro-context.

The research, then, follows Ihlen and Verhoeven's (2012) suggestion that the fundamental starting point for constructivists is the *micro studies of individual actions*, and only after considering the micro level can we move to the macro perspectives of systems theory. Interpersonal interactions thus are the unit of analysis in this research. We understand texts and textual analysis in an inclusive sense (Fairclough, 2009) as including written texts, interviews, and videoed multiparty interactions that can combine the verbal, the non-verbal, and visual images.

Consequently, we use a combination of methods for data collection and analysis. Our research employs traditional methods alongside newer ones afforded by video and audio technologies, in the belief that *no single type of data can give a full picture*. Combining methods and tools allows for triangulation and for meaning to be produced through the inter-relationships between and within the data sets. The combination of data affords the option to concentrate on the micro level detail or step back and take a broader, social viewpoint (Flewitt, Hample, Hauck, & Lancaster, 2009).

The data were gathered on videotape during ethnographic-style field-work designed to shed light on the "ecology" (Gumperz, 2001, p. 221) of the practice of public relations. Detailed fieldnotes were kept and semi-structured interviews were carried out with key participants. In total, 100 hours were spent in an in-house media relations department and a public relations agency, respectively, and further interviews were carried out with PRPs in other organizations as a way of corroborating some of the findings.

Breaking New Ground: Video Ethnography

Ethnographic methods are deemed appropriate for a detailed exploration of professional practice (Kawulich, 2005), and here, video ethnography was employed to gather data. This method was complemented by in-depth interviews and the examination of products resulting from the observed professional interactions. Importantly, the use of video ethnography proved a groundbreaking approach to research in public relations (Sissons, 2015a,b). In the past decade or so, ethnography has been identified as a valid approach to increasing our understanding of public relations in practice, with L'Etang (2005) calling for more ethnographic research. Only a few researchers have responded to this call, notably Edwards (2009), who examined power relations in a corporate affairs department in a passenger-transport company, and Daymon and Hodges (2009), who conducted cross-cultural ethnographic research in three public relations departments in Mexico City. The current study, however, is believed to be the first where such data were captured on video, allowing the interactions to be replayed many times during analysis to allow for greater understanding and reflection on what was occurring between the participants.

One of ethnography's strengths is that it involves researchers consciously taking themselves out of their own environment and *moving into the world of the people being studied.* This allows the researcher to experience the environment "first hand" (Agar, 2008, p. 31) and enables him or her to focus on how the study's participants enact their professional lives, how they communicate with others, and how they act and react in specific situations. Thus, a researcher can analyze their influences, beliefs, and meaning-making processes which can—in part—explain public relations products, thereby charting a group's professional routines, philosophies, hierarchies, and approaches to others.

For one of us, this meant concentrated periods in selected workplaces, which allowed time for her to familiarize herself with the habits and practices of the group, establish relationships, and observe the phenomena under investigation. Because it is a lengthy process, ethnographic study is necessarily restricted to a small number of cases with the aim of providing a detailed description including an explanatory-interpretive account of each to illuminate elements of the participants' lives (in this study it was their working lives). This is a process that can best be described as *participant observation,* which Agar (2008) called an "awkward term" that refers to the ethnographer's need, if they are to gather the necessary information, to "establish relationships with people, participate with them in what they do, and observe what is going on" (p. 31). This view is supported by Schensul, Schensul, and LeCompte (1999), who wrote that participant observation involves spending time and building rapport with the people in whom the researcher is interested. The "details of human activity" (Agar, 2008, p. 31) that a participant observer witnesses, allow the gaps in understanding between the researcher and the researched to close, awareness and knowledge to be built about workplace events, the meaning of interactions among participants, and what they perceive to be important.

In their guide for fieldworkers, DeWalt and DeWalt (2010) proposed that participant observation is all about *gaining understanding* of another group of people. They added that it "includes the use of information gained from participating and observing through explicit recording and analysis" (DeWalt & DeWalt, 2010, p. 2). They listed the key elements of participant observation as follows: (1) immersion in the group for an extended period, (2) learning the language of those being studied (in our case the professional language), (3) taking part in a wide range of the daily activities, both routine and extraordinary, of those being studied, (4) using everyday conversation as an interview technique, observing the participants in informal activities, (5) recording these observations, and (6) using both tacit and explicit information in analysis and writing.

Participant as Observer

While participant observation began as a method for observing "others' lives from an outsider viewpoint" (Kawulich, 2005, p. 3), it has increasingly been found to be useful for studying groups in one's own culture, which as a former journalist and a PRP, we considered the groups being studied to be. As insiders, it is easy to overlook taken-for-granted practices and not recognize their significance for theory-building, but participant observation through video ethnography provided opportunities for reflection on those practices and allowed for the identification of significant events.

Although some meetings that were observed occurred inside offices or off-site, the researcher was always based in the main office area, making it possible to follow Fine's (2003) advice that participant observation was at its most effective when the researcher observed the group being studied in settings that enabled him or her to "explore the organized routines of behavior" (p. 41).

Fieldnotes were kept alongside the making of the video recordings. These notes were crucial as they augmented and/or explained the video data, as well as providing material on which to base follow-up interviews with participants as needed. Tuchman (1991) argued that it was this ability to gain extra explanation about events or interactions that have been observed that made this sort of data so valuable, "such data transform the 'non-observable' into the 'observable'" (p. 87).

Despite the added difficulties a camera brings to gaining access to participants, it proffered important benefits. Among these was the ability to record the actions of the people being studied as they went about their professional lives. The recordings were a detailed and accurate record of the interactions and situations the researcher observed, as well as a reminder of who was speaking when and an exact note of what they said. In addition, the recordings provided detailed non-verbal information of who was looking where, their posture, proxemics (how close people were positioned in relation to one another), and gestures. This data could be replayed as often as necessary during the analysis, with the ability to slow down the video, play it frame by frame, or, at times, stop it, allowing close study, transcription, and fine-grained analysis. As researcher Tim Dant (2004) remarked, considering these benefits, it is surprising that more scholars do not employ video in their research.

However, video has limitations. First, the data captured is limited to that which was seen through the camera lens. Anything occurring outside of that small square, or in another part of the office, goes unrecorded. Also, as Pink (2007) stated, ethnographers must always remember that video data gathered in fieldwork is a *representation* rather than a visual fact and that the data refer to a *version of reality*. For that reason, triangulation and the wider context are important.

Second, in isolation, video data cannot tell the researcher if a professional practice, event, or a particular interaction is commonplace (perhaps emblematic), or whether it is out-of-the-ordinary. This is knowledge that comes through immersion in the group required by participant observation, as well as from follow-up conversations or interviews with the participants. Having said that, video recordings can be replayed to the people being studied so that they can review an event and be asked what thoughts and feelings they recollect. More broadly, a researcher can show a participant any part of the video data relevant to them and check their analysis and interpretation of an event or interaction with those involved. Further, video data allow (with the permission of the participants) the researcher to make visual transcripts of an interaction that can accompany their published interpretations, allowing other researchers to judge the validity of those findings.

Analysis is helped if the video data gathered is of good quality. The co-author's background as a BBC television reporter proved useful here, but we also drew on DuFon (2002), who advocated filming an entire event, for example, a meeting, or complete sequences of activities to capture the structure of an event and any hierarchies involved. She argued that in studies such as the one here, capturing whole events is crucial to understanding the professional practices enacted by the participants.

[T]he interpretation of the meaning of any given utterance is influenced by what has come before. Having a recording of only parts of an event could make it difficult to judge the appropriateness of a comment, question or response.

(DuFon, 2002, p. 46)

DuFon acknowledged that determining the boundaries of an event can be problematic, and therefore recommended pressing the record button the moment the researcher realized an event was about to start. When recording a meeting, for example, ideally filming would begin a few minutes before the participants arrived, and continue until after everyone (apart from the researcher) had left the room. In addition, for context, the researcher should always pan the entire room at some point to show the layout of the meeting. DuFon also recommended that researchers not change any part of the setting or manipulate the participants for the purposes of the camera. Filming should, therefore, record the event as is, rather than follow a "script" of sort.

Crossing the Rubicon: Gaining Access

The process we undertook to gain access to the public relations offices involved in this research is worth noting. Previous researchers have remarked on the difficulty faced by ethnographers gaining access to newsrooms (Paterson, 2008; Reich, 2006, 2009; Stokes, 2013), while so few ethnographic studies have been carried out in public relations offices as to indicate either a reluctance on the part of researchers to seek access or public relations departments to grant it. Stokes (2013) stated that people in the media industries demonstrate a wariness of academics and have a tendency to believe that their own practices are ordinary and not subject to question. An added complication in our study was the plan to record our observations on video.

The first overtures to potential participants were made informally and to people who were already known to us. These tentative approaches were followed up by email and included an explanation of the research along with the protocols that had been approved by the Auckland University of Technology's Ethics Committee (AUTEC) and which would be observed during fieldwork.

Once a response had been received, and if the organization was amenable, a meeting would be arranged either with a manager or with the person who we were hoping would become the main participant. Thus, a combination of *purposeful* and *convenience sampling* was used (Palinkas, Horwitz, Green, Wisdom, Duan, & Hoagwood, 2013). Purposeful sampling is the identification of individuals or organizations that are information rich, that is, they contain the necessary knowledge and expertise about the phenomena of interest (Suri, 2011). The two public relations departments involved in the study were approached because they were prominent organizations locally, and represented two key types of professional public relations practice: in-house and consultancy. Convenience sampling, which involves the researcher selecting participants who are reachable and available (Palinkas et al., 2013; Suri, 2011), or in this case agreed to give the researcher access, was necessary because of the recognized difficulties already mentioned in gaining access for the purposes of video ethnography.

Surprisingly, permission to enter the public relations departments was gained remarkably quickly. The organizations were open and welcoming, and extensive access was afforded to employees, meetings, and relevant documentation. In return, it was agreed that the names of all but one of the organizations be changed and that the names of all the people involved be changed.

Understanding the Culture: Semi-structured Interviews

In addition to video ethnography, the research employed video- or audiotaped semi-structured interviews with 12 key participants, namely six journalists and six PRPs, as well as a further 26 interviews with participants not directly involved in the study.

These interviews explored the working practices of the participants as well as their professional identities. The interviews were conducted as open-ended sociolinguistic interviews that should be viewed and carried out as a "conversational encounter" (Wood & Kroger, 2000, p. 72) between the researcher and the interviewee. They took place in familiar settings, sometimes in the office, at other times in more informal settings, such as cafés, and used broad topics as a guide instead of set questions. We followed Saville-Troike's (1989) recommendation that interviews be only loosely structured and use open questions, with no predetermined answers, at natural points in the conversation. This, Saville-Troike argued, is the most appropriate interview method for collecting data about communication within a community. The method was also influenced by Minichiello, Aroni, and Hayes (2008), who wrote,

> The content of the interview is focused on the issues that are central to the research question, but the type of questioning and discussion allows for greater flexibility than does the survey-style interview. This may reduce the statistical comparability of interviews within the study, but provides a more valid explanation of the informant's perceptions and constructions of reality.
>
> (p. 51)

The 26 additional semi-structured interviews were recorded with PRPs and journalists from organizations not directly involved in the study.

These interviews focused on the interviewee's role and responsibilities within the organization and how (if at all) their working practices have changed in recent years. It also sought their opinion about what had influenced changes in their practice. Finally, they were questioned about how they perceived their relationship with other communication professionals. As this book is about public relations and relationships within this field, only the interviews with the PRPs are reported on here.

Significant Moments: Selecting the Data

When it came to analyzing the data, the research followed Gumperz (2001), who emphasized the selection for analysis of representative samples from among the ethnographic data. We also drew on Gitlin (1980), who advised a "preliminary interrogation" of the data to select the strips or, as Gitlin described them, the moments that "matter" (pp. 303–304). In line with Gitlin's instructions, the selections were informed by our knowledge of the broader sociopolitical context in which the people being studied were operating.

We decided not to follow Agar (2008, p. 33), who also uses the term "strip" (taken from the idea of a film strip) to refer to ethnographic data. In his approach, a *strip* results in what he calls *rich points* and does not necessarily contain examples of representative behavior, as is the case with our analysis. For Agar, strips highlight the times when the ethnographer cannot make sense of an encounter and hence needs to alter the way they look at it, or "modify the original frames" they have brought to the analysis (Agar, 2008, p. 34). Instead, we chose a different approach, using the *critical incident technique* to select our strips of data for analysis and to help us to identify the moments that matter (Flanagan, 1954; Keatinge, 2002; Tripp, 1993). The technique originated with Flanagan (1954), who described an incident as "any observable human activity that is sufficiently complete in itself to permit inferences and predictions to be made about the person performing the act" (p. 327).

To qualify as critical, the ethnographer must see the event as having both a *clear purpose* and *sufficiently definite consequences* that its effects are obvious. In choosing the critical incidents or strips of data to analyze, Keatinge (2002) was influential. He advocated changing the name from critical to *revelatory* or *significant* in order to work with incidents that are more universal. Consequently, the incidents analyzed in this research had to conform to three key criteria:

1   The entire incident had to have been captured, as explained earlier.
2   The incident had to be an interesting and/or colorful example of a significant aspect of public relations practice.
3   This aspect of public relations practice had to have been seen routinely in the data.

In other words, the strips of data chosen were interesting examples identified as indicative of public relations practice observed during the research.

Going Multimodal: Analyzing the Data

The ethnographic data and the interviews were analyzed *multimodally*, that is, all the relevant communicative modes involved in the interaction were analyzed. These included *speech* (Jucker, 1986; Schegloff, Jefferson, & Sacks, 1977; Schiffrin, 1987), *non-verbal actions*, such as *posture* and *proximity* (Goffman, 1964; Norris, 2004), *gaze* (Goffman, 1964; Kendon, 1967), and *manual gesture* (Goldin-Meadow, 2003; McNeill, 1992, 2005). By understanding the constellation of actions, we posit that we can more fully grasp the intangible meaning of an interaction.

Language/speech is analyzed using *conversation analysis* (Jucker, 1986; Schegloff et al., 1977; Schiffrin, 1987), which considers how those involved organize their talk-in-interaction through, for example, turn-taking, or how they solve problems through, for example, repair talk (Schegloff et al., 1977).

It is only relatively recently that researchers have begun to recognize and acknowledge the advantages of studying interactions multimodally. In the 1990s, Gumperz and Berenz wrote that when people interact, they do so using talk and non-verbal signals that provide feedback throughout the conversation, indicating to interlocutors how the interaction is progressing:

> Conversing in turn rests on speakers' and listeners' interpretation of verbal and nonverbal signs or contextualization conventions that is, systems of cues that guide conversational management.
> (Gumperz & Berenz, 1993, pp. 91–92)

Despite this clear pointer to the need for a more multifaceted approach to understanding interactions, it was still almost a decade before researchers began showing an increased focus on multimodality and some began to use visual research methods routinely (Sissons, 2012).

The use of video ethnography in the current research provided us with data from which we were able to select significant or critical incidents representing:

- Formal workplace interactions including meetings to discuss ongoing issues and strategic message planning;
- Informal interactions between colleagues of equal status and between senior and junior colleagues;
- Data on work flow and normative workplace practices;

- PRPs interacting with clients;
- Interviews that related to specific experiences, situations, or interactions that had been witnessed during the period of data collection. These provided explanations, opinions, and/or further information about the situations or interactions.

Such data involving interactions between PRPs, their colleagues, clients, and journalists have been rarely available to researchers. Therefore, this study differs from the earlier ones in that it offers more comprehensive evidence than has been obtainable before, covering back-stage interactions seldom visible to outsiders. By analyzing these (critical) interactions we gain unique insights into public relations relationships and how strategic decisions within the practice are negotiated, providing us with empirical evidence to drive theory-building within the discipline.

Overview of the Structure of the Book

Each chapter in this book addresses a different aspect of relationships in public relations practice, ranging from the relationships among PRPs themselves to relationships between PRPs and journalists and, the much discussed "organization-public relationship."

We begin with an overview of some of the key theories of interpersonal relationships and communication in Chapter 2, focusing on the main aspects identified during the research and pre-empting some of the discussion around organization-public relationships. Of particular interest is how relationships are formed, maintained, and, at times, ended. What strategies are used to form relationships, and how are relationships maintained? What do these interpersonal relationships look like, and how do they play out in practice?

In this chapter, we discuss the personal influence model as central to public relations practice as well as the role and impact of impression management. Importantly, we consider concealment and deception in interpersonal relationships. A PRP can only exert influence if she has built trust with others, which happens when others believe her actions to be genuine and her intentions to be beyond reproach. However, there are times when information is distorted, concealed, or simply withheld. These forms of deception require further scrutiny if we are to explore the practice of public relations as it *is*, and not how it might be or should be.

In Chapter 3, we change gears, and explore what we call *mediated relationships*, that is, relationships mediated through technologies. In the 21st century, most (if not all) relationships are mediated through some form of technology. The most common and prolific is email, a tool that has been in common use now for more than 20 years. Many practitioners continue to lament the use of email, preferring to make contact through a richer medium of communication such as the telephone or face-to-face. In this chapter, we explore in detail an example of an email exchange, highlighting challenges facing emailers such as conventions around politeness and the expression of anger or frustration.

In considering mediated relationships, Chapter 3, also addresses the use of social media platforms. Although much has been written about social media's potential for dialogue and conversation, little has been written that explores social media as sites of enactment. In this chapter, we discuss topics not often addressed in public relations scholarship and textbooks, namely (mediated) impression management, ambient awareness, and privacy. We present the idea of mediated relationships as a way to think about enactment through and on social media.

Chapters 4–7 address in more detail the specific relationships we argue dominate public relations practice: the *PRP-PRP relationship* (Chapter 4), the *PRP-client relationship* (Chapter 5), the *PRP-journalist relationship* (Chapter 6), and the *organization-public relationship* (Chapter 7). The order of these chapters is quite deliberate; its intention is to show the relationships in order of importance, spiraling out from the very personal relationship in the office to, ultimately, the diffuse and intangible relationship the organization is said to have with its publics.

Addressing the PRP-PRP relationship in Chapter 4, we consider the types of relationships that develop in the workplace. Of specific interest is the power that is enacted within relationships where there is no formal hierarchical power. We propose that the power present is ambient power, that is, power that is low-key and that lies on the periphery. We show how practitioners enact power and manage conflict while adhering to politeness and civility, thereby preserving their relationships with colleagues.

Like the PRP-PRP relationship, very little has been written about the PRP-client relationship. In Chapter 5, we provide a rare window into interactions between PRPs and their clients, and highlight meetings as crucial sites for meaning-making. Again, the incidents or events illustrate how PRPs plan their interactions with clients, navigate difficult talk, and move the client towards a decision while remaining civil throughout.

Chapter 6 highlights the sometimes-strained relations between PRPs and journalists. Recent global events, including claims of an increase in so-called "fake news," have again catapulted this relationship to the forefront, requiring us to re-examine it, especially if we wish to maintain a democratic society. With changes to the newsroom, journalists increasingly turn to PRPs for information, while PRPs continue to rely on journalists for third party endorsement and publicity. Equally, PRPs often attempt to keep their clients out of the news if it may result in negative publicity. Thus, the relationship between these content siblings is often a delicate balancing act.

Chapter 7 addresses the idea of organization-public relationships, and, here, we explore some of the key arguments involved. We investigate how PRPs view these relationships by observing how they talk in their meetings, and how they strategize communicating with their organization's public/s.

Chapter 8 concludes by integrating some of the key insights gained from this research, pointing towards directions and areas for further research and theory-building, as well as making suggestions as to what should be recognized as skills and expertise in public relations practice.

References

Agar, M. (2008). *The professional stranger: An informal introduction to ethnography* (2nd ed.). Bingley: Emerald Group.

Cotter, C. (2001). Discourse and media. In D. Schiffrin, D. Tannen, & H. E. Hamilton (Eds.), *The handbook of discourse analysis* (pp. 416–431). Malden, MA: Blackwell Publishing.

Countries – Geert Hofstede. (2016). Geert–hofstede.com. Retrieved 25 August 2016, from www.geert-hofstede.com/countries.html.

Dant, T. (2004). Recording the habitus. In C. Pole (Ed.), *Seeing is believing? Approaches to visual research* (Studies in Qualitative Methodology, Vol. 7, pp. 41–60). Bingley: Emerald Group.

Daymon, C., & Hodges, C. (2009). Researching the occupational culture of public relations in Mexico. *Public Relations Review, 35*(4), 429–433. doi:10.1016/j.pubrev.2009.06.006.

DeWalt, K. M. M., & DeWalt, B. R. (2010). *Participant observation: A guide for fieldworkers* (2nd ed.). Walnut Creek, CA: Rowman & Littlefield, Md.

Domingo, D., & Paterson, C. (Eds.). (2011). *Making online news: Newsroom ethnographies in the second decade of internet journalism* (Vol. 2). New York: Peter Lang Publishing.

DuFon, M. (2002). Video recording in ethnographic SLA research: Some issues of validity in data collection. *Language Learning & Technology, 6*(1), 40–59.

Edwards, L. (2009). Symbolic power and public relations practice: Locating individual practitioners in their social context. *Journal of Public Relations Research, 21*(3), 251–272. doi:10.1080/10627260802640674.

Fairclough, N. (1989). *Language and power.* London: Longman.

Fairclough, N. (1995a). *Critical discourse analysis: The critical study of language.* Essex: Longman.

Fairclough, N. (1995b). *Media discourse* (3rd ed.). New York: Hodder Arnold.

Fairclough, N. (2009). A dialectical-relational approach to critical discourse analysis in social research. In R. Wodak & M. Meyer (Eds.), *Methods of critical discourse analysis* (2nd ed., pp. 162–187). Thousand Oaks, CA: Sage Publications.

Fairclough, N. (2016). A dialectical-relational approach to critical discourse analysis in social research. In R. Wodak & M. Meyer (Eds.), *Methods of critical discourse studies* (3rd ed., pp. 86–109). London: Sage Publications.

Fine, G. A. (2003). Towards a peopled ethnography: Developing theory from group life. *Ethnography, 4*(1), 41–60. doi:10.1177/1466138103004001003.

Flanagan, J. C. (1954). The critical incident technique. *Psychological Bulletin*, 51(4), 327–358. doi:10.1037/h0061470.

Flewitt, R., Hample, R., Hauck, M., & Lancaster, L. (2009). What are multi-modal data and transcription? In C. Jewitt (Ed.), *The Routledge handbook of multimodal analysis* (pp. 40–53). Abington, Oxon: Routledge.

Frey, R. A., & Powell, L. A. (2005). Beyond left–right ideology in the study of justice perception: Interdependent and independent distributive Worldviews in Jamaica and New Zealand. *Journal of Cross–Cultural Psychology*, 36(1), 117–146. doi:10.1177/0022022104271429.

Geertz, C. (1973). *The interpretation of cultures*. New York: Basic Books.

Gitlin, T. (1980). *The whole world is watching: Mass media in the making and unmaking of the New Left*. Berkeley, CA: University of California Press.

Goffman, E. (1964). The neglected situation. *American Anthropologist*, 66(6_PART2), 133–136. doi:10.1525/aa.1964.66.suppl_3.02a00090.

Goldin-Meadow, S. (2003). *Hearing gesture: How our hands help us think*. Cambridge, MA: Belknap Press of Harvard University Press.

Gumperz, J. (2001). Interactional sociolinguistics: A personal perspective. In D. Schiffrin, D. Tannen, & H. Hamilton (Eds.), *The handbook of discourse analysis* (pp. 215–228). Malden, MA: Blackwell Publishing.

Gumperz, J., & Berenz, N. (1993). Transcribing conversational exchanges. In J. Edwards, & M. Lampert (Eds.), *Talking data* (pp. 91–120). New Jersey: Lawrence Erlbaum Associates.

Heath, R. L. (2013). The journey to understand and champion OPR takes many roads, some not yet well traveled. *Public Relations Review, 39*, 426–431. doi:10.1016/j.pubrev.2013.05.002.

Heracleous, L. (2004). Interpretivist approaches to organizational discourse. In D. Grant, N. Phillips, C. Hardy, L. Putnam, & C. Oswick (Eds.), *Handbook of organizational discourse* (pp. 175–192). Beverly Hills, CA: Sage Publications.

Holmes, J., & Stubbe, M. (2015). *Power and politeness in the workplace: A Sociolinguistic analysis of talk at work*. Abingdon: Routledge.

Hong, B. (2014). National cultural indicators in New Zealand. *Cultural Trends, 23*(2), 93–108. doi:10.1080/09548963.2014.897450.

Hutton, J. G. (1999). The definition, dimensions, and domain of public relations. *Public Relations Review*, 25(2), 199 211. doi:10.1016/s0363-8111(99)80162-3.

Ihlen, Ø., & van Ruler, B. (2007). How public relations works: Theoretical roots and public relations perspectives. *Public Relations Review, 33*, 243–248. doi:10.1016/j.pubrev.2007.05.001.

Ihlen, Ø., & Verhoeven, P. (2012). A public relations identity for the 2010s. *Public Relations Inquiry, 1*(2), 159–176. doi:10.1177/2046147X11435083.

Jucker, A. (1986). *News interviews*. Amsterdam, The Netherlands: John Benjamins.

Kawulich, B. (2005). Participant observation as a data collection method. *Forum: Qualitative Social Research*, 6(2), 1–19.

Keatinge, D. (2002). Versatility and flexibility: Attributes of the critical incident technique in nursing research. *Nursing and Health Sciences*, 4(1–2), 33–39. doi:10.1046/j.1442-2018.2002.00099.x.

Kendon, A. (1967). Some functions of gaze–direction in social interaction. *Acta Psychologica, 26*, 22–63. doi:10.1016/0001-6918(67)90005-4.

Ki, E.-J., & Shin, J.-H. (2015). The status of organization–public relationship research through an analysis of published articles between 1985–2013. An appeal for further research. In E.-J. Ki, J.-N. Kim, & J. A. Ledingham (Eds.), *Public relations as relationship management: A relational approach to the study and practice of public relations* (2nd ed., pp. 28–45). London: Routledge.

L'Etang, J. (2005). Critical public relations: Some reflections. *Public Relations Review, 31*(4), 521–526. doi:10.1016/j.pubrev.2005.08.011.

L'Etang, J. (2013). Public relations: A discipline in transformation. *Sociology Compass, 7*(10), 799–817. doi:10.1111/soc4.12072.

Lewis, R. D. (1999). *Cross cultural communication: A visual approach* (2nd ed.). Hampshire: Transcreen Publications.

Love, T., & Tilley, E. (2014). Acknowledging power: The application of Kaupapa Māori principles and processes to developing a new approach to organisation–public enactment. *Public Relations Inquiry, 3*(1), 31–49. doi:10.1177/2046147X14521198.

Macnamara, J. (2012). The global shadow of functionalism and excellence theory: An analysis of Australasian PR. *Public Relations Inquiry, 1*(3), 367–402. doi:10.1177/2046147x12448581.

McNeill, D. (1992). *Hand and mind: What gestures reveal about thought.* Chicago, IL: University of Chicago Press.

McNeill, D. (2005). *Gesture and thought.* Chicago, IL: University of Chicago Press.

Minichiello, V., Aroni, R., & Hays, T. (2008). *In–depth interviewing* (3rd ed.). Sydney, Australia: Pearson Education Australia.

Moreno, Á., Verhoeven, P., Tench, R., & Zerfaß, A. (2014). Increasing power and taking a lead—What are practitioners really doing? Empirical evidence from European communications managers. *Revista Internacional de Relaciones Públicas, 7*(4), 73–94. ISSN: 2174-3681.

Norris, S. (2004). *Analyzing multimodal interaction: A methodological framework.* New York: Routledge.

Palinkas, L. A., Horwitz, S. M., Green, C. A., Wisdom, J. P., Duan, N., & Hoagwood, K. (2013). Purposeful sampling for qualitative data collection and analysis in mixed method implementation research. *Administration and Policy in Mental Health and Mental Health Services Research, 42*(5), 533–544. doi:10.1007/s10488-013-0528-y.

Pink, S. (2007). *Doing visual ethnography: Images, media, and representation in research.* Thousand Oaks, CA: Sage Publications.

Population clock. Statistics New Zealand. (December 6, 2016). Retrieved from www.stats.govt.nz/tools_and_services/population_clock.aspx.

Reich, Z. (2006). The process model of news initiative: Sources lead first, reporters thereafter. *Journalism Studies, 7*(4), 497–514. doi:10.1080/14616700600757928.

Reich, Z. (2009). *Sourcing the news: Key issues in journalism—an innovative study of Israeli press.* Cresskill, NJ: Hampton Press.

Saville-Troike, M. (1989). *The ethnography of communication: An introduction* (2nd ed.). New York: Blackwell Publishing.

Schegloff, E. A., Jefferson, G., & Sacks, H. (1977). The preference for self correction in the organization of repair in conversation. *Language, 53*(2), 361. doi:10.2307/413107.

Schensul, S., Schensul, J., & LeCompte, M. (1999). *Essential ethnographic methods: Observations, interviews, and questionnaires (Ethnographer's toolkit).* Walnut Creek, CA: AltaMira Press.

Schiffrin, D. (1987). *Discourse markers.* Cambridge: Cambridge University Press.

Sissons, H. (2012). Journalism and public relations: A tale of two discourses. *Discourse & Communication, 6*(3), 273–294. doi:10.1177/1750481312452202.

Sissons, H. (2015a). *Whose news? Investigating power relations between journalists and public relations practitioners* (Doctoral thesis). Auckland University of Technology, Auckland, NZ.

Sissons, H. (2015b). Lifting the veil on the PRP–client relationship. *Public Relations Inquiry, 4*(3), 263–286. doi:10.1177/2046147x15614686.

Skilling, P. (2013). Egalitarian myths in New Zealand: A review of public opinion data on inequality and redistribution. *New Zealand Sociology, 28*(2), 16–43.

Statistics New Zealand. (2014). *2013 Census QuickStats about culture and identity.* Retrieved from www.stats.govt.nz.

Stokes, J. (2013). *How to do media and cultural studies.* London: Sage Publications.

Suri, H. (2011). Purposeful sampling in qualitative research synthesis. *Qualitative Research Journal, 11*(2), 63–75. doi:10.3316/qrj1102063.

Titscher, S., Meyer, M., Wodak, R., Vetter, E., & Jenner, B. (2000). *Methods of text and discourse analysis: In search of meaning.* London: Sage Publications.

Tracy, K., Martinez-Guillem, S., Robles, J., & Casteline, K. (2011). Critical discourse analysis and (U.S.) communication scholarship. In C. T. Salmon (Ed.), *Communication yearbook No 35* (pp. 241–286). New York: Routledge.

Trenwith, L. (2010). The emergence of public relations in New Zealand from 1945 to 1954—The beginnings of professionalisation. *New Zealand Journal of Applied Business Research, 8*(1), 51–62.

Triandis, H. C. (2006). Cultural aspects of globalization. *Journal of International Management, 12*, 208–217. doi:10.016/j.intman.2006.02.010.

Tripp, D. (1993). *Critical incidents in teaching: Developing professional judgement.* New York: Routledge.

Tuchman, G. (1991). Qualitative methods in the study of news. In K. B. Jenson & N. Jankowski (Eds.), *A handbook of qualitative methodologies for mass communication research* (pp. 79–92). London: Routledge.

Van Dijk, T. A. (1988). *News as discourse.* Mahwah, NJ: Lawrence Erlbaum Associates.

Van Dijk, T. A. (2001). Critical discourse analysis. In D. Schiffrin, D. Tannen, & H. E. Hamilton (Eds.), *The handbook of discourse analysis* (pp. 352–371). Malden, MA: Blackwell Publishing.

Waymer, D. (2013). Democracy and government public relations: Expanding the scope of "relationship" in public relations research. *Public Relations Review, 39*(4), 320–331. doi:10.1016/j.pubrev.2013.07.015.

Williams, M. (2000). Interpretivism and generalisation. *Sociology, 34*(2), 209–224. doi:10.1177/s0038038500000146.

Wodak, R., & Meyer, M. (2001). *Methods of critical discourse analysis.* London: Sage Publications.

Wood, L., & Kroger, R. (2000). *Doing discourse analysis: Methods for studying action in talk and text.* California: Sage Publications.

World Values Survey (2015). *Cultural map—WVS wave 6 (2010–2014).* Retrieved from www.worldvaluessurvey.org/WVSContents.jsp.

Zaharna, R. S. (2016). Beyond the individualism–collectivism divide to relationism: Explicating cultural assumptions in the concept of "relationships." *Communication Theory, 26*, 190–211. doi:10.1111/comt.12058.

2 Relationships and Relationship Building

> Seldom, very seldom, does complete truth belong to any human disclosure; seldom can it happen that something is not a little disguised or a little mistaken.
>
> —Jane Austen (1775–1817), Author of "Emma"

The Neglected Relationship

This book explores relationships, and in particular, the professional relationships that public relations practitioners (PRPs) develop during their work. In Chapter 1, we described relationships as being at the core of all public relations activity and crucial to effective public relations. In this chapter, we investigate what is meant by "relationships" in public relations scholarship and consider some of the key theories concerning interpersonal relationships that are shaping the field. We also continue to set out how we believe public relations scholarship needs to develop to better reflect and influence current practice. What does it really mean to "have a relationship," and what does this relationship look like? How do we create, maintain, and, yes, *end* relationships?

Relationships—whether personal or professional—are complex. We have relationships because we are human; we work at them because we have a vested interest in their success. Much of what we do in our lives, and in the workplace, can only be achieved through relationships, and therefore they are necessary for productivity (Myers, 2010). The late Paul Dryden, past CEO of the Public Relations Institute of New Zealand (PRINZ), once commented that relationships were integral to the practice of public relations, and a practitioner who did not have the ability to build relationships had no business being in public relations. A similar view was echoed years later by U.S. Fulbright Specialist, Dr. Rebecca Gilliland Deemer (Personal Communication, 2016).

But, while relationships are necessary, and can be a rewarding aspect of the PRP's job, they are also fraught with political play, issues of confidentiality, and deception, and therefore require a range of skills to navigate effectively. Yet, few—if any—public relations textbooks explore the role and function of *interpersonal* relationships in public relations. Most highlight their significance but provide no or very little insight into how practitioners can develop the ability to navigate these relationships intelligently or strategically. Too often in public relations practice and education this ability is taken for granted, assuming the new entrant intuitively knows how to develop and maintain effective relationships. As Ledingham (2015) pointed out, even though PRPs *should* have interpersonal skills to navigate the complexity of relationships, these skills are seldom taught. This is especially important if we are to consider the personal influence model as a necessary and viable model for public relations practice.

We argue that relationships in public relations comprise layers, spiraling outwards from close interpersonal relationships between peers (the "inner circle"), who make strategic decisions about public relations messages or products, to interactions PRPs have with groups of publics (the "outer circle") to hear their concerns and to convey these concerns to senior management. As Grunig (2015) stated, having constructive relationships allows the organization's publics to bring their misgivings to the decision-makers of that organization and provides them with an opportunity to respond to those concerns. But this cannot happen if practitioners, who usually bring these concerns to decision-makers, have not gained the trust of their senior management or that of their publics—if they are unable to navigate complex and messy interpersonal relationships. Accepting that relationships in public relations comprise layers means accepting that nebulous and intangible organization-public relationships cannot exist without more discernible interpersonal relationships, and that, without understanding interpersonal relationships and interpersonal communication, PRPs cannot fulfil their roles effectively.

What is a "Relationship"?

Public relations scholarship habitually conflates different types of relationships, and particularly, interpersonal relationships with organization-public relationships. At times, a relationship is simply understood to be some sort of connection (in the most abstract way) between material *things* or people and has little to do with what we understand communication or interpersonal connection between people to be. Lattimore, Baskin, Heiman, Toth, and Van Leeuwen (2004), for example, suggested, "Both systems theory and situational theory are considered *theories of relationships*" (p. 47, original emphasis).

At other times, intangible and diffuse relationships are seen as something to be managed in order to influence the organization's reputation:

> To manage relationships with groups and individuals that have a stake in the company is to manage the sum of those relationships, something called reputation.
>
> (Doorley & Garcia, 2015, p. 3)

Indeed, as we will discuss in Chapter 7 of this book, scholars have argued that reputation and relationships with publics are interlinked, and therefore how organizational members interact with others will affect how those others perceive the organization.

Regardless, the current situation in public relations literature is no different to 20 years ago, when Broom, Casey, and Ritchey (1997) lamented, "public relations literature is replete with references to *relationships* without defining the concept and without indicating how to measure them" (p. 84, original emphasis).

There is no doubt that relationships "have always been the elephant in the room in public relations practice and theory" (Grunig, 2015, p. xxvii). It is a concept that has been used as a *primitive term*, that is, a term where the meaning is treated as a given (Broom et al., 1997), not unlike how Taylor and Kent (2014) described the ideograph "enactment." Indeed, Coombs and Holladay (2015) stated that the concept "relationships" in public relations can be treated as such an *ideograph*, which lies at the intersection between rhetoric and ideology (McGee, 1980). "People are conditioned to follow ideographs—they become guides for action or reasons for behavior" (Coombs & Holladay, 2015, p. 693), and indeed, people believe they know what the concept means and that "everyone" shares this understanding. But, as scholars such as Doan and Bilowol (2014) and Zaharna (2015) have discussed, "relationships" and "relationship-building" are not understood in the same way across all cultures, and we should therefore not assume that their meaning is shared universally.

Outside the field of public relations, interpersonal relationships have been studied widely by scholars from philosophers to psychologists. But, even in psychology, interpersonal relationships were not studied as a dedicated topic until the 1980s (Jackson-Dwyer, 2014), which roughly corresponds to the time that the idea of relationships was brought to the attention of public relations scholars through Mary Ann Ferguson's 1984 paper, in which she argued that *relationships* should be the focus of public relations (Grunig, 2015). Relationships, she proposed, were what set the discipline apart from other related disciplines such as journalism (Grunig, 2015)—a radical idea at a time when public relations was still closely associated with mass communication and publicity. So, what does it mean to have a relationship?

Relationships Are Things We Do

An interpersonal relationship refers to "an emotional or other connection between people" (Berko, Rosenfeld, & Samovar, 1997, p. 254) that results in the parties exerting "strong, frequent and diverse effects on one another over an extended period of time" (Jackson-Dwyer, 2014, p. 1). Typically, all parties are aware that they have a link or an association, or that they are involved in some way or another. When that relationship is formed, there is an expectation that they must "take each other into account" when making decisions (Adler, Rosenfeld, & Proctor, 2007, p. 234; Berko et al., 1997, p. 254), which suggests that the parties have some influence or power over one another, regardless of how minuscule that influence might be. (Power and, more specifically, power between PRPs is discussed in Chapter 4.)

Relationships are things we *do*, Jackson-Dwyer (2014) stated, and thus not things we *possess*. Because we do not possess them, we cannot exert control over the relationships themselves or the other parties, which scholars should take note of when transposing the principles of interpersonal relationships to organization-public relationships without deeper reflection. Not only would the exertion of control (through management practices) lead to a potential struggle for power, but it could be perceived as unethical, because presumably, in a relationship we have *free will*, that is, the power to act at our own discretion. (The issue of control is again addressed in Chapter 7.)

Following a critical theory approach, Curtin, Gaither, and Ciszek (2016) proposed that relationships in the practice of public relations are an expression of a Foucauldian notion of power, and that meaning is derived from these relationships as articulations of the cultural economic model of public relations practice. These relationships can be modified by the context in which they arise, and are "forged in and through the articulation process; they are the manifestations of the temporary linkages formed" (p. 43). Important here is not only the idea that power is embedded within relationships, but that relationships are linkages that are short-lived, which does not mean that they cannot be a powerful tool for PRPs.

Communication Is Integral

Situated within interpersonal relationships is the idea of interpersonal communication, which Berger (2015) described as "the study of social interaction between people" (p. 498). *Interpersonal communication theory* "seeks to understand how individuals use discourse and non-verbal actions to achieve a variety of instrumental and communication goals" within that relationship (Berger, 2015, p. 498), not unlike the approach we take in this book when we explore the critical interpersonal interactions PRPs have with their peers, clients, and journalists. These relationships—identified through empirical research, using video ethnography (as discussed in Chapter 1)—differ from Sallot's (2013) proposed areas of application of interpersonal communication theory in public relations, which she described as:

> (1) *client/organization practitioner relations*, in which practitioners interpret the external environment to the organization; (2) *journalist/media gatekeeper practitioner relations*, in which practitioners

facilitate publicity about the organization; and (3) *members of target publics practitioner relations*, in which practitioners interpret the organization's intents and actions to the public.

(p. 477, emphasis added)

Essentially, an interpersonal relationship can be viewed as a dance where "two people move together in a coordinated display" (Berko et al., 1997, p. 261). It is only when the dance is exceptionally well-choreographed or completely out of step that we sit up to take notice. In other words, we may notice the *exceptions* rather than the mundane, everyday interactions. This is, of course, what makes this book unique: it is in the mundane, everyday interactions where we find value and meaning, and which tell us about the practice of public relations and the relationships on which it hinges.

No Single Relationship Is the Same

An interpersonal relationship is highly personal and idiosyncratic in nature; it is the parties themselves that shape the relationship, determine its rules, the behavioral norms, and the expectations that govern it. What we do, and how we do it, then, will depend on how we define the relationship we have, and how this relationship is structured. In other words, the *interactional rules* are determined by the expectations that accompany the *roles* parties play, and the *relational structure* (Berko et al., 1997).

This is not to deny that the relationship can be influenced by external factors such as societal or professional culture, but it does mean that relationships vary greatly in purpose, complexity, and communicative style. In an ideal situation, parties agree explicitly or implicitly about the nature of their relationship (Berko et al., 1997) and the social norms and expectations that govern it (Adler et al., 2007). Very often, these norms have to do with what we regard as "standards of politeness or decorum, such as acknowledging the presence of others" (Hargie, 2017, p. 485). This suggests that there must be some agreement about the fundamental rules of the relationship: what is acceptable, and what is not; who makes the decisions and when? Are these decisions shared or unilateral? Questions such as these are complicated by infusing our expectations with cultural assumptions (Zaharna, 2015). In our analysis of PRP-client relationships in Chapter 5, for example, we found that parties expected a certain level of formality and confidentiality. We also found that there are various strategies for saving face during meetings (see also Sissons, 2016a,b) and that PRPs consciously and deliberately plan their interaction with clients.

Types of Relationships

The most frequent type of interpersonal relationship that PRPs have, are *role relationships*. These are relationships determined by their roles, that is, the position they hold in an organization and the communicative interactions that form part of that (Berko et al., 1997), such as PRP-PRP, PRP-client, and PRP-journalist relationships. Sometimes, these role relationships grow gradually into *acquaintance relationships* and *good friend relationships* as familiarity and trust increase (Berko et al., 1997).

It is not unusual to find role relationships moving to acquaintance relationships when parties remain in a shared context or space over a longer period, and in some cases, the critical incidents in this book reflect this development. A PRP-client relationship can thus potentially develop into an acquaintance relationship, and perhaps even into a (good) friend relationship if each party feels comfortable in the other's presence and enjoys their company for longer periods of time (see Berko et al., 1997).

When people first meet, there is a level of uncertainty that is only reduced as parties get to know each other and when rules—and expectations—are established. As uncertainty within the relationship lessens, and self-disclosure is reciprocated, the relationship's complexity and idiosyncrasy are increased. Thus, as they become better acquainted, parties are likely to assert their identities and develop a unique, joint relationship identity within the boundaries of that connection. They may share common experiences and context, and their communication is likely to be focused on those shared experiences, opinions, and attitudes (Berko et al., 1997). As Berko et al. pointed out, when parties feel that their idiosyncrasies are accepted, they are more willing to engage in self-disclosure—although personal information remains reserved for relationships that have entered the friend stage. Arguably, then, the closer the relationship, the higher the potential levels of influence within that relationship. While a multitude of relationships is regarded as an asset (Paliszkiewicz & Mądra-Sawicka, 2016), the strength of those relationships is equally, if not more, important than their number.

Power Is Embedded in Relational Structures

Berko et al. (1997) identified three relational structures based on the distribution of power or influence within a relationship, namely a *symmetrical, complementary* or *parallel structure*. A *symmetrical relational structure* suggests that power or influence is equally distributed, and the independence of each participant is stressed. In a *complementary relational structure*, one party may be dominant, but each has specific duties and obligations. As can be surmised, power is unequally distributed within these types of relational structures. However, many relationships are *hybrids* of these two. Berko et al. (1997) referred to this hybrid as a *parallel relational structure*.

Although understanding power in a relationship is important for managing that relationship and the associated politics, it is not always easy or even possible to identify *where* the power in a relationship lies, or whether parties have a closer relationship than merely a role or acquaintance relationship. Observed interactions at a given time do not always provide the necessary insight, and in many professional and workplace relationships power is equally distributed and governed by a different set of rules. In her study of work relationships, Sias (2009), for example, identified peer-coworker relationships or simply *peer relationships*, which she described as people in "relationships at the same hierarchical level who have no formal authority over one another" (p. 58). This does not suggest that parties have no influence over each other but rather, that influence is low-key and ambient, as we found in our research. These peer relationships are discussed in more detail in Chapter 4.

Borrowing from psychotherapy, Broom et al. (1997) also identified the *transference relationship* and the *real relationship*. The transference relationship develops through the "displacement of feelings from previous relationships" to the other party (Broom et al., 1997, p. 89) as opposed to the real relationship that develops and exists between the parties through, for example, the *actual* (experienced) behaviors and feelings towards each other. The real relationship is not unlike Grunig's (2015) suggestion of *experiential relationships* that influence the organization's reputation (discussed in more detail in Chapter 7). A typical example of a transference relationship is where a journalist enters a professional (role) relationship with a PRP having had negative experiences in the past with other PRPs. These feelings and expectations are then transferred into this new role relationship.

It is important to note *that not all interaction involves a relationship, yet all relationships require interaction.* This is perhaps the greatest challenge for public relations scholars who propose that organizations have "relationships" with their publics. Much of what is suggested to be a relationship is nothing more than ritualistic interaction, where organizations send out one way messages or respond mechanically to requests or comments from their publics. Nowhere is it more noticeable than when organizations enter the social media domain responding to publics by copying and pasting standard responses to, mainly, complaints. As Berko et al. (1997) and Adler et al. (2007) pointed out, rituals or mechanized exchanges do not constitute a relationship; the latter involves so much more. Relationships are complex, messy and in a constant state of flux (Berko et al., 1997). Heath (2013) agreed, stating that relationships are "multidimensional, multilayered, and subject to motivation for conflict and aggression" (p. 426). To fully understand the complexities of relationships and relationship-building in public relations, it is necessary to cover the *full* spectrum of human behavior, whether good or bad, including the use of deception and power play, as well as the development and ending of relationships.

The Phases in Relationship Building

There is much talk about relationship *management* in public relations, and yet, the question remains whether we can truly "manage" relationships. Relationships are not "things" we can own or possess, as already mentioned. They are *intangible* (Adler et al., 2007), and thus, the idea of managing relationships appears to be incongruous with the nature of interpersonal relationships. Yet, public relations scholars have attempted to find ways of measuring relationships in their effort to provide evidence of the value of public relations work to an organization. But, if we were to assume that we can purposefully create and maintain (or manage) relationships, we must also accept that we can purposefully *end* relationships. In doing so, practitioners should understand the phases of interpersonal relationship development. Indeed, all interpersonal relationships, whether personal or professional, go through phases and have beginnings, middles and ends—much like a story. By employing the metaphor of a narrative, we can view relationships as journeys. Some are scenic, some are enjoyable, and others are a challenge.

According to the developmental model of relationships, they begin when parties come together, initiate a relationship, and gradually move towards a stage where the relationship is maintained (Adler et al., 2007). If this maintenance is not effective, the relationship goes into decline. When this happens, the relationship parties make an effort to differentiate themselves from each other, use avoidance strategies and, eventually, terminate the relationship altogether. Most relationships, however, function in the "maintenance" phase, which suggests a level of stability even though relationships move back and forth through various stages.

Drivers for Establishing a Relationship

Most relationships begin with some form of *attraction* or seeing someone as appealing (Berko et al., 1997). In professional relationships, this "attraction" can take many forms, ranging from shared values to recognizing the potential for a working partnership. The appeal of the other person can be enhanced by seeing them as similar to ourselves, or simply by being in the other's proximity. For example, one PRP we followed for our research often described clients in ways that identified shared values, including twice describing clients as "one of the good guys."

> Well, I really like Sean. I think because we deal with a lot of boards and Chairmen and CEOs—and he is genuinely one of the good guys.

About another CEO, he said:

> Richard is like Sean, he is another one of the good guys.

Although he did not elaborate on what he meant by "one of the good guys," it is inferred that he viewed the two clients as likeable, and that he not only appreciated their fundamental values, but believed they shared common beliefs that guided their professional practice. The positive comments also suggest that these professional relationships have the potential to move beyond mere role relationships to "friends" or "likeable acquaintances." A relationship with them would, therefore, cost little but could potentially provide personal rewards, which Berko et al. (1997) referred to as the *economic model of relationships*. Such rewards can be *intangible* (information and insight into the industry) or *tangible* (future contracts), and are driven by *personal motives*, which can include getting others to do something for you, expressing concern for them, or providing distraction from work demands (Berko et al., 1997).

Another factor that drives people to enter a relationship is *proximity* because, to interact and enter a relationship, participants need to be in the others' presence (Berko et al., 1997), that is, they must be near in space and time. Of course, the concept of "proximity" has taken on a different shape in the contemporary world of computer-mediated communication, as discussed in Chapter 3. Social media, for example, is aimed at bringing people "closer" together and thus increasing proximity (Theunissen, 2015), but this scenario is not always played out, as some social spaces contain negative behaviors such as name-calling, insults, and "trolling" that can damage relationships.

Similarity also drives the process of relationship building. While the adage that opposites attract may hold true, we tend to favor those who are similar to us in age, opinions, socioeconomic status, and so forth (Berko et al., 1997). Jackson-Dwyer (2014) added that we like those who like us, which she called the *reciprocity effect* whereby relationship formation becomes a self-fulfilling prophecy.

Perceived similarity drives many of our decisions to engage with others and has been of key interest to scholars of dialogic communication, who point towards a central tenet of dialogue being to engage with many diverse voices rather than restricting enactment to those who think and act as we do (Heath, Pearce, Shotter, Taylor, Kersten, & Zorn, 2006). Yet, it appears easier to develop a relationship and build trust with those with whom we have something in common. For example, in our research, a PRP who was involved in creating a public relations campaign for a client in financial distress, expressed disapproval that the client's marketing manager was only 24 years old. He added, "so we just pulled together a whole team of gray hairs like us." It was clear the PRP felt more comfortable working with people of similar age to himself, who he believed had the background to prepare them for the situation. He appeared unconvinced that the much younger marketing manager had the relevant know-how or experience to assist with the campaign.

   Interpersonal relationships also sometimes develop to *enhance one's self-esteem* (Berko et al., 1997). Indeed, many people enjoy building relationships with those they deem as the most important or smartest people in the room because by association, their own status—and therefore self-esteem—is improved. PRPs, too, displayed some of these drivers for relationship building. Here is one of our participants talking about the board members of one of his clients:

> Martin Sidcup[1], he's the General Manager of the fund. Sam Green, who we know well, is also on that Board and so is Ryan Smith, the Chancellor of ((name)) University, Vice-Chancellor, and ex-Treasury. Dead set genius. Watching him and Sam bounce off each other for a day and a half is quite fascinating. And they have got…Kevin Brown, who is the Chairman, is a really smart property guy and he's been at the heart of a lot of big deals.

Developing Personal Influence

PRPs, aware of the importance of *personal influence* in gaining legitimacy in the profession, may deliberately develop networks (relationships) with key players in the industry. Valentini (2010), for example, wrote that "in order to be part of the dominant coalition, PR practitioners must exercise influence and at the same time use influence tactics and strategies to help shape organizational choices, ideology, and practices" (p. 154). Influence, however, is notoriously difficult to identify.

   For example, in an interview, one of our participants described how he was attempting to guide a client in a new enterprise, especially in her choice of advertising companies, but also by putting forward a suggestion for a board member, because, he said, she would need "good people around her."

> Giles ((another client)) has put her in touch with us because we are the experienced guys in the crunchy end of the PR business. And so we have got some contacts in ad and branding land that we will put her on to. And this is really hers, but we will open some doors and Simon is one of the best money guys going around and very strategic and that sort of thing, so that is why I think he will be a good fit for her.

We can see that the PRP is using his own networks and personal influence to help his client increase hers—a process that is implicit. As Parker (2013, p. 50) said,

> Influence is an inherently difficult thing to observe, and even more difficult to measure. To do so, we need to isolate the element exerting influence and the resulting 'action, behavior, opinions etc.' caused by it.

In Chapter 4, we attempt to do just that when we analyze the interactions between three colleagues to identify what we refer to as "ambient power," that is power that is intangible and on the periphery of interaction.

Interestingly, the idea of personal influence was first introduced in 1995 by J. E. Grunig, L. A Grunig, Sriramesh, Huang, and Lyra as one of two "additional patterns of public relations practice" (p. 164). Later, Sriramesh (1996/2009) showed it to be a practice model for Indian public relations. The model, which has often been hailed as the "fifth model" to complement the four models identified by Grunig and Hunt (1984), is perceived to be based on culture. It is a relational strategy that is linked to the cultural variable of power distance (Taylor, 2004) and highlights the link between interpersonal relations and personal influence (Grunig et al., 1995).

At the time of his research, Sriramesh found that the practitioners he studied spent time and effort to establish and maintain interpersonal communication and relationships with, for example, journalists by providing hospitality and brokering influence with the aim of seeking favors in return. This suggests that the model relies on *reciprocity* in the relationship, and is, to some extent, based on the *social exchange theory* discussed in Chapter 7.

Reciprocity relies on unspoken conventions that the other will return the favor, and is a strategy of *seeking compliance* (Adler et al., 2007). It is, therefore, a relationship development and maintenance strategy. Indeed, our research found that building and maintaining relationships based on reciprocity was important, especially for the PRP-journalist relationship, which, as we discuss in Chapter 6, is becoming increasingly significant.

A PRP we spoke to, for example, described how his "very close relationship" with a national journalist worked. He used the example of a media release he had sent to the journalist and that had just been published:

> He ran an image which we sent him through. It's a small piece, but clearly there's a lot of value in that copy and more importantly the image for our client…He's not sought any verification of the facts included within the press release, but why should he really? We have a very close relationship and we've never jeopardized that, we would never compromise that. So he knows that the content we are providing him with is always factually correct.

Evident here is the trust that is inherent in the relationship—the PRP's track record has resulted in confidence that the information is factually correct, and that, by implication, the PRP is ethical in his communication and interaction.

For journalists, having a good working relationship with PRPs covering the areas they report is increasingly important (Sissons, 2014). An extreme example was a beauty editor for a Sunday supplement, who (perhaps not surprisingly) informed us that all her contacts were PRPs and these were crucial in providing content for her pages.

> It [the relationship] is quite even, like I couldn't do those beauty pages without them [PRPs] because you need to know what's new and it is quite helpful, especially with pictures and images. We don't have a picture editor anymore here and so if I need an image for something I've written about, they'll send me a high-res image or a CD—so I do need them.

It is evident that these networks of personal influence and relationships are beyond the domain of the organization as they are highly particular and individual (Valentini, 2010). While the organization gains publicity from the content published in the Sunday supplement or online story, *the interaction is between the journalist and the PRP*, and not the journalist and the organization as is often alluded to in scholarship, and thus, the interpersonal relationship between the parties is key to gains in publicity and reputation. Understanding, therefore, the development and maintenance of interpersonal relationships and being skilled in interpersonal communication should be an important part of public relations training. As Valentini (2010) found in her analysis of Italian PRP-journalist relationships, many practitioners are hired for the quality and extensiveness of their personal networks. Consequently, she proposed that having such networks should be recognized as public relations expertise.

Managing Impressions

Developing networks of influence requires making good impressions on those we meet, and therefore impression management is integral to developing personal influence. Predictably, much of public relations work is about creating favorable impressions as an attempt to manage or control the perceptions that others form about a person or organization (Paliszkiewicz & Mądra-Sawicka, 2016). In practice, this enhances the practitioner's legitimacy and increases confidence in her ability to deliver what she promises. In the earlier example, the PRP's track record allowed him to develop an image of reliability and trustworthiness. In another example, one of the participants in our research explained how she paid special attention to her grooming when meeting a male client who she knew was impressed by, and more likely to take guidance from, an attractive woman than from a plain or badly groomed one.

Creating a favorable impression is an important initial strategy to build a relationship. It is created during an introductory conversation when parties show *cooperativeness* and appear *considerate*. Once someone has shown positive traits, we attribute other positive traits to them, filling any potential gaps—and there are usually many—to gain a complete impression of the other (Wood, 1993). This process is called the *implicit personality theory*, which proposes that we integrate information about the situation and the behavior of the other person to make a general judgment of that person (Wood, 1993). Thus, first impressions count.

Another key strategy in creating a favorable impression is *self-disclosure,* which involves "explicitly sharing personal information with another person" (Solomon & Theiss, 2013, p. 79). According to *self-disclosure theory*, strangers will disclose enough to establish an appropriate level of intimacy in the relationship (McKinney & Donaghy, 1993) or, we would argue, reciprocal liking, as discussed earlier. Self-disclosure allows parties to show cooperativeness by following the rules of conversation and behaving according to the other party's norms (Berko et al., 1997). It can be seen, then, as a reciprocal act that is a key factor in establishing and maintaining the relationship.

Caring, on the other hand, is displayed by showing interest through engaging in discussion, asking questions and listening thoughtfully, that is, by *paying attention*, while *memorability* is created by communicating one's most dynamic and interesting self (Berko et al., 1997). According to Berko et al. in collective societies such memorability is established by focusing on one's role in the family, the team or society. They added that creating a favorable impression is accompanied by the process of *seeking affinity*, or getting others to "like you and feel positive towards you" (Berko et al., 1997, p. 312).

Men and women differ in the strategies they use to seek affinity, Berko et al. asserted. Women, for example, tend to avoid showing off but pay attention to their appearance, as we saw in the earlier example where the PRP admitted to taking particular care with her grooming when meeting a specific client. Women also encourage others to talk, and generally follow a strategy of being dependable, encouraging and supportive, while being more inclined to disclose personal information (Berko et al., 1997).

Men, on the other hand, follow a strategy of telling the other person how wonderful they are, aim to present an interesting self, present themselves as leaders, offer favors, highlight past accomplishments, tend to initiate encounters, and focus on things they have in common (Berko et al., 1997). The latter played out in our research during an all-male meeting between a PRP, the CEO and the legal counsel of a client. The client was in financial difficulties and was facing an investigation by the Trustee. But, despite the seriousness of the situation, the meeting included a considerable amount of banter. Among the light-hearted back-and-forth was some leg-pulling about the PRP's colorful sweater, which was labeled a "Range Rover sweater." The car theme had been a feature of the meeting with several jokes around the CEO's love of cars and motorbikes, prompted by a comment in a recent media article about his collection of fast cars. The PRP pointed out that the article had "missed a few acquisitions along the way" including "the Panamera." The legal counsel quipped, "The Panamera only lasted about three weeks." The PRP added, "Perhaps we should tell them you've also got a Mini" to which the legal counsel responded, "That only lasted about a week." Then the conversation moved to the CEO's interest in trail bikes. Here the PRP mentioned he used to represent a major motorbike manufacturer, thereby moving from common interests to past accomplishments:

> 'cos I love bikes…no one else would ride them so they'd give me all their bikes and I'd go for a play at the weekends. It was brilliant and they're such an easy thing to ride.

Relationships Are Not Free of Persuasion

Dialogue is often seen as integral to relationship management. Kent and Theunissen (2016) wrote that "The strength of dialogue as a public relations tool…is its ability to facilitate interpersonal exchanges, research, and maintaining relationships" (p. 4047). However, this does not mean that relationships are free of persuasion. *Seeking compliance*, which is described as the "active process to direct and influence your communication partner's behavior" (Berko et al., 1997, p. 314), is generally accepted as integral to relationship development.

According to Berko et al. (1997), "*mutual* influence is a defining characteristic of relationships" (p. 314, emphasis added). Such attempts to seek compliance from the other party can, thus, be seen as a tactic we use to *persuade* or influence others to think or act in a desired way (Adler et al., 2007). Compliance seeking can, therefore, be part of an effective PRP's repertoire to assert her personal influence to achieve the outcome she wants.

According to Adler et al. (2007), there are over sixty ways in which we seek compliance from others. While we can enhance our knowledge of these strategies, the fundamental skills to influence others develop in early childhood. Examples range from *direct requests*, *indirect appeals*, *reciprocity*, *reward and punishment*, *maintenance of face*, and *relational appeals* (Adler et al., 2007). The earlier instance of the beauty editor relying on PRPs for her content is an example of reciprocity, and thus creates relationships through which influence is extended.

Direct requests are just that: asking directly for assistance or permission to do something. *Indirect appeals*, on the other hand, often come in the form of hints, hoping the other party will infer our real intent. Of course, there is always the risk that they won't, and our appeal will come to naught. Regardless, indirect appeals are useful where a direct request may be perceived as too confrontational or result in an awkward situation (Adler et al., 2007).

Direct and indirect requests were evident throughout our ethnographic research with practitioners. In one of these examples, a PRP is on the phone, discussing media coverage with a client, who in the past has been reluctant to approach the media, but who now needs to gain public support for his organization going forward. The PRP and the client are discussing letting the media know about a business deal that has just been successfully concluded. The PRP attempts to convince the client by way of a "suggestion" that the client let the local paper know about the deal, as they have talked about it with the paper before and now that it is concluded, the paper should be told. He cautiously attempts to coax the client into informing the newspaper, employing hedges ("maybe") and padding language ("one of the things"). The vagueness of padding (as well as hedging) language is often used to soften the impact of what is said (Machin & Mayr, 2012):

> Maybe you should do something with the local paper again? Just yeah, uhm. One of the things with this, Martin, is you need to be a bit consistent about it and because you've said to them, "well we are going for this," you kind of have to let them know the result of this, even if it's just a quick call.

Here the PRP hedges the request as a "suggestion" using the modal verbs, "maybe" and "should," to soften its impact and urgency, resulting in it being less direct and demanding. But his tactful attempt to influence the client is unsuccessful. The latter responds that he does not have time to talk with journalists at the moment, even on the phone, and he does not want another story published. The PRP then changes tack, explaining that the reporter will want to follow up on the story whether the client likes it or not:

> So you could probably just do it with a phone call, just saying, "just to give it to you." Yeah it will lead to another story, but it will lead to another story whether he calls you or you call him. But you know, it's kind of good for the relationship if you were to say to him "we got what we were after," rather than him having to chase you.

Modality, or the mode in which something is expressed, shows how speakers see themselves in relation to others. Here, the PRP uses *low modality* ("could"), which avoids being direct or specific, and the modal adverb "probably," which indicates uncertainty. Doing so suggests to the client that the PRP is not certain a phone call will be enough, and may, in fact, lead to the reporter wanting a face-to-face interview, but the PRP does not want to state that outright to the already reluctant client. *High modality* can be seen in constructions such as "will" as in "will lead to another story" (Machin & Mayr, 2012), illustrating that he (the PRP) is confident in his belief that the reporter would want another story. Combining low and high modality can be viewed here as strategy of influence: while the PRP leaves room for uncertainty, he also confirms what he believes will be the outcome of the action, hoping to prompt the client into action.

Other compliance-seeking strategies involve *reward and punishment,* which provide a clear and unambiguous pay-off (Adler et al., 2007). For compliance, there may be a monetary reward, a friendlier relationship, or, perhaps, a future contract. On the other hand, punishment for not complying can be the removal of a service or a contract or a refusal to cooperate. For the PRP-journalist relationship (see Chapter 6), a refusal to cooperate can mean a loss of access to information—the lifeblood of a journalist's work.

In one of our examples, a PRP explained how a client, who was involved with a company facing receivership, was on a plane looking through some documents, without realizing that the person sitting next to him was reading the documents over his shoulder and taking notes. Those notes ended up forming the basis of a news story in a national newspaper. Before publishing the story, the journalist approached the client, and the PRP tried to explain that some of the documents did not relate to others, meaning the story was wrong on several points. This argument was not accepted by the news organization and the story was published. Relating the incident, the PRP used a negative colloquialism that his client was "pretty brown" on the organization.

> Peter's relationship with Noel Salter, who wrote the story: Noel won't be getting another story out of Peter, which is bad for Noel, because Peter's on 10 or 11 boards. I see this morning he's popped up on another one, some new investment fund he's involved in.

However, in what could be thought of as a reciprocal arrangement—or way of making it up to the businessman—the news organization subsequently ran a profile piece in the weekend paper about Peter, written by a different reporter, suggesting that while compliance is sought and punishment is meted out for non-compliance, strategies to maintain a long-term working relationship are commonplace.

Withholding information is one strategy to punish those that are non-compliant, information overload is another. A PRP related that if a journalist wrote about her organization in a way that she regarded as unfair—perhaps by taking information or quotes out of context or by angling a story negatively—then a way to punish them was not to refuse to respond to their enquiry, but rather, to respond fulsomely, with large amounts of information.

Sometimes we like to be a bit tricky with our responses to people—just give them the most boring, long-winded information that they have to trawl through purely because we know it's going to take them ages to go through and that's just fun and games, that's how you play it. So, if you want to play hard ball, we can play just as well.

But punishment and reward are not the only ways of seeking compliance. Other strategies include the maintenance of face and relational appeals (Adler et al., 2007). *Face maintenance*, for instance, relies on stroking egos or ensuring that the other's status in the organization or society is not diminished. Its purpose is to seek compliance through socially desirable ways that make parties feel good, or better, about themselves. *Relational appeals* rely on respect or affection within that relationship and are, therefore, bound to the state of the relationship.

Adler et al. (2007) proposed that strategies in seeking compliance are culture bound. According to them, parties in the United States often provide reasons or explanations when seeking compliance while in cultures that rely on being connected (collectivist) and a sense of duty, parties will invoke shared beliefs or obligations. As an island in the Asia-Pacific region, New Zealand appears to straddle the collectivist and individualist principles, seeking compliance through invoking shared obligations and sometimes expressing reasons for seeking compliance. For example, a 2014 drunk driving advertisement relied heavily on connectedness. In an effort to stop a group of drunken young men from driving, an older man walks up and states that since he has spoken to them, his fate is connected with theirs and they now have a duty towards him not to drive drunk (NZ Transport Agency, 2014).

Concealing and Deceiving

The thought of deceiving a party with whom we have some form of relationship seems counter intuitive to effective relationship building; we expect our interpersonal interactions and relationships to be free of concealment and deception. Yet deception is an integral part of human relationships (Burgoon & Levine, 2010).

Conventional wisdom tells us that effective relationship maintenance requires *self-disclosure* because it allows participants to get to know each other by (truthfully) revealing information about themselves (Berko et al., 1997). But, if we apply the principles of dialectics then self-disclosure must be balanced with non-disclosure, and, worse, deliberate deception.

To understand non-disclosure, we should appreciate that self-disclosure is a cultural construct: what and how much we disclose will depend on our culture (Adler et al., 2007). In Taiwan and Japan, for example, parties will go to extremes to hide unfavorable information about *in-group* members such as family and friends to *out-group* members (Adler et al., 2007), and it is, therefore, likely that deception will occur within professional relationships when friends and family are involved.

Furthermore, even when we do disclose personal information, not all self-disclosure is equally revealing. According to the *social penetration model*, the *breadth* (range of topics), and *depth* (how much) of the information we reveal determines how much self-disclosure takes place (Adler et al., 2007). The hard reality is that disclosing the truth can have "risky, potentially unpleasant consequences" (Adler et al., 2007, p. 286), and therefore many err on the side of non-disclosure, or if we wish: *deception.*

Deception Comes in Many Disguises

Deception comes in a "variety of guises," ranging from "flat-out lies, elaborate fabrications, misdirection and exaggerations, to evasions, equivocations, concealments, omissions, strategic ambiguity and deflections, spoofing and phishing, to more subtle misdirection, and camouflage" (Burgoon & Levine, 2010, p. 202). According to Burgoon and Levine, mixing true with false information is not uncommon, but *omission, evasion,* and *strategic withholding of information* appear to be the most common forms of deception.

In Chapter 3, we discuss the case of an email exchange that is centered on a request for information by a journalist. At first, the information was deliberately withheld by the organization. Eventually, it was released when it was too late to be of value. A similar process of deception occurred in a phone call between a PRP and a journalist (Chapter 6), when the PRP omits telling the journalist that he does not want the CEO to speak to her while pretending that he is surprised she hasn't been able to get an interview. Equally, in Chapter 7, in one of the meetings, the PRPs are at pains to discuss the disclosure of accurate information albeit controlled and framed to benefit the organization. It would, therefore, be fair to argue that disclosure as opposed to concealment, and transparency as opposed to deception, are recognized in practice albeit not always enacted.

Exaggerations and untruths can be used as tools to enhance relationships, and to make one appear more like the other party (Adler et al., 2007). A practitioner, for example, may exaggerate her experience to impress a potential client or future employer, or may lie or tell "untruths" to gain power.

Deception can be described as *knowingly* and *intentionally* misleading another person, which rules out "self-delusion, accidental transmission of faulty information, or faulty conclusions by receivers that are of their own doing" (Burgoon & Levine, 2010, p. 202). Ironically, most people tend to accept obvious lies without challenging them (Adler et al., 2007).

Approximately one-third of all conversations contain some form of deception, and such deception does not only occur in face-to-face communication, but also "in telephone conversations, voice mails, e-mails, chats, and other forms of mediated communication" (Burgoon & Levine, 2010, p. 201). Indeed, face-to-face communication—while often preferred where there is a low level of societal trust (Taylor, 2004)—is not a foil against being deceived, partly because we are subject to an inherent bias towards believing the other person to be honest, and partly because we are just bad at picking up cues of deception.

According to the interpersonal deception theory (IDT),

> deception is a goal-directed, intentional, and strategic activity; that deceivers attempt to adapt to whatever feedback and suspicions they perceive receivers are communicating so as to appear credible and evade detection. Receivers in turn are not passive recipients of senders' messages. They have their antenna (albeit often subconsciously) and may engage in active or indirect strategies to ferret out the true state of affairs. Thus, deceptive episodes are not static.
>
> (Burgoon & Levine, 2010, p. 205)

While it may appear unpalatable, effective public relations work is likely to contain some form of deception or concealment, such as strategically and knowingly withholding or omitting information or evading embarrassing questions. Paradoxically, some of the foundations for this reality are laid in the professional codes of conduct, such as the one by the Public Relations Institute of New Zealand (PRINZ), which states that practitioners have a professional duty not to disclose confidential information, and to safeguard "the confidences and privacy rights of present, former and prospective clients and employers" while at the same time being expected to "avoid deceptive practices" ("PRINZ code of ethics," 2016). Thus, a paradox is created: while they are encouraged to avoid deception, PRPs can find themselves practicing a form of legitimized deception by *not* disclosing information.

Adler et al. (2007) pointed out that every communicative interaction has a *content* (information being exchanged) and *relational* dimension (how they feel about each other). Deception can occur within any of these dimensions. The question is, in a professional relationship, does it do more damage when the deception relates to the content or when it relates to the state of the relationship? And, is it possible that deception may serve as a strategy to strengthen relationships?

If we consider that deceiving or concealing is part of all interpersonal interaction and a human phenomenon, we should consider the possibility that in some instances, it would be ethical to conceal. We could argue, for example, that to remain *civil* in the workplace (see Fritz, 2014) practitioners may need to refrain from disclosing dislike for a coworker or a client. Adler et al. (2007), for example, referred to the "benevolent lie," which is intended to spare another person's feelings or to protect relationships by lying to one person in order to honor a commitment to someone else. Indeed, lies told to friends and family were more often benevolent than self-serving as opposed to telling lies to strangers.

Civility and the Long Tail of the Truth Bias

People generally over-estimate their ability to detect deception: *confidence* in their ability is not correlated with the *actual* ability to detect it (Burgoon & Levine, 2010). That said, according to Burgoon and Levine, most people can accurately detect deception at least half of the time.

The reason we are not more successful lies in our inherent *truth bias,* that is, the tendency to judge a message as truthful rather than as deceptive. The truth bias is more active in face-to-face communication, when people are relationally closer and not primed to be distrustful (Burgoon & Levine, 2010). While face-to-face interaction allows us to build closer relationships through trust, and New Zealand (Bhargava, 2010), and Croatian (Taylor, 2004) PRPs, for example, often prefer face-to-face contact, the truth bias primes us to give the other participant the benefit of doubt (Burgoon & Levine, 2010). The realities of this dialectic in interpersonal relationships could be seen in several cases throughout our research. Having built a relationship with a journalist, a coworker or a client, and having developed a level of confidence and trust, allows the skilled PRP to evade controversial issues or to strategically withhold information. Sissons (2016a), for example, described two instances where PRPs were involved in deception. The first involved a PRP reporting a public meeting about a road-building project to a journalist that appeared to deliberately underestimate the strength of opposition to the proposals, and the second showed a PRP managing to delay the release a report that would reflect negatively on his client (in the face of the Ombudsman's disapproval) to a time when minimal public discussion of the report would be assured. This latter example is discussed in the next chapter.

A contributing factor to deception is the existence of *professional civility*, that is, formal politeness and courtesy in the workplace. Indeed, *politeness theory* is based on the premise that, as members of society, we base our behavior and interaction on a so-called "model person" who is competent and rational, and who works towards maintaining their own, and others', face needs (Schnurr, 2013). Therefore, we *expect* a certain level of civility or politeness in our interactions with others. Coworkers do not need to like each other, but they should show their care for their organization through their civility, Fritz (2014) argued, adding that civility is an ethical requirement. Therefore, the quality of the communication reflects the kind of relationship that exists between the parties (Adler et al., 2007), as well as the state of that relationship (Theunissen, 2015).

Because it is the civil thing to do, we give the other person the benefit of doubt and miss potential cues that suggest deception. Burgoon and Levine (2010) speculated that there does not seem to be "any strong, cross-situation behavioral cues that would make high accuracy possible," and when cues *are* available, we pay attention to those that "lack diagnostic utility" (p. 203) by applying inaccurate but common beliefs about detecting lies. For example, we may believe that a person avoids eye contact when lying, which we know to be a poor indicator, that is, if we are familiar with cross-cultural communication. Therefore, relying on such unscientific beliefs or *diagnostic cues* is likely to lead the communicator astray. Furthermore, we are what Burgoon and Levine (2010) called "cognitive misers" relying on "mental shortcuts called heuristics" (p. 202) to draw conclusions and these conclusions are often incorrect. The implicit personality theory (Wood, 1993) discussed earlier in the chapter also applies: if we assume others to be truthful, we will not even entertain that they are lying, and while suspicion can lower the truth bias, it will not fully eliminate it (Burgoon & Levine, 2010).

Thus, the PRP's reputation and track record become valuable (and risky) assets in the profession (hence the need for impression management). If the practitioner has not overtly deceived another party before and has a reputation for being a "straight shooter," it may be easier to mislead on specific occasions. Consequently, deception and detection become a strategic and complex dance. But, as Burgoon and Levine (2010) pointed out, lies do not remain hidden, and while we rarely detect deception on the spot, it is often detected *after the fact* through inconsistencies with prior knowledge, information obtained from third parties and physical evidence. It is, therefore, an interactive process, and our ability to detect lies is greatly enhanced by our communication skills, familiarity with the other person's background and communication patterns, and our ability to recognize how their interaction deviates from the anticipated communication pattern.

Ending a Relationship

While relationships end for a variety of reasons, ending relationships is not a topic that is frequently addressed—if at all—in public relations scholarship. The implication is that once a relationship has been built, it needs to be maintained and never ends. Indeed, Ledingham (2013) discussed taking corrective action to prevent the demise of the relationship between an organization and its publics. Yet, relationships end.

Sometimes the end is heralded by goals having been fulfilled and no new goals having been established, or because the patterns of interactions have become too rigid and boring. Certainly, the "death of a relationship evokes a strong response often accompanied by heightened defensiveness" (Berko et al., 1997, p. 318).

Relationships can end suddenly or it can be a protracted process. As Berko et al. (1997) suggested, there may have even been attempts to repair the relationship, and in some cases, a new, restructured relationship emerges. At other times, the relationship is terminated completely and irrevocably. Occasionally, both parties end the relationship; other times it is the wish of only one party. In both cases, either party may use direct or indirect strategies to break away. Reducing disclosure of one's self is a typical (indirect) strategy (Solomon & Theiss, 2013) to distance or detach oneself emotionally from the other, and corresponds with strategies of allowing the relationship to fade.

In interpersonal relationships, strategies are generally oriented to the self *or* the other. Self-orientation may include *taking control away* from the other (making the end a fait accompli), *withdrawal* (such as being very constrained during meetings), *escalation of cost* (it takes more effort to be with them; they are busy, have a lot of meetings, etc.), or *attributional conflict* (it's the other person's fault). It may involve other strategies such as a *"state-of-the-relationship" talk* where the relationship is discussed, *pseudo de-escalation*, such as seeing a little less of each other for a while, a (rational) *negotiated farewell*, or simply *"fading away"* where parties see increasingly less of each other and disclose less (Berko et al., 1997). As mentioned, the latter can be seen as a distancing behavior.

Distance, Kolbe (2013) argued, can take various forms, such as physical or psychological, and serve various purposes (a topic we take up again in Chapter 3). Physical distancing, for example, can occur in an attempt to *reduce intimacy* (Hargie, 2017). Although distancing, or *disengagement* (Theunissen, 2018), is often perceived as problematic, it is at times the ethical and appropriate approach to take in a relationship, and should, therefore, be recognized as a valid strategy for relationship management. A PRP-client relationship may end, for example, because the contract has ended and no new work is required. Equally, a PRP-PRP relationship may end because one or both take up new roles elsewhere. While contact may be maintained between people who have built a strong acquaintance relationship, even a friend relationship, the rules for interaction are likely to have changed. The relationship has thus become *restructured*, and cannot continue in the same way as before.

Conclusion

Relationships are complex and require skills and communication competency to manage. Building, maintaining and amicably ending relationships should be acknowledged as valuable skills in public relations practice. Having said this, it should be noted that the idea of deliberately and consciously building and maintaining relationships is not a universal one. In their analysis of South Korean public relations practice, Jo and Kim (2004) referred to the concept *yon* as "related to the belief that relationships are formed, maintained, and terminated by uncontrollable external forces" (p. 294). Consequently, these practitioners would experience relationships differently to, for example, New Zealand practitioners. But if we were to see relationship-building as integral to public relations, then understanding interpersonal relationship theory is a requirement for appreciating the inherent challenges facing "organization-public relationships" (see Chapter 7).

Regardless, much of the traditional interpersonal communication and relationship theory has been based on face-to-face interaction. As we move further into the 21st century, we find technology to be playing an increasing role in the mediation of relationships and communication, and we would argue that nowadays, *all* relationships are mediated to some extent through technology. This is a topic we take up in the next chapter.

Note

1 All names have been changed to protect the privacy of research participants.

References

Adler, R. B., Rosenfeld, L. B., & Proctor, R. F. (2007). *Interplay. The process of interpersonal communication* (10th ed.). Oxford: Oxford University Press.

Berger, C. R. (2015). Interpersonal communication. In W. Donsbach (Ed.), *The concise encyclopedia of communication* (pp. 498–501). West Sussex: John Wiley & Sons.

Berko, R. M., Rosenfeld, L. B., & Samovar, L. A. (1997). *Connecting: A culture–sensitive approach to interpersonal communication competency* (2nd ed.). Fort Worth, TX: Harcourt Brace College Publishers.

Bhargava, D. (2010). *The use of Internet in public relations and its impact on the practice: a New Zealand perspective* (Master of Communication Studies thesis). Auckland University of Technology, Auckland, NZ.

Broom, G. M., Casey, S., & Ritchey, J. (1997). Toward a concept and theory of organization–public relationships. *Journal of Public Relations Research*, 9(2), 83–98. doi:10.1207/s1532754xjprr0902_01.

Burgoon, J. K., & Levine, T. R. (2010). Advances in deception detection. In S. W. Smith & S. R. Wilson (Eds.), *New directions in interpersonal communication research* (pp. 201–220). Thousand Oaks, CA: Sage Publications.

Coombs, W. T., & Holladay, S. J. (2015). Public relations' "Relationship Identity" in research: Enlightenment or illusion. *Public Relations Review*, 41(5), 689–695. doi:10.1016/j.pubrev.2013.12.008.

Curtin, P. A., Gaither, T. K., & Ciszek, E. (2015). Articulating public relations practice and critical/cultural theory through a cultural–economic lens. In J. L'Etang, D. McKie, & N. Snow (Eds.), *The Routledge handbook of critical public relations* (pp. 41–53). London: Routledge.

Doan, M., & Bilowol, J. (2014). Vietnamese public relations practitioners: Perceptions of an emerging field. *Public Relations Review*, 40(3), 483–491. doi:10.1016/j.pubrev.2014.02.022.

Doorley, J., & Garcia, H. F. (2015). Reputation management. In J. Doorley & H. F. Garcia (Eds.), *Reputation management: The key to successful public relations and corporate communication* (3rd ed., pp. 1–44). London: Routledge.

Fritz, J. M. H. (2014). Organization as other. In R. C. Arnett & P. Arneson (Eds.), *Philosophy of communication ethics. Alterity and the other* (pp. 266–286). Madison, WI: Fairleigh Dickinson University Press.

Grunig, J. E. (2015). Foreword. In E.-J. Ki, J.-N. Kim, & J. A. Ledingham (Eds.), *Public relations as relationship management: A relational approach to the study and practice of public relations* (2nd ed., pp. xxiii–xxvii). London: Routledge.

Grunig, J. E., Grunig, L. A., Sriramesh, K., Huang, Y-H., & Lyra, A. (1995). Models of public relations in an international setting. *Journal of Public Relations Research, 7*(3), 163–186. doi:10.1207/s1532754xjprr0703_01.

Grunig, J. E., & Hunt, T. T. (1984). *Managing public relations.* New York: Holt, Rinehart and Winston.

Hargie, O. (2017). *Skilled interpersonal communication: Research, theory and practice* (6th ed.). London: Routledge.

Heath, R. L. (2013). The journey to understand and champion OPR takes many roads, some not yet well traveled. *Public Relations Review, 39*(5), 426–431. doi:10.1016/j.pubrev.2013.05.002.

Heath, R. L., Pearce, W. B., Shotter, J., Taylor, J. R., Kersten, A., & Zorn, T. (2006). The processes of dialogue. *Management Communication Quarterly, 19*(3), 341–345. doi:10.1177/0893318905282208.

Jackson-Dwyer, D. (2014). *Interpersonal relationships.* London: Routledge.

Jo, S., & Kim, Y. (2004). Media or personal relations? Exploring media relations dimensions in South Korea. *Journalism & Mass Communication Quarterly, 81*(2), 292–306. doi:10.1177/107769900408100205.

Kent, M. L., & Theunissen, P. (2016). Elegy for mediated dialogue: Shiva the destroyer and reclaiming our first principles. *International Journal of Communication, 10*, 4040–4054.

Kolbe, D. G. (2013). Virtually there: The paradox of proximity. In R. Morrison & H. Cooper–Thomas (Eds.), *Relationships in organizations: A work psychology perspective* (pp. 171–192). London: Palgrave Macmillan.

Lattimore, D. L., Baskin, O. W., Heiman, S., Toth, E., & van Leeuven, J. (2004). *Public relations: The practice and the profession* (5th ed.). Boston: McGraw–Hill Higher Education.

Ledingham, J. A. (2013). Relationship managing theory. In R. L. Heath (Ed.), *Encyclopedia of public relations* (2nd ed., pp. 781–783). Thousand Oaks, CA: Sage Publications.

Ledingham, J. A. (2015). Managing relationship management. In E.-J. Ki, J.-N. Kim, & J. A. Ledingham (Eds.), *Public relations as relationship management: A relational approach to the study and practice of public relations* (2nd ed., pp. 46–60). London: Routledge.

Machin, D., & Mayr, A. (2012). *How to do critical discourse analysis: A multimodal introduction.* Los Angeles, CA: Sage Publications.

McGee, M. C. (1980). The "ideograph": A link between rhetoric and ideology. *Quarterly Journal of Speech, 66*(1), 1–16. doi:10.1080/00335638009383499.

McKinney, D. II., & Donaghy, W. C. (1993). Dyad gender structure, uncertainty reduction, and self–disclosure during initial interaction. In P. J. Kalbfleisch (Ed.), *Interpersonal communication: Evolving interpersonal relationships* (pp. 81–116). Hillsdale, NJ: Lawrence Erlbaum Associates.

Myers, K. K. (2010). Workplace relationships and membership negotiations. In S. W. Smith, & S. R. Wilson (Eds.), *New directions in interpersonal communication research* (pp. 135–158). Thousand Oaks, CA: Sage Publications.

NZTransportAgency. (2014, December 18). *Local legends.* Retrieved from www.youtube.com/watch?v=H8F6ydrdD1o&feature=youtu.be.

Paliszkiewicz, J., & Mądra-Sawicka, M. (2016). Impression management in social media: The example of LinkedIn. *Management, 11*(3), 203–212.

Parker, A. (2013). Understanding social capital. In R. Brown & S. Waddington (Eds.), *Share this too: More social media solutions for PR professionals* (pp. 49–58). Malden, MA: John Wiley & Sons.

PRINZ code of ethics. (2016). Retrieved from www.prinz.org.nz/Attachment?Action=Download&Attachment_id=1039.

Sallot, L. M. (2013). Interpersonal communication theory. In R. L. Heath (Ed.), *Encyclopedia of public relations* (2nd ed., pp. 476–479). Thousand Oaks, CA: Sage Publications.

Schnurr, S. (2013). *Exploring professional communication: Language in action.* New York: Routledge.

Sias, P. M. (2009). *Organizing relationships. Traditional and emerging perspectives on workplace relationships.* Los Angeles, CA: Sage Publications.

Sissons, H. (2014). Negotiating the news. *Journalism Studies, 17*(2), 177–198. doi:10.1080/1461670x.2014.973147.

Sissons, H. (2016a). Negotiating the news. *Journalism Studies, 17*(2), 177–198. doi:10.1080/1461670x.2014.973147.

Sissons, H. (2016b). Journalists versus public relations practitioners: Power and agency at a media conference. *Australian Journalism Review, 38*(2), 31–45.

Solomon, D., & Theiss, J. (2013). *Interpersonal communication: Putting theory into practice.* New York: Taylor & Francis.

Sriramesh, K. (1996/2009). Power distance and public relations: An ethnographic study of Southern Indian organizations. In H. M. Culbertson & N. Chen (Eds.), *International public relations: A comparative analysis* (pp. 171–190). New York: Lawrence Erlbaum Associates.

Taylor, M. (2004). Exploring public relations in Croatia through relational communication and media richness theories. *Public Relations Review, 30*(2), 145–160. doi:10.1016/j.pubrev.2003.09.003.

Taylor, M., & Kent, M. L. (2014). Dialogic enactment: Clarifying foundational concepts. *Journal of Public Relations Research, 26*, 384–398. doi:10.1080/1062726X.2014.956106.

Theunissen, P. (2015). The quantum entanglement of dialogue and persuasion in social media: Introducing the Per–Di Principle. *Atlantic Journal of Communication, 23*(1), 5–18. doi:10.1080/15456870.2015.972405.

Theunissen, P. (2018/in press). The philosophy and ethics of enactment. In K. A. Johnston & M. Taylor (Eds.), *The handbook of communication enactment.* Malden, MA: Wiley–Blackwell.

Valentini, C. (2010). Personalised networks of influence in public relations. Strategic resources for achieving successful professional outcomes. *Journal of Communication Management, 14*(2), 153–166. doi:10.1108/1363254101 1034600.

Wood, R. (1993). Deceptive schemata: Initial impressions of others. In P. J. Kalbfleisch (Ed.), *Interpersonal communication: Evolving interpersonal relationships* (pp. 150–184). New York: Lawrence Erlbaum Associates.

Zaharna, R. S. (2015). Beyond the individualism–collectivism divide to relationalism: Explicating cultural assumptions in the concept of "Relationships." *Communication Theory, 26*(2), 190–211. doi:10.1111/comt.12058.

3 Mediated Relationships

> One of the great ironies of the social media era is that some of the least social people in the world created it.
>   —Sarah Lacy (1975–), American journalist

A Changing World

While all relationships have an interpersonal component, as discussed in the previous chapter, this does not necessarily require the participants to be physically present in an interaction. In fact, nowadays, relationships are increasingly mediated by technology. It is this element of relationships that we turn to next in this chapter.

According to Greenfield (2003), it takes about two generations for a technology to be optimized and filter through all institutions and functions of society, and computer technology is a classic example of this phenomenon. Greenfield argued that, for the first 25 years (to the 1970s), computer or internet technology followed a similar development trajectory to that of electricity: it was unreliable and inefficient with no discernible impact. Then, during the 1980s its development accelerated. It was still expensive and unreliable, but, thanks to the development of personal computers, towards the end of the 1980s more and more people starting purchasing computers. For the latter, perhaps the most significant innovation came in 1989 when Tim Berners-Lee developed the world-wide web. Once this communication protocol became public in 1991, it opened the floodgates for developers, inventors, and entrepreneurs to exploit the potential of internet technology.

Fast forward to today and computer or internet technologies mediate much of our personal and professional lives through what is colloquially called "social media" or "the internet." Most of us have numerous communication devices that allow us to connect with people in our immediate proximity and those further afield, including those we have never met in person. Platforms and applications, ranging from Facebook, Twitter, LinkedIn, Snapchat, WhatsApp, and Skype abound. The number of applications, in particular, is continuously growing and their functions evolving, and a generation of Millennials is growing up in this networked society, taking for granted how relationships are created, conducted, and ended using technologies. Indeed, in New Zealand social media use is the most prevalent among younger users, declining noticeably with age (Crothers, Smith, Urale, & Bell, 2016).

Connecting

In a recent Pew Research survey conducted among 2,003 American adults, Olmstead, Lampe, and Ellison (2016) found that "workers" used social media for various purposes, including to connect with friends and family (27%), make or support professional connections (24%), strengthen or build relationships with coworkers (17%) and learn more about them (17%). Despite their willingness to engage with social media, only a relatively small number of employees have incorporated specific social media platforms such as Facebook (19%), LinkedIn (14%) or Twitter (3%) into their work. When they do use them, Olmstead et al. (2016) found, it was mostly for networking or finding jobs (78%), staying in touch with others in their field (71%), connecting with experts (56%), getting to know their coworkers personally (51%) or for purely information-seeking purposes (46%).

Still, a New Zealand survey on 1,377 respondents over the age of 16 years highlighted that *face-to-face meetings* and *writing letters* remained popular forms of keeping in touch, with 93% of participants engaging in these activities (Crothers et al., 2016). This did not mean that users were not active on social media or social networking sites. Indeed, while checking emails was by far the most common and frequent form of online communication across all ages, with nearly 90% checking emails at least once a day, 82% also posted comments on social networking sites, 73% posted videos or photos and 13% posted audio. According to Crothers et al. (2016), some 25% did so daily. Furthermore, *browsing* was perceived to be the most common form of entertainment with nearly 90% of participants engaging in this as a daily activity.

Comparing the 2015 internet survey findings with those in previous years, Smith, Bell, Miller, and Crothers (2016) noted an increase in the number of internet users who go online during an average work day. This number had increased from 65% in 2011 to 87% in 2015, and there was a steady increase in those who perceived the internet as "important," with participants reporting increasing confidence in using the internet. When considering social networking sites, here too perceived importance had increased, more than doubling since 2009, with more than half regarding these sites as important (Smith et al., 2016). As we will see later in this chapter, the increased confidence in using the internet and perceived importance of being connected holds implications for *ambient awareness* (awareness of others through social media use) in expanding personal influence and maintaining relationships.

As the internet continues to pervade our lives and shape how we interact with others, we can expect changes in how we develop, maintain and end relationships. For example, learning about colleagues through social networks can be a double-edged sword: 29% of American adults in the 18 to 29-year age group said it *lowered* their opinion of their coworkers while 23% said it *improved* their opinion of them (Olmstead et al., 2016). These numbers were distinctly lower for those in the oldest age group of American working adults (50-64 years)—perhaps because they spent less time on social networking sites or perhaps because they did not give it as much credence as their younger counterparts. In this older age group, 9% said it lowered their opinion of their colleagues as opposed to the 6% who said it improved their opinion. Nonetheless, 51% of the employees that used social media in their everyday work felt that it allowed them to see far too much of their coworkers (Olmstead et al., 2016). Taking this research into consideration, it is evident that professional relationships mediated through social networking sites or social media require more attention than they have been afforded thus far in public relations scholarship.

Conversing

Certainly, the internet, social media, and the diversification of social networking sites have changed how public relations practitioners (PRPs) communicate with their publics, how they gather information, craft, and distribute their messages, and perceive the value of their work.

Coombs and Holladay (2015) believed that the growth of social media has bolstered the use of and interest in relationships in public relations; it has reinforced the notion in public relations scholarship *that organizations are in conversations with their publics*. The idea that PRPs are in conversations with groups of people, however, is not limited to scholarship alone; it has also taken hold in practice. Rob Brown, managing partner of Rule 5, a public relations agency in the United Kingdom that works with social media wrote:

> [...] public relations practitioners are uniquely placed to take advantage of a world where conversation and dialogue have largely supplanted top-down, one-way messaging. Our skills are firmly rooted in debate, discussion and the art of persuasion.
>
> (Brown, 2013, p. 7)

This belief that PRPs *converse* with publics has the consequence that public relations scholarship has become more strongly associated with interpersonal relationships (Coombs & Holladay, 2015) even though, as we will see in Chapter 7, likening organization-public relationships to interpersonal relationships is fraught with difficulties.

In a warning to public relations scholarship's optimistic embracement of social media and its potential to "nourish" relationships, Valentini (2015) proposed that social media does not always present opportunities. At times, it can even be risky to use. The trouble, she said, lies in *how* practitioners use social media and the *purpose* for its use, as well as scholarship's inability to *reconcile the rhetorical with the relational*. Indeed, as we discussed in Chapter 2, many public relations activities in building relationships are rhetorical and persuasive in nature such as seeking compliance or affinity; suggesting that they are not, would be akin to suggesting that relationships are predictable, linear, and simplistic.

The risks of social media use are also recognized in the marketing literature. Malthouse, Haenlein, Skiera, Wege, and Zhang (2013), for example, wrote that social media connects and empowers customers, challenging the traditional notion of customer relationship management. It also enables customers to move beyond the standard passive relationship with an organization, to one where they can exchange information with other customers and compare services or products with those offered by competitor organizations, ultimately empowering them (Labrecque, Esche, Mathwick, Novak, & Hofacker, 2013). This networked environment of more active users makes it harder for companies to manage the information that customers receive about a service or product, and at the same time, it allows customers to "talk back" to the company, ask questions and even challenge claims (Schultz, Malthouse, & Pick, 2012).

All Relationships are Mediated

This chapter is about *mediated relationships*, and since it is not a term that is commonly used in public relations scholarship, it is important to elucidate what we mean by "mediated relationships."

The concept "mediated," as we use it, can be seen much like the term as it is used in "mediated communication." That is, it can have various meanings ranging from interpersonal communication mediated through a medium such as a telephone or a computer to mass communication mediated through channels such as television, radio, and newspapers (see Chandler & Munday, 2016). Adler, Rosenfeld, and Proctor (2007), for instance, argued that communication mediated through computers can increase the *amount* and *quality* of interpersonal communication. For example, much computer-mediated communication is asynchronous allowing the receiver time to consider a response and the space to reply at his or her convenience. If immediacy is required, there are tools that allow interaction in real time for example through "chat" applications, while users who wish to do so, can quickly and easily share information in multimedia forms, adding to the potential richness of any communication. The same could be argued about relationships mediated through social media technologies: the always-on quality of social media increases the perceived proximity (in time and space) of users, potentially enhancing their familiarity with and knowledge of each other, and thereby enhancing ambient awareness. The "pervasive and ubiquitous nature of our contemporary media ecosystem" results, Beckett and Deuze (2016) wrote, in people's everyday lives being "lived *in,* rather than *with* media" (p. 1, emphasis added).

"Mediated" can also be seen as a form of interpersonal communication taking place (being mediated) through a third (and not necessarily human) party, or it can—more radically—refer to the idea of "the *mediatedness* of all human communication" (Chandler & Munday, 2016, emphasis added), inferring that all forms of language (verbal and nonverbal) act as mediators for communication.

This idea of mediatedness is not unlike Scollon's (1998, 2001) argument—drawing on Wertsch, 1991—that all discourse (written or spoken communication) is mediated, and while we do not equate a mediated relationship to mediated discourse, there are elements that are of value in understanding our notion of mediated relationships. For example, we argue that *all relationships are mediated*, and, in the 21st-century, *all relationships are, to a certain degree, mediated through technology*. This is particularly marked in public relations practice, where practitioners use a variety of communication modes, tools, and sites to communicate with colleagues, clients, journalists, and publics.

This, of course, holds implications for how we practice public relations because, as Carr (2010) pointed out, the more we use computers or internet-based technology as a medium, "the more we mold ourselves to its form and function" (p. 209). Technology is designed for a specific purpose and in a specific way, which will extend possibilities (such as gaining access to information and being in touch with people geographically dispersed), but also imposes limitations through its form and function. Citing McLuhan, Carr (2010) said, "Whenever we use a tool to exert greater control over the outside world, we change our relationship with that world" (p. 212). For example, by using platforms such as LinkedIn, we change our relationships with the world around us, including our clients, publics, and colleagues, by amplifying certain aspects of ourselves (e.g., our work experience) and connections while diminishing other aspects (e.g., family lives and hobbies). More troubling for our discussion on relationships and relationship building, "the most intimate and personal human activities can be turned into ritualistic behavior" (Carr, 2010, p. 218), such as clicking "like" to acknowledge a "friend's" Facebook post in an acknowledgement that it has been "seen" *without actually liking it.*

Rethinking Social Media

In explaining the idea of mediated discourse analysis, Scollon (1998; 2001) identified five concepts that are central: (1) the mediated action,

(2) the site of enactment, (3) the mediational means, (4) the social practice and (5) the nexus of that practice. We can use these insights to explain our understanding of mediated relationships.

First, mediated actions are focused on the social actors *as they are acting*. These actions are, therefore, inherently social, and inseparable from the people and the objects that are used to act. It is consequently unproductive, Scollon (2001) proposed, to work with "abstract representations" (p. 3) of social actions, and we could argue, that in the same way, it would be unproductive to study relationships—as Broom, Casey, and Ritchey (1997) suggested—as independent constructs (see Chapter 7) since *relationships are tied uniquely to those who enact those relationships*, regardless of the medium used.

Second, Scollon's (2001) site of enactment represents the *social space* in which this mediated action takes place. He highlights that these sites are created by the mediated (and social) actions that occur real-time; these actions are irreversible and unfinalizable. They are points in history. In other words, if we were to see social media or "the internet" as a site of enactment, then this site is *created through the actions of those who interact in these spaces*. Equally, a site of enactment can be a face-to-face meeting, an email, a tweet, or a telephone call. What is important is that the actions that create these sites are never completed nor are they reversible, meaning that an act, once done, cannot be undone. (As many organizations have learned when attempting to delete their social media posts—see Ott & Theunissen, 2014). It is also impossible to engage once-off and "hope for the best"—an important point if we were to see these sites of enactment as places where relationships are built or maintained through, for example, dialogue. Therefore, for public relations practice, we must acknowledge the existence of *sites of relational enactment*.

Third, mediational means can comprise external objects and internal psychological constructs; they are the tools which people use to carry out mediated action. Scollon (1998; 2001) discussed mediational means as being the *material* and *cultural objects* that include the participants' movements such as gestures or utterances. These mediational means, we argue, are used to *enact the relationship and express the state of the relationship in practice*, and can vary from nonverbal communication in face-to-face situations to internet-based applications, such as WhatsApp, Snapchat or Messenger.

Fourth, for a mediated action to take place, we need to consider the juncture between practice, social structure, and the mediational means. This intersection, Scollon (2001) argued, creates various social groups, histories, and identities. To understand *relationships* in public relations, therefore, we need to consider the context or social structure. By definition, this results in *every relationship being unique*, which holds implications for public relations practice and scholarship, reaffirming the complexity of relationship formation and maintenance. Too often, public relations scholarship assumes that relationships are linear and predictive, which disregards their inherent complexity and uncertainty (Willis, 2015). Arguing that each relationship is unique will, by implication, complicate attempts to manage and measure these relationships, and will require a higher order of skill set than is currently acknowledged in public relations practice and education. In other words, practitioners need to find ways to measure abstract concepts and communicate the value of these, rather than counting the number of responses on a Facebook page or the number of Twitter followers as representative of a "relationship."

Last, all practices are linked, thereby creating a nexus of practice. Using the example of "having a coffee," Scollon (2001) explained that the pricing practices, ordering practices (standing in queue, asking for a "coffee with milk" as opposed to "flat white," etc.), drinking practices (sitting at a table or having a take-away cup), and physical spacing practices (tables, chairs, etc.) are linked and cannot be discussed in isolation. Using Scollon's example of the nexus of practice, we argue that a *nexus of relationship practice* exists in public relations practice, where roles, rules, people, place, and content establish and result from an interaction. Over time, these interactions establish a pattern or history that is unique to, in this case, an occupation, an industry, or a society.

A Relationship is Co-Constructed

While all relationships are mediated in some or other form, in contemporary society, all relationships are mediated to some degree through technology. Public relations practice, therefore, cannot exist without technologically mediated relationships. If we assume that currently, this meditation takes place increasingly through what we colloquially call "social media," then we must refrain from seeing social media and the use of social networking sites as merely extra tools in the PRP's arsenal. Rather, these are sites of relational enactment, and each site is created through the actions of those that interact in the space. The implication of this perspective is that PRPs do not carry sole responsibility for the relationships that are created on and enacted through social media, these are co-constructed relationships. Hence, PRPs share the responsibility with their clients, publics, organizations, and journalists. And these actions are not one-off, but are ongoing, reflecting that *a relationship is a process and not a product*. It is an idea that builds on Jenkins' (2006) argument that media convergence caused a paradigm shift from medium-specific content towards content disseminated and accessed on multiple channels, which resulted in a more participatory and collaborative environment and, "ever more complex relations between top-down corporate media and bottom-up participatory culture" (p. 243). It also builds on

Kent's (2013) call for a shift in thinking, and that "social media should be reenvisioned as interpersonal and group communication tools, and not a replacement for a weakened mass media" (p. 341).

Relationships are tied uniquely to those that enact the relationships, and thus, "relationships" cannot be studied or measured as "independent constructs" that are separate from their interlocutors; they cannot be reduced to simple predictive formulae where specific actions will lead to desired reactions or results. As Willis (2015) stated, the ability of scholars and practitioners alike to *predict* the progression of a relationship is far from perfect.

Facebook messages, emails, websites, and so forth, are mediational means that allow us to enact the relationship and express the state, specifically the character and health, of the relationship in practice. This holds implications for practitioners who engage in social media surveillance or environmental scanning: understanding the context and content of the messages allow for a more accurate assessment of the circumstances and current state of the relationship. As we discussed in Chapter 2, all interpersonal communication has a relational and content dimension, and message formulation involves, therefore, more than merely sharing information. It shares information about the state of the relationship. Persuasive messages, for example, are more likely to happen at the early stages of the relationship when trust is relatively low because dialogue requires higher levels of trust to take place (Theunissen, 2015). Therefore, while social media or the internet was hailed in its early stages for its dialogic potential (Kent & Taylor, 1998; 2002), this potential may not be fully achieved because of low levels of trust and the presence of *distance*.

Distance and Proximity

Social media and technology-mediated communication have a significant impact on relationships. In 2007 Adler et al. argued that computer-mediated communication (CMC) can increase the amount and quality of interpersonal communication because of its asynchronous nature. But characteristics such as synchronicity can also reduce distance and increase *proximity*, which, as we have seen in Chapter 2, is required to make relationships work—we need to be in each other's *presence* in order to interact. Proximity, however, can come in various forms, ranging from social to physical proximity.

Kolbe (2013) discussed *distance* as the opposite of proximity, which he proposed, involves more than how far or how near we are physically to those around us. Indeed, technology has significantly changed the perception of nearness, he argued. Distance is a "dynamic, multidimensional condition of perceived remoteness or isolation" (Kolbe, 2013, p. 178), which *can* include geographical separation, but also technical issues relating to technology, delays or barriers such as speed, cost or physical disconnects, connective absences, spatial, and temporal distance, and other connective gaps that may result from inter-group differences or cultural and philosophical differences. Essentially, the experience of distance is multidimensional, based on our *objective experience* of the physical world and our *subjective perceptions* of this world combined with *idiosyncratic factors*, or those factors that are unique to us, such as our psychological condition (Kolbe, 2013). Kolbe referred to this technology-aided distance as *connective distance*: we are connected, yet distant. At any point in time and with the touch of a button, we can contact a person within our network, regardless of how far they are physically from us. Consequently, time and space become compressed and, combined with the ability to communicate synchro-nously, result in the *network effect* (Kolbe, 2013). Smartphones, instant messaging, and Skype are typical examples of the phenomenon. This idea is related to the concept of *telepresence*, which has been used to explore issues of shared space or presence in a remote environment (Draper, Kaber & Usher, 1998), for example using teleconferencing (Hiltz, Johnson & Turoff, 1986; Mühlbach, Böcker, & Prussog, 1995).

However, being connected is no longer the challenge; being *discon-nected* is (Kolbe, 2013), a sentiment echoed by Carr (2010) who pointed out that ubiquitous technology—while having numerous advantages—is causing us to become distracted. He lamented, "the more distracted we become, the less able we are to experience the subtlest, most distinc-tively human forms of empathy, compassion, and other emotions" (Carr, 2010, p. 221).

Empathy, compassion, and other human emotions are integral to forming and maintaining relationships. Recently, displaying empathy has been acknowledged for its potential in aiding an organization's goals (see Yeomans, 2016). But, it requires reflection (Hargie, 2017), and being continuously connected (through technology) prevents us from having time to reflect (Carr, 2010). If our experiences are "numbed" by tech nologies, then, perhaps technologies do not always mediate relationships in a positive way, and we should heed Valentini's (2015, p. 175) warning that "There is a lack of critical reflection on the implication of this [so-cial media use] for the public relations profession, for the organizations that public relations professionals often represent, and for publics."

In a world where it's easy to connect with others, *attention* is now what we demand most from others (Kolbe, 2013), both giving and de-manding it. It has become a scarce resource. Attention is what signals to others that we have an interest in them, want to hear what they have to say, and learn more about them. Attention is fundamental to relation-ship building (Kolbe, 2013), and *paying attention* to the other person essentially increases one's *appeal* or attractiveness by showing care, as discussed in Chapter 2.

But we have become subject to so much information that information overload has become a concern for the maintenance of relationships. Which information is important and what do we need to pay attention to?

Contemporary internet technology has provided us with the tools to discover information, filter relevant material and distribute information to ensure that "we are forever inundated by information *of immediate interest to us*" (Carr, 2010, p. 170, emphasis added). What was meant to make us more productive has resulted in us being persistently (physically) connected, yet remaining (psychologically) distant. And, because we have little time for reflection or paying attention—key factors in building and maintaining relationships—we rely on automated filters and algorithms, which consequently influence our thinking and shape the way we see the world. These algorithms "grant their privilege instantaneously to the new and popular" (Carr, 2010, p. 171), i.e., that which is "trending." By implication, these algorithms tell us what and who we should pay attention to, and what we need to do to have others pay attention to us, that is, manage the impression we make on others.

However, gaining attention is one thing, gaining *appropriate* attention is another. Hence, having a clear understanding of how internet technology shapes how we perceive the world, and how it functions, enables the practitioner to approach it more critically, and assess its value, as a medium for relationship development and maintenance.

When Phil Vine left his reporter's job in television to join the interest group, Greenpeace, what worried him was the loss of the audience that television news guaranteed him. This concern was soon allayed, as within a week of joining Greenpeace they got news, and exclusive pictures, of the world's largest seismic survey vessel working off the New Zealand coast. Rather than hand the pictures over to the mainstream media, Phil edited them into a one-minute, 20-second news story and put it on the group's Facebook site. It received more than 2 million views. He said, "I was bowled over. I mean, you wouldn't even hope to get that [number of viewers] on TV3 or TVNZ."

He explained that Facebook, aided and abetted by Twitter and Instagram, has been essential to how Greenpeace has maintained its relevance and its effectiveness when campaigning. Social media, he said, allow the organization to connect disparate groups of people and organize them. For example, the seismic survey story triggered a public debate on the effect of seismic testing on whales and dolphins.

> Facebook and the green movement in NZ is pretty strong. It's grown up with Facebook. We're quite an old organization now—30 years old. So Facebook is the thing that's grown up with us, I suppose.
>
> (Personal Communication, 2017)

Mediated Impression Management

In Chapter 2, we discussed the process of managing impressions in inter-personal, face-to-face settings with participants, and we highlighted its importance for developing personal influence. Because social network-ing sites are sites of relational enactment that differ from face-to-face interactions, any attempt to manage one's image on these sites will take a different shape. For example, managing impressions through social me-dia usually involves controlling information, photos, videos, and other (mediated) material (Paliszkiewicz & Mądra-Sawicka, 2016), such as tweets, Facebook posts, and LinkedIn profiles. In their study of impres-sion management through LinkedIn, Paliszkiewicz and Mądra-Sawicka (2016) pointed out that the presence of a photograph of the user (a visual image) makes that person appear more appealing. Equally, they argued, spelling and grammar mistakes in an online profile can be more det-rimental than errors in a paper version of a Curriculum Vitae, simply because the online site's visibility quickly gives a negative impression to recruiters visiting the profile.

Essentially, the *impression management model* comprises two key players: the person who engages in the impression management behav-iors (the *"actor"*) and the people who interact with the person in that setting (the *"audience"*) (Paliszkiewicz & Mądra-Sawicka, 2016). This idea goes back to Goffman's (1959) concept of impression management. Goffman wrote that people who come into the presence of others are like actors on a stage. How they express themselves, that is, how they use their performances to communicate their personal characteristics, as well as their motivations and objectives, will determine what impression others have of them. Goffman wrote that the audience attends to all ver-bal and non-verbal actions to form an impression of another. Hence for a performance to be successful, an actor must control the setting, their script and such, as the roles they prepare will be subjected to scrutiny by the audience for believability and authenticity. Goffman's framework is useful here. Although we are talking about mediated communication and relationships, his ideas still apply. The stage could be a face-to-face meeting with a client or a colleague; equally, it could be a web page or a social networking site such as Twitter or Snapchat. In each of these settings the impression created by the PRP, including how well they nav-igate the setting, the images and words they use (grammar, spelling, fluency) will be subject to scrutiny by the intended audience and create a perception in the minds of the audiences. "Actors look good when they display traits and behaviors compatible with social values and expecta-tions" (Mohamed & Gardner, 2004, p. 132).

Citing Mohamed, Gardner, and Paolillo (1999), Paliszkiewicz and Mądra-Sawicka (2016) highlighted typical tactics used by organizations (if we assume them to be entities similar to individuals) to manage their image ranging from direct tactics to defensive tactics. *Direct tactics*, which involve presenting information about skills, abilities, and accomplishments, can be seen on social networking sites such as LinkedIn, where members present their qualifications and work experience. *Indirect tactics*, which involve managing information about people and events with which one is associated, would include vetting one's contacts, images or "tags" online. *Assertive tactics* surface when people or organizations see opportunities to boost their image, such as tweeting about an issue that they know will place them in a certain light. *Defensive tactics* are tactics that involve minimizing or repairing damage such as deleting an offensive comment or insensitive post or posting an apology or explanation (see Smith and Sissons, 2016, for a discussion of the defensive tactics used by a news organization following an online and front-page, hard-copy error).

When we join a community, we must select and present the "appropriate pieces of information" (Paliszkiewicz & Mądra-Sawicka, 2016, p. 204) to project an image consistent with that community so that we can achieve acceptance and will be seen as credible (Goffman, 1959). LinkedIn—like other social networking sites—provides a pre-set structure and communicative affordances to help us to manage our impressions (Paliszkiewicz & Mądra-Sawicka, 2016) thereby confirming Carr's (2010) assertion that technology affects how we communicate, think about, and interact with others. Populating it with the required information, such as a photograph, limiting recommendations to trustworthy people (because we are judged by the "company we keep"), adding credible people to our network, and joining relevant groups, provide an avenue to manage our online image (Paliszkiewicz & Mądra-Sawicka, 2016). These structures and tools are akin to what Carr (2010) referred to as "a script in the form of an algorithm that someone else has created for us," and although they are helpful, they do "mechanize the messy processes of intellectual exploration and even social attachment" (p. 218). Managing the image we project and judging others' approachability, authenticity or presence, is thereby scripted for us; our relationships are mediated and shaped through technology.

When discussing LinkedIn as a site for impression management, Paliszkiewicz and Mądra-Sawicka (2016) stated that we make judgments about users' trustworthiness and credibility, as well as their social and professional attractiveness, through what we see on this and other social networking sites. They said that, "Images help to increase social presence in electronic communications" (p. 207), but added the caveat that in professions like public relations, the *number of connections* is equally important as it shows that the PRP has the ability to develop and maintain a network of personal influence, thereby echoing Valentini's (2010) call for the recognition of network development as expert knowledge in public relations.

Ambient Awareness

Connecting online through social media, socially and professionally, results in a phenomenon referred to as "ambient awareness." Simply put, ambient awareness can be described as "The awareness of the world gained by accessing social media" (Ince, 2016). More specifically, it refers to the *peripheral social awareness* that is generated through social media posts, updates, and browsing. For example, when we add people to our LinkedIn network, follow them on Twitter, or add them to our Facebook "friend" list, we recognize their *social presence* in that space, thereby reducing "distance."

This social presence has a quality of "being there," allowing us to create an awareness of each other through social media and make "person-judgments" about the other while we browse (Levordashka & Utz, 2016, p. 148). Making these judgements is important for relationship-building, as it may provide us with cues that the other person is approachable and a potential source of information (Levordashka & Utz, 2016), which, in public relations practice, allows the PRP to expand her *personal influence* (as discussed in Chapter 2) and increases the likelihood that she can fulfill key aspects of her role. Mikela Dennison, Marketing Manager at Te Pa Wines, described enactment through social media as an opportunity to gain insight into the work and views of, for example, journalists:

> Social media provides a window into the people behind the press, and creates an invaluable opportunity to connect with media professionals, their views, and interestingly, also enhances their own [PRP's] reach by following or engaging with emerging journalists on Twitter and reaching out to them via tweets or direct messages to arrange a coffee or pitch a story, as well as checking out the more personal and nuanced comments that seasoned journos will often add when sharing an article (theirs, or others).
>
> (Personal Communication, 2017)

Dennison's comments highlight the relationship potential that ambient awareness through social networking sites can bring. Indeed, Leonardi (2015) linked ambient awareness specifically to communication and being exposed to messages shared among people. He believed it to be "the awareness that an individual has about the communications occurring among those around them" (p. 758) and is a direct result of technology being configured to "push" messages to users' newsfeeds. In Leonardi's view, ambient knowledge leads to metaknowledge in the workplace or knowledge about "who knows who" and "who knows what" that is obtained while observing other people's communication. He linked this to the emerging *theory of communication visibility*, which he identified as still needing to be empirically tested.

Levordashka and Utz's (2016) study of Twitter users indicated that the most common reported awareness involved personality, humor, hobbies, and career. The latter two, they pointed out, disclose what members of a network are interested in and knowledgeable about. Such an awareness allows users "to develop a cognitive map of who knows what" in their social media network (Levordashka & Utz, 2016, p. 154), and is, therefore, an extension of peer-to-peer networks as highlighted by Sias (2009) (see Chapter 4). This knowledge, however, takes time to develop (Leonardi, 2015).

In face-to-face situations, there is a *physical presence* that allows participants to pick up verbal and other cues from each other, and to develop an awareness of, for example, the other's emotional state (Levordashka & Utz, 2016). As mentioned, these same cues also allow us to detect deception, but on social networking sites, such physical cues are missing and we must rely on the participants' social presence to draw conclusions about their approachability and potential as an information source. In this situation, ambient awareness acts "as a basis for first impressions and results in a sense of familiarity, both of which can make a target appear more approachable" (Levordashka & Utz, 2016, p. 153). There is a caveat built into this: we must remain vigilant that interactions through social networking sites are subject to *impression management*. Thus, users attempt to manage the impression they create, and sometimes misrepresent themselves, which can result in deception. This deception is aided by, among other things, our inherent *truth bias* (as discussed in Chapter 2).

In their study of Twitter users' ambient awareness, Levordashka and Utz (2016) identified a positive correlation between the frequency of media use and ambient awareness. They postulated that the finding supported the *electronic propinquity theory*, which proposes that users who are familiar with a specific medium will gain more benefit from its use. To apply this to public relations practice, practitioners who are frequent users of social networking sites are more likely to understand its cues and the rules that govern it, and will thus be in a more strategic position to use it as a site of relational enactment and relationship building. They will also be in a better position to create personal (and organizational) ambient awareness through social media. As Levordashka and Utz (2016, p. 154) stated, "Awareness of who knows what offers a potential solution to the problem of locating valuable information without needing to post public or widely shared requests." Implicit in their statement is, however, an aspect that is often ignored. While the size of the PRP's online network provides an indication of her ability to build networks and connect with others, this is not the whole picture. Schoenmaker (2016) pointed out that *connecting* is not the same as *relating*, and therefore is only a precursor to relationship building and maintenance. For example, a PRP may know many people but as we suggested in Chapter 2, the *strength* of that connection is also of importance.

Ambient awareness provides an alternative understanding of social media's impact on relationship-building. Too often, discussion among public relations scholars laments the lack of "using social media to its full potential" as a dialogic or relationship-building medium. Waters and Jamal (2011), for example, expressed their disappointment that Twitter is not used as "symmetrical communication," but rather as a medium to share information and convey one-way messages. They acknowledged that it demonstrates the *willingness* to share information, but argued that it falls short of attempting any form of *conversation*. Perhaps then, it is not that social media and social networking sites are not living up to their potential, but rather that we are imposing a dated framework on paradigmatically different sites of relational enactment.

Deception, Self-Disclosure and the Myth of Privacy

In Chapter 2, we discussed self-disclosure and deception in interpersonal relationships. In mediated relationships, these aspects take on a slightly different form. Deception is, by its very nature, more commonly and easily executed in an online environment where images and text can be manipulated and massaged, and the skills for detecting deception are still lacking (Sissons & Varoli Piazza, 2016). In 2007, Adler et al. specified that about 27% of survey respondents had engaged in deceptive behaviors while online. A surprising number of people, for example, had presented themselves as members of the opposite sex. Adler et al. pointed out that personal web pages—like other forms of communication— provide opportunities for these creators to construct and manage their online identities by deciding what to include or exclude from their web pages. Very importantly, they added, "people are more likely to prefer mediated channels when their own self-presentation is threatened" (Adler et al., 2007, p. 77).

Ho, Hancock, Booth, and Liu (2016) reiterated that in (computer-mediated) deception, "the availability and influence of physical cues is re duced when compared with face-to-face (F2F) communication," adding that the only available cues are the person's "written words" (p. 395). This lack of cues, we argue, not only contributes to the problems users have in detecting deception, but also to the *illusion of privacy and anonymity* that permeates social media use. Because we can interact in a way where (we believe) no-one can see us or know what we do, there is a prevailing illusion that what we do online is private, even anonymous. While it may be true for some who use anonymizing sites or tools, for the average person it is not; everything can potentially be mined for data and turned into information (Carr, 2010). In fact, few people have any idea of the level of knowledge other people or organizations have about them and what this means for their privacy. Acquisti, Brandimarte, and Loewenstein (2015) cited a survey in which 62% of respondents were shown to mistakenly believe that if a website posted a privacy policy this meant the organization could not share their personal information without permission. In other words, a privacy policy that few ever read, creates the *illusion* that users are protected.

Former Wall Street Journal reporter Julia Angwin set out to investigate how much Google really knew about her and learned, to her discomfort, that they could provide her with all of her searches since 2006—a total of 26,000 searches a month. Such a mass of data provides an accurate picture of our online behavior, especially when married with information already available through our other social media accounts such as Facebook and Twitter (Angwin, 2014).

Problematizing the issue of *self-disclosure* and computer-mediated interviews, Lucas, Gratch, King, and Morency (2014) highlighted research that shows that computer-mediated interviews are perceived to be more *anonymous* than face-to-face interviews. They found when participants interacted with a virtual human (VH), which can mimic social behaviors designed to elicit feelings of rapport, such as *listening* (a key attribute of dialogue—see de Bussy, 2010) and human gestures, participants disclose more of themselves. They posited that the use of VHs enables us to gain crucial and beneficial (in this case health) information from participants.

In the online environment, however, the illusion of privacy and anonymity may have a significant impact on relationship formation and maintenance. For example, anonymity (especially on social networking sites) is known to increase self-disclosure, which can be rewarding to individuals (leading to social validation, releasing of stress, and gaining support), but it can also be inherently risky, increasing vulnerability, loss of privacy and negatively affecting reputation (Ma, Hancock, & Naaman, 2016). Further, anonymity makes it difficult to build communities or develop relationships. Kang, Brown, and Keisler (2013) wrote that building trust or getting credit for one's contribution to a group was hindered by anonymity. Despite this, they found more than half of their interviewees remained anonymous or used fictitious profiles on social networking sites, even when posting original artwork, photos or written work, as they wanted to avoid any links to their offline life. Their reasons for wishing to avoid links to "real" life ranged from not wanting to be seen asking for help in a support group to not wishing to be associated with a fan fiction site. Kang et al. (2013) found people preferred anonymity when engaging in activities that would make them seem socially undesirable or needy. Therefore, anonymity could be said to help certain groups of people access support in ways they would not feel able to on non-anonymous platforms, where they believed they would violate self-presentation goals (Ma et al., 2016).

In other ways, privacy (rather than anonymity) is important to people when connecting with others. For example, the monitoring of a romantic partner through social media has been found to have a negative effect on a relationship (Elphinston & Noller, 2011) and yet checking up on a partner was the second most commonly reported act on Facebook (Tokunaga, 2011).

Overall, what is observed is referred to as the *personalization-privacy paradox*, which is increasingly seen in situations where personal information is collected and used through mobile devices.

> The one-on-one direct relationship established between a smartphone and its user enables identification, differentiation, and interaction with individual consumers and offers an opportunity to provide personalized information without time or location constraints.
>
> (Lee & Rha, 2016, p. 454)

Lee and Rha studied the use of location-based mobile commerce and the factors affecting consumers' psychological and behavioral reactions to the personalization-privacy paradox. They found that people's attitudes depended on the amount of involvement they had with the technology, their level of trust towards the technology/company along with how confident a person was in their ability to protect their personal privacy and their readiness to use technology.

True and Trusted: The Use of Email

In 1997, Berko et al. mused about the role of email in beginning and maintaining relationships, pointing out that this—which is now taken for granted—had become yet another means to meet our fellow human beings. Today, despite the growth of social networking sites and instant messaging, email remains the most popular form of communication in the business world. To sign up to anything online (including social networking sites, instant messaging, and internet shopping) one must have a valid email account (The Radicati Group, 2016). According to The Radicati Group, which tracks the use of email, instant messaging, mobile instant messaging, social networking, and mobile email worldwide, in 2014 business users sent and received on average 121 emails a day. The company predicted that this would grow to 140 emails a day by 2018; the sheer number reflecting Carr's (2010) observations that we are never disconnected.

Conventional (perhaps outdated) thinking proposes that computer-mediated communication (CMC) limits the potential for relationship-building and identity management because media, such as instant messaging and email, appear to lack the "richness" of other channels, such as face-to-face communication (Adler et al., 2007). But this perceived lack of richness can also be an advantage, as Adler et al. (2007) pointed out. Emailers and instant messengers can choose the desired level of clarity, seriousness, humor, logic, or emotion, and one can say difficult things without forcing the receiver to respond immediately, which permits the receiver to ignore the message rather than give an unpleasant response. This can, of course, be very useful in public relations where remaining silent can allow for more *control* over the message and the image. Equally, it affects the rules that govern mediated relationships.

In our research, we found the email medium being used much in the ways described in this chapter. Several PRPs told the researchers that choosing to interact via email rather than by phone, for example, with members of the media helped them to keep control of the messaging and hence manage an organization's image more easily. Emails allowed for a considered response to questions or criticisms, as time could elapse between receiving an email and responding, unlike in synchronous communications, such as telephone calls and face-to-face meetings. Thus, it enables the enactment of distance while remaining connected and is, therefore, a valuable tool for relationship management. It is this *distancing*, we would argue, that enables control over the relationship.

Further, an email response could potentially address only the issues the PRP wishes, in the clarity and depth deemed appropriate, and unlike with a phone or face-to-face conversations an immediate challenge or follow-up question is not possible (see Sissons, 2015 for a discussion of a PRP-journalist email exchange). Email communication also creates a precise record of what is said by both sides, limiting opportunities for quotes to be inaccurately reported or taken out of context, which PRPs interviewed for this research said was reassuring.

However, critics point to email communication allowing for behavior by PRPs that could be interpreted as deliberate obfuscation and/or delay in communications with interested publics. In our research, such an interpretation was made by a journalist about communications over email following an information request to a local authority and eventually resulted in the journalist complaining to the Ombudsman[1] about what he believed was a deliberate delay.

Radio reporter, Matt, a specialist local government reporter, had requested information under New Zealand's Local Government Official Information and Meetings Act 1987 (LGOIMA) through his regular local authority contact and media relations officer, Stuart. He had already been in contact with Stuart, first by phone and then email, about a report being prepared by the authority of its handling of a major sporting event that ran over six weeks earlier that year. The council had faced serious criticism over its mishandling of crowds at the opening night celebrations, and Matt was trying to discover what decisions had been made by elected representatives and officials in the build-up to the event, and whether they now accepted mistakes were made.

He asked Stuart by email "to set the clock ticking" straight away, as under the Act requests must be answered within 20 working days. He also included in the email that he believed the information he required might be found in "reports to and minutes from the [name of]."

Twenty days later, Stuart and the authority had still not responded to the request, and so Matt complained to the Ombudsman. As a result, two weeks later the authority responded to Matt advising him that it was "refusing your request under section 17(d) of the Local Government Official Information and Meetings Act (LGOIMA) (Government, 2015) as the information requested will soon be publicly available."

By "publicly available," the authority claimed, "a comprehensive and independent post-event review will cover most, if not all, of the information you have requested." By "soon" they meant approximately six weeks from the correspondence, as the report was expected to be completed "by the middle of December."

When Matt approached the authority on December 8 to follow up on the progress of the report, he was advised that it would now not be released until December 22, which was one working day prior to the Christmas shutdown. Again, he complained to the Ombudsman that this was unacceptable, as it would be more than three months after the initial request and would allow "almost no follow-up reporting of what was a significant event." He claimed the authority must have the information he required, but was deliberately and unjustifiably withholding it:

> In my view [name of city] Council should be required ASAP to release the requested information, which has presumably been collated to form part of the report which remains a work in progress.

A Relationship Strained

Following the Ombudsman's intervention, the authority agreed to release the information. However, on receiving the material on December 15, Matt found vital sections were missing. He emailed the council the same day with a message contained entirely in the subject line:

> Subject: Oops, sorry, in each case, THE WHOLE OF PROGRAM PERFORMANCE REPORT appears to be missing, ta Matt.

Matt's email was forwarded at 4:01 pm to an in-house lawyer at the authority. Just over an hour later, at 5:12 pm, he received a response from the manager of that department.

> Dear Matt,
> I am looking into this. It appears that some information may have been withheld for reasons of commercial sensitivity.
> I will get back to you tomorrow by when I expect that I have finished my enquiries. I will also confirm the position to the Office of the Ombudsmen [sic].
> Best wishes,
> Pamela

Matt responded to this email at 5:52 pm,

> Hi Pamela,
> OK thanks. A partial deletion where there are grounds, is of course appropriate. It does seem that the entire reports are missing for each of the monthly meetings.
>   Look forward to hearing the outcome tomorrow.
>
> Ta
Matt

Pamela responded the following day (December 16):

> Dear Matt,
> The deletion in the document dated June 22 was made on the basis that it would unreasonably impact upon the commercial position of a person who supplied or is the subject of the information. The Whole of Program Performance Reports was withheld due to the need to maintain the effective conduct of public affairs through the free and frank expression of opinions and/or on the basis of commercial sensitivity.
>   The reasons for withholding the information should have been contained in my letter to you of December 14 and I apologize that this did not happen.
>   I will be sending the complete documents to the Office of the Ombudsmen [sic] as they still hold an open file in relation to your original complaint. The Ombudsmen [sic] has already been sent a copy of the material that we disclosed to you. If you are dissatisfied with the grounds upon which the information was withheld, please direct your complaint to the Office of the Ombudsmen [sic].
>
> Regards,
Pamela

If we look at this email interaction in more detail, we see how a site of relational enactment, such as an email thread, can be used by the parties for their communication or relational aims. As already mentioned, in the first email Matt uses the *subject line for his entire message.*

The reason for this is probably two-fold: the subject line is the first visible part of an email and therefore signals to the recipient the content of the email. This, along with the name of the sender, allows the recipient to decide whether and how quickly to respond (Sappleton & Lourenço, 2015). Matt was keen to receive a response quickly and to ensure that his message stood out among the hundred plus other emails in the recipient's inbox. He may have also wished there to be no opportunity for the recipient to say she did not receive the message or did not have a chance to read the contents.

His use of "Oops sorry," frames this exchange initially as an apology. "Oops" is commonly followed by what is known in *speech act theory* as an illocutionary force indicating device (IFID) associated with apologies, such as "sorry" (Lutzky & Kehoe, 2016). Upon closer inspection, there are several problems with this "apology." First, apologies should have four components to be recognized as apologies: the *offender*, the *offended*, the *offense* and the *remedy* (Deutschmann, 2003). In this case, the offender is the local authority, the offended is Matt, the offense is failing to attach the reports, and the remedy would, presumably, be sending those reports as soon as possible along with an apology for not doing so initially. However, in this interaction, it is the *offended*—and not the offender—who is *apologizing* (Deutschmann, 2003).

Obviously, on occasion an offended person has to point out the offense to the offender if it has not been recognized (Deutschmann, 2003), and this perhaps is the case here, but we would argue there is more going on. Matt's apology could be classed as a "parasitic apology" (Galatolo, Ursi, & Bongelli, 2016), as it is not the main aim of the interaction, rather it is used as a subsidiary activity. In phone conversations, these sorts of apologies usually occur at the start of the call, before the speaker moves on to the main reason for calling, for example, "I am sorry for disturbing you, but I wanted to ask…." We can see something similar happening in this email, but, while Matt's apology appears to conform to a parasitic apology, it also possibly conforms even more to what Deutschmann (2003) refers to as a "face attack apology."

Face attack apologies are made following "breach of consensus" offenses, which include acts, opinions or personal characteristics that the speaker (or emailer in this case) does not like or approve of (Deutschmann, 2003, p.74). The specific offense here could be seen as a "breach of expectation" offense, because following the Ombudsman's order to provide the documents, Matt had expected them to arrive, and they did not thereby breaking the unspoken rules that govern this relationship (as discussed in Chapter 2).

Face attack apologies lack the sincerity of a genuine apology and are either categorized as *challenging* or *sarcastic*. In this case, it is sarcastic. Although sarcasm is usually communicated in tone and we cannot hear Matt's voice, his use of "oops," as if *he* had made a mistake along with the exaggerated stressing of what was missing from the documents suggests this is a sarcastic message. The use of capital letters in the section that specifically refers to the missing documents is used for emphasis and can be equivalent to a person raising their voice or shouting in face-to-face or telephone interactions. Perhaps he also wanted to use the subject line (as is commonly the case) as a way of reflecting his stance (Skogs, 2013), which is displeased. Therefore, Matt's message was framed as an apology, but was, in fact, a reproach and meant to be taken as such. Given the history of the interactional context of the email, it is also likely to be meant as a further complaint.

We could, therefore, argue that at this point in the interaction, the author of the email has decided to abandon the tacit rules of *politeness* (see Chapter 2) and express his frustration. Using capitals becomes a *face threatening act* (FTA), that is, an act that threatens the recipient's "face" or her desire to be appreciated by others (Schnurr, 2013). According to Schnurr (2013) *complaints*, *disagreements*, *disapproval*, and *criticism* are all face-threatening acts—their seriousness calculated on the social distance between the parties, their perceived status distance, and how threatening an act is in a particular culture. Because face threatening acts express negative emotions, which are "approach emotions" (Dillard & Nabi, 2006), they drive the author to approach the source of his frustration: the authority that is denying him access to the needed information. Therefore, while understandable, the action is not meant to build relationships although there is some effort to maintain this relationship.

It was just over an hour later when Matt received a response from the manager of legal services, indicating his email had been referred up to supervisory level. The response appears to have three aims: to communicate to Matt that his email has been received and is *being given attention* (keeping in mind here the earlier discussion that attention is an antecedent for relationship building); as a *disarmer* (Deutschmann, 2003) in anticipation that he will not be given the information, as it may have been withheld for a reason acceptable under the LGOIMA; and that he will hear back from the authority the following day ("tomorrow") as will the Ombudsman.

The email is formally worded, indicating that Pamela is interacting as a "role-filler" (Bean & Johnstone, 1994, p. 60) in her professional role as manager of the authority's legal services. She also uses the first-person singular "I" to take responsibility for actions required in response to the email, thus displaying as the manager "an orientation to [her] specialist identity" (Kangasharju & Nikko, 2009, p. 108), and reaffirming the relationship as a "role relationship" (see Chapter 2).

The first sentence of her response has two important performative verbs: the phrasal verb "look into," which communicates the receiver, Pamela, is acting on the email, and "withhold," which alerts Matt to the possibility (as mentioned) of there being reasons for the deletion.

What is interesting about this email thread is that since Matt complained to the Ombudsman, written communication with him has been passed to the legal team, and so it could reasonably be expected that they are aware of the position being taken by the authority's communications team. Yet, Pamela softens her assertion that the document has been withheld for commercial sensitivity reasons by hedging using the modal verb "may," which indicates doubt as if she does not have all the information.

Matt's reply acknowledges Pamela's assertion that under the Act it is reasonable that some commercially sensitive material be deleted from the record. However, he uses the term "partial deletion." He then reiterates that "entire reports" have been deleted from the material provided of each monthly meeting. Matt is careful not to judge why this might have occurred and uses the modal verb "seem" to indicate that he may be mistaken—perhaps they haven't been withheld but are "missing" for another reason such as human error, thereby softening the earlier face-threatening act.

Matt's informality of language, shown by his use of "Hi Pamela," "OK thanks," and sign off "Ta," contrasts with the formality of Pamela's language. He may have chosen a more informal mode as less face-threatening and he perhaps wished to keep the interaction on a friendly footing thereby preserving their working relationship. It could also reflect that in email discussions, participants often see themselves as being engaged in conversation (Harrison, 2002), and these interactions use many of the rules of conversation making them a hybrid of the oral and written forms of interaction (Harrison, 2002; Yates & Orlikowski, 1993). Matt's use of "Hi" and the first name of his recipient implies familiarity, but it is also appropriate to the more egalitarian and colloquial forms typical of online communication (Harrison, 2002) and New Zealand culture.

Another common email form can be seen in the incomplete first sentence of Matt's email— "OK thanks"—which reads like the reply in a verbal conversation. Yates and Orlikowski (1993) found incomplete sentences are common in email messages that respond to previous messages. At the end of the email, Matt reminds Pamela that he is expecting her to come back with a response, as promised, the next day, before signing off with "Ta Matt."

Pamela responded the afternoon of the following day (December 16). Again, her approach is formal and she gives two legal reasons for the deletions in the material supplied to Matt. It appears that Pamela does not recognize the need to explain further or to use any expressions associated with apology ("regrettably," "unfortunately") to Matt for the continued withholding of the deleted material. She does, however, apologize for not informing him of the authority's reasons in her previous correspondence. This is significant considering that part of Matt's original complaint to the Ombudsman was that the withholding of the information was unexplained. However, if we are to take Pamela's earlier email at face value, then she did not explain as she was unsure of the reasons herself. This is noteworthy as the reasons are legal ones associated with the 1987 Act, and so we have to assume the communications team has not kept the legal team informed of why the material was being withheld. The wording of the sentence containing the apology is interesting as it first accepts that an explanation for withholding the information should have been contained in the letter that accompanied the material. Pamela then uses the conjunction "and" to link this obligation to her apology—"and I apologize that this did not happen."

According to Holmes (1990) keeping another person waiting or causing delay is a legitimate reason for an apology. However, while Pamela accepts responsibility for not informing Matt in a timely manner about the deletions, she does not take responsibility for the deletions themselves. This is further evidence that the decision involved the communications team and its wish to control the message by releasing its report in a media event on December 22. Such an interpretation of the behavior of the communications team is understandable and is not conducive to good relations with interested parties. From this, it is reasonable to deduce that obfuscation and delay in communications is at times considered by PRPs a price worth paying for protecting the reputation of a client.

Conclusion

In this chapter, we noted the increasing popularity of online communications for developing and maintaining relationships. In fact, so pervasive is the technology that it has altered the communicative behavior of users, including that of PRPs. At the same time, users, including PRPs, have adapted the tools to their purposes, as we saw in the examples.

The ubiquity of the technology leads us to argue that while all human relationships are mediated through mediational means or tools such as language and gesture, in the 21st century all relationships are to some extent also mediated through technologies such as mobile phones, internet-based applications, and various social media.

We also argue that the pervasiveness combined with the always-on quality of social media has created an ambient awareness in users of the online behaviors of other users. This ambient awareness has the potential to improve the quality as well as the quantity of relationships because of the perceived proximity in time and space between users that the social media technologies afford.

However, it is clear that the possibilities of social media and social networking sites as sites of relational enactment between PRPs and members of their publics are not yet fully utilized. We found many PRPs are still using social media (and other online communication tools) to try to manage and control their relationships, seeking compliance rather than embracing the potential of more active, and perhaps critical, users.

Note

1 Among other services, the Ombudsman in New Zealand (where this research was conducted), "handles complaints against government agencies" (Ombudsman. Fairness for all, 2017) and fulfills an important role in managing the government's relationship with its constituents.

References

Acquisti, A., Brandimarte, L., & Loewenstein, G. (2015). Privacy and human behavior in the age of information. *Science, 347*(6221), 509–514.

Adler, R. B., Rosenfeld, L. B., & Proctor, R. F. (2007). *Interplay: The process of interpersonal communication* (10th ed.). Oxford: Oxford University Press.

Angwin, J. (2014, February 24). *If you think you're anonymous online, think again.* Retrieved January 10, 2017, from npr all tech considered, www.npr.org/sections/alltechconsidered/2014/02/24/282061990/if-you-think–youre–anonymous–online–think–again.

Bean, J. M., & Johnstone, B. (1994). Workplace reasons for saying you're sorry: Discourse task management and apology in telephone interviews. *Discourse Processes, 17*(1), 59–81. doi:10.1080/01638539409544859.

Beckett, C., & Deuze, M. (2016). On the role of emotion in the future of journalism. *Social Media and Society, 2*(3), 1–6. doi:10.1177/2056305116662395.

Broom, G. M., Casey, S., & Ritchey, J. (1997). Toward a concept and theory of organization–public relationships. *Journal of Public Relations Research, 9*(2), 83–98. doi:10.1207/s1532754xjprr0902_01.

Brown, R. (2013). Digital PR is dead: Social goes mainstream. In R. Brown & S. Waddington (Eds.), *Share this too: More social media solutions for PR professionals* (pp. 3–10). Hoboken, NJ: John Wiley & Sons.

Carr, N. G. (2010). *The shallows: What the internet is doing to our brains.* New York: Norton, W. W. & Company.

Chandler, D., & Munday, R. (2016, April 19). *Mediated communication.* Retrieved December 20, 2016, from Oxford Reference, www.oxfordreference.com.ezproxy.aut.ac.nz/view/10.1093/acref/9780199568758.001.0001/acref-9780199568758-e-1691.

Coombs, W. T., & Holladay, S. J. (2015). Public relations' "Relationship Identity" in research: Enlightenment or illusion. *Public Relations Review, 41*(5), 689–695. doi:10.1016/j.pubrev.2013.12.008.

Crothers, C., Smith, P., Urale, P. W. B., & Bell, A. (2016). *World Internet Project New Zealand. The internet in New Zealand 2015.* Retrieved from http://icdc.aut.ac.nz/__data/assets/pdf_file/0003/635835/WIPNZ-Report-060515.pdf.

de Bussy, N. M. (2010). Dialogue as a basis for stakeholder enactment: defining and measuring the core competencies. In R. L. Heath (Ed.), *The Sage handbook of public relations* (2nd ed., pp. 127–144). Thousand Oaks, CA: Sage Publications.

Deutschmann, M. (2003). *Apologising in British English.* Umeå, Sweden: Umeå University.

Dillard, J., & Nabi, R. (2006). The persuasive influence of emotion in cancer prevention and detection messages. *Journal of Communication, 56*(1), S123–S139.

Draper, J., Kaber, D., & Usher, J. (1998). Telepresence. *Human Factors, 40*(3), 354–375.

Elphinston, R., & Noller, P. (2011). Time to face it! Facebook and the implications for romantic jealousy and relationship satisfaction. *Cyberpsychology, Behavior, and Social Networking, 14*(11), 631–635.

Galatolo, R., Ursi, B., & Bongelli, R. (2015). Parasitic apologies. *Discourse Processes, 53*(1–2), 97–113. doi:10.1080/0163853x.2015.1056694.

Goffman, E. (1959). *The presentation of self in everyday life*. New York: Anchor Books.

Government, N. Z. (2015, September 2). Local Government Official Information and Meetings Act 1987 No 174 (as at 26 March 2015), Public Act 5 Principle of Availability—New Zealand legislation. Retrieved January 23, 2017, from www.legislation.govt.nz/act/public/1987/0174/latest/DLM122285.html#DLM122285.

Greenfield, S. (2003). *Tomorrow's people: How 21st century technology is changing the way we think and feel*. London: Allen Lane/Penguin Books.

Hargie, O. (2017). *Skilled interpersonal communication: Research, theory and practice, 5th edition* (6th ed.). London: Routledge.

Harrison, S. (2002). *The discourse structure of email discussions* (PhD thesis). University of Central England, Birmingham, United Kingdom.

Hiltz, S., Johnson, K., & Turoff, M. (1986). Experiments in group decision making: Communication process and outcome in face–to–face versus computerized conferences. *Human Communication Research, 13*(2), 225–252.

Ho, M., Hancock, J., Booth, C., & Liu X. (2016). Computer–mediated deception: Strategies revealed by language–action cues in spontaneous communication. *Journal of Management Information Systems, 33*(2), 393–420.

Holmes, J. (1990). Apologies in New Zealand English. *Language in Society, 19*(2), 155. doi:10.1017/s0047404500014366.

Ince, D. (2016, July 11). Ambient awareness. Retrieved December 20, 2016, from Oxford Reference, www.oxfordreference.com.ezproxy.aut.ac.nz/view/10.1093/acref/9780191744150.001.0001/acref-9780191744150-e-4440?.

Jenkins, H. (2006). *Convergence culture: Where old and new media collide*. New York: New York University Press.

Kang, R., Brown, S., & Kiesler, S. (2013). Why do people seek anonymity on the internet? Informing policy and design. In *Proceedings of the ACM Conference on Human Factors in Computing Systems* (CHI '13). New York: ACM Press.

Kangasharju, H., & Nikko, T. (2009). Emotions in organizations: Joint laughter in workplace meetings. *Journal of Business Communication, 46*(1), 100–119. doi:10.1177/0021943608325750.

Kent, M. (2013). Using social media dialogically: Public relations role in reviving democracy. *Public Relations Review, 39*(4), 337–345. doi:10.1016/j.pubrev.2013.07.024.

Kent, M. L., & Taylor, M. (1998). Building dialogic relationships through the World Wide Web. *Public Relations Review, 24*(3), 321–334.

Kent, M. L., & Taylor, M. (2002). Toward a dialogic theory of public relations. *Public Relations Review, 28*(1), 21–37. doi:10.1016/s0363-8111(02)00108-x.

Kolbe, D. G. (2013). Virtually there: The paradox of proximity. In R. Morrison & H. Cooper-Thomas (Eds.), *Relationships in organizations: A work psychology perspective* (pp. 171–192). London: Palgrave Macmillan.

Labrecque, L., Esche, J., Mathwick, C., Novak, T., & Hofacker, C. (2013). Consumer power: Evolution in the digital age. *Journal of Interactive Marketing, 27*(6), 257–269.

Lee, J. M., & Rha, J. Y. (2016). Personalization-privacy paradox and consumer conflict with the use of location-based mobile commerce. *Computers in Human Behavior, 63*, 453–462.

Leonardi, P. M. (2015). Ambient awareness and knowledge acquisition: Using social media to learn "who knows what" and "who knows whom." *MIS Quarterly*, *39*(4), 747–762.

Levordashka, A., & Utz, S. (2016). Ambient awareness: From random noise to digital closeness in online social networks. *Computers in Human Behavior*, *60*, 147–154. doi:10.1016/j.chb.2016.02.037.

Lucas, G. M., Gratch, J., King, A., & Morency, L.-P. (2014). It's only a computer: Virtual humans increase willingness to disclose. *Computers in Human Behavior*, *37*, 94–100. doi:10.1016/j.chb.2014.04.043.

Lutzky, U., & Kehoe, A. (2016). "Oops, I didn't mean to be so flippant." A corpus pragmatic analysis of apologies in blog data. *Journal of Pragmatics*. doi:10.1016/j.pragma.2016.12.007.

Ma, X., Hancock, J., & Naaman, M. (2016). Anonymity, intimacy and self-disclosure in social media. In *2016 CHI conference on human factors in computing systems* (pp. 3857–3869). New York: ACM.

Malthouse, E., Haenlein, M., Skiera, B., Wege, E., & Zhang, M. (2013). Managing customer relationships in the social media era: Introducing the social CRM house. *Journal of Interactive Marketing*, *27*(4), 270–280.

Mohamed, A., & Gardner, W. (2004). An exploratory study of interorganizational defamation: An organizational impression management perspective. *Organizational Analysis*, *12*(2), 129–145.

Mühlbach, L., Böcker, M., & Prussog, A. (1995). Telepresence in videocommunications: A study on stereoscopy and individual eye contact. *Human Factors*, *37*(2), 290–305.

Olmstead, K., Lampe, C., & Ellison, N. B. (2016, June 22). *Social media and the workplace*. Retrieved December 20, 2016, from www.pewinternet.org/2016/06/22/social-media-and-the-workplace/.

Ombudsman. Fairness for all. (2017). Ombudsman.parliament.nz. Retrieved from www.ombudsman.parliament.nz/.

Ott, L., & Theunissen, P. (2014). Reputations at risk: Enactment during social media crises. *Public Relations Review*. doi:10.1016/j.pubrev.2014.10.015.

Paliszkiewicz, J., & Mądra-Sawicka, M. (2016). Impression management in social media: the example of LinkedIn. *Management*, *11*(3), 203–212.

Sappleton, N., & Lourenço, F. (2015). Email subject lines and response rates to invitations to participate in a web survey and a face-to-face interview. The sound of silence. *International Journal of Social Research Methodology*, *19*(5), 611–622. doi:10.1080/13645579.2015.1078596.

Schnurr, S. (2013). *Exploring professional communication: Language in action*. New York: Routledge.

Schoenmaker, S. (2016). Commentary: Connecting, responding and engaging, not yet relating online. *Prism*, *13*(1). www.prismjournal.org/homepage.html.

Scollon, R. (1998). *Mediated discourse as social interaction: Ethnographic study of news discourse*. London: Longman.

Scollon, R. (2001). *Mediated discourse: The nexus of practice*. New York: Routledge.

Sias, P. M. (2009). *Organizing relationships: Traditional and emerging perspectives on workplace relationships*. Los Angeles, CA: Sage Publications.

Sissons, H. (2015). Lifting the veil on the PRP-client relationship. *Public Relations Inquiry*, *4*(3), 263–286. doi:10.1177/2046147x15614686.

Sissons, H., & Varoli Piazza, C. (2016, July). *Hidden truth: Improving verification skills in the classroom and the newsroom.* Paper presented to the World Journalism Education Congress, Auckland, New Zealand.

Skogs, J. (2013). Subject line preferences and other factors contributing to coherence and interaction in student discussion forums. *Computers & Education*, *60*(1), 172–183. doi:10.1016/j.compedu.2012.07.005.

Smith, P., Bell, A., Miller, M., & Crothers, C. (2016). *World Internet Project New Zealand. Internet trends in New Zealand 2007–2015.* Retrieved from http://icdc.aut.ac.nz/__data/assets/pdf_file/0003/707295/WIPNZtrends–07–15.pdf.

Smith, P., & Sissons, H. (2017). Social media and a case of mistaken identity: A newspaper's response to journalistic error. *Jalism*, 1–17.

The Radicati Group Inc (2016). *Email statistics report, 2016–2020.* The Radicati Group. Retrieved from www.radicati.com/wp/wp-content/uploads/2016/01/Email_Statistics_Report_2016-2020_Executive_Summary.pdf.

Theunissen, P. (2015). The quantum entanglement of dialogue and persuasion in social media: Introducing the Per-Di principle. *Atlantic Journal of Communication*, *23*(1), 5–18. doi:10.1080/15456870.2015.972405.

Tokunaga, R. (2011). Social networking site or social surveillance site? Understanding the use of interpersonal electronic surveillance in romantic relationships. *Computers in Human Behavior, 27*(2), 705–713.

Valentini, C. (2010). Personalised networks of influence in public relations. *Journal of Communication Management*, *14*(2), 153–166. doi:10.1108/13632541011034600.

Valentini, C. (2015). Is using social media "good" for the public relations profession? A critical reflection. *Public Relations Review*, *41*(2), 170–177. doi:10.1016/j.pubrev.2014.11.009.

Waters, R. D., & Jamal, J. Y. (2011). Tweet, tweet, tweet: A content analysis of nonprofit organizations' Twitter updates. *Public Relations Review*, *37*(3), 321–324. doi:10.1016/j.pubrev.2011.03.002.

Wertsch, J. V. (1991). *Voices of the mind: A sociocultural approach to mediated action.* London: Harvester Wheatsheaf.

Willis, P. (2015). Preach wine and serve vinegar: Public relations, relationships and doublethink. *Public Relations Review*, *41*(5), 681–688. doi:10.1016/j.pubrev.2014.02.004.

Yates, J., & Orlikowski, W. (1993). *Knee-Jerk Anti-Loopism and Other E-Mail Phenomena: Oral, Written, and Electronic Patterns in Computer-Mediated Communication.* Report, MIT Sloan School.

Yeomans, L. (2016). Imagining the lives of others: Empathy in public relations. *Public Relations Inquiry*, *5*(1), 71–92.

4   PRP-PRP Relationships[1]

> Power works, not through [...] some rule-bound logic imposed from above, but through the experience of the space itself, through its ambient qualities.
>
> —Allen, 2006, p. 442

Unchartered Territory

In the previous chapter, we discussed how the *sites of relational enactment*—that is the spaces where people interact, including PRPs, their clients, and publics—are increasingly being mediated through technology. In the next few chapters, we move to examining the relationships themselves. We first look at what we consider to be the most important of a public relations practitioner's (PRP's) professional relationships, that with their peers.

Little has been written about the relationships between PRPs themselves and how these relationships and the communication that takes place within these relationships influence the practice and profession of public relations. As Hodges (2006) pointed out, PRPs "will live in some sort of relationship to other practitioners" (p. 85), and it is within these relationships that meaning about the occupation and its place and function within the organization and wider society is formed. Relationships and relationship communication, therefore, become sites of meaning-making and occupational culture.

Indeed, interaction between peers is a major influence on workplace behavior (Sias, 2009), and to understand public relations work, as well as its effect on society, we must first understand these peer relationships or—as we call them—PRP-PRP relationships. Akin to Sias' (2009) description of peer [co-worker] relationships, we define PRP-PRP relationships here as: relationships between public relations practitioners who have no formal authority over each other and who operate at the same hierarchical level within an organization.

This chapter follows the interactions of an in-house PRP, Kate, during her routine work day. It highlights two critical incidents that represent how she uses verbal and nonverbal interpersonal interaction to manage relationships between herself and her colleagues.

Peer relationships

According to Kram and Isabella (1985), peer relationships offer many career-enhancing and psychosocial benefits. Career-enhancing functions include information sharing, job-related feedback and career strategizing while psychosocial benefits involve confirmation, emotional support, personal feedback, and friendship. The presence of *mutuality* increases the benefits for both parties. As Kram and Isabella (1985) highlighted,

> Within the context of a relationship of this kind, information sharing gives both individuals technical knowledge and perspective on the organization that better enable them to get their work done. In addition, through career strategizing, individuals can discuss their career options and dilemmas, finding in a peer a medium for exploring their own careers. Finally, peers give and receive feedback concerning work-related matters that lets them evaluate their own experiences.
>
> (p. 117)

It is within these exchanges that practitioners construct meaning about their own practice and its value for the organization and society at large. The role and place of ethics, for example, is constructed within these micro-interactions, and it is here that *occupational culture* is created. As Holmes and Stubbe (2015, p. 2) pointed out, "Co-workers typically take a great deal for granted; they share common assumptions, common reference systems, and use the same jargon or system of verbal shortcuts."

In addition, they often share experiences, background knowledge and may hold similar values and attitudes towards their work (Holmes & Stubbe, 2015). It is these similar values, knowledge, and experiences that influence the decisions made in sites of relational enactment and meaning-making, such as meetings. The professional culture that is collectively constructed in such meetings influences the nature of communication on behalf of the organizations, and how they might deal for example with "dissident" publics, as we will see in Chapter 7.

Three Types of Peer Relationships

There are three types of peer relationships that manifest themselves during organizational interaction: the *information peer,* the *collegial peer* and the *special peer* (Kram & Isabella, 1985). Kram and Isabella presented these relationships on a continuum of trust and self-disclosure with the information peer on the one end (low levels of trust and self-disclosure) and on the other end, the special peer with high levels of trust and self-disclosure. In the middle is the collegial peer. In her book *Organizing Relations: Traditional and Emerging Perspectives on*

Workplace Relationships, Sias (2009) proposed that nearly all peer relationships start out as information peers—some develop further; others do not. Consequently, PRPs are likely to have significantly fewer special peer relationships than information peer relationships. And, as with any interpersonal relationship (see Chapter 2), the strength of the relationship is increased when it is *reciprocal,* that is, when both parties provide support and contribute to the development of the relationship.

Special peer relationships are akin to being "best friends." These relationships are characterized by high levels of trust, intimacy, self-disclosure and support (Sias, 2009). Such colleagues can talk openly and honestly about almost any topic (work-related and personal), which allows them not only to strategize about their careers and build confidence and competency, but also to manage work-life demands.

In contrast, *information peer relationships* are much more superficial, and communication is limited to task and work-related topics. In these relationships, there are significantly lower levels of trust and self-disclosure. However, they are essential for networking and staying in-the-know, and, we would argue, are essential for developing a network of *personal influence* (see Chapter 2). Indeed, Sias (2009) emphasized that, while these relationships are typical for early career professionals, they remain essential throughout one's career.

Career success is dependent on information for competent decision-making, and this information is transferred through the networks a professional has developed. While Sias (2009) referred here to face-to-face relationships, where colleagues generally share the same physical space, that is, are in proximity to each other, information peer relationships are also created—and mediated—through technologies and social networking sites, such as LinkedIn, Twitter, and Facebook. Levordashka and Utz (2016), for example, proposed that *ambient awareness* (see Chapter 3) allows Twitter users to identify potential sources of information. Often, users have not met any of these sources in person, and sometimes these networks are created and maintained solely online.

Collegial peer relationships rank in-between special peer and information peer relationships. In these collegial peer relationships, there are moderate levels of trust, emotional support, and self-disclosure. Discussions within these relationships involve a wider range of topics that include work and non-work or personal topics. In addition, these relationships are generally more complex than information peer relationships, and it is through these relationships that recognition in the workplace is gained as well as the identification of opportunities for professional advancement. In other words, they enable, more so than information peer relationships, opportunities for career strategizing.

Most professionals have a range of relationships with varying levels of "closeness," trust and self-disclosure. As Sias (2009) suggested, having a range of relationships is essential for career development, and, of course, being able to develop these relationships should be acknowledged as expertise in public relations (Valentini, 2010). This is particularly relevant if we are to consider the *power* that accompanies the idea of having *personal influence* (see Chapter 2 for a discussion on personal influence).

Peer Relationships and Power

More than ten years after Edwards (2006) identified a lack of development in our understanding of power in public relations, the concept remains under-developed. In fact, limited research has been done to theorize power "beyond the traditional definitions of individual commodity" (Place, 2012, p. 439). For example, traditionally, scholarly discussions about power privileged those in roles of formal authority, while communication between peers or colleagues was dismissed as idle chitchat that served no work-related purpose (Sias, 2009). It was only after the "interpretative turn" in the 1980s that scholarship increasingly focused on "unobtrusive forms of control and influence" (Sias, 2009, p. 67). This unobtrusive, yet ever-present, form of power we have labeled here as *ambient power*, based on the analysis of micro-interactions between PRPs in their place of work.

Indeed, power, and how it is enacted in peer relationships, is barely touched on in public relations training and scholarship. As Macnamara (2012) highlighted, most public relations textbooks skim over issues of power, and many do not discuss it at all. Indeed, where it *is* addressed in scholarship, it is often directed at the meso (organizational) and macro (societal) level. Yet, "exerting control requires participating in peer relationships" (Sias, 2009, p. 67)—hence the focus in this chapter is on micro-interactions between colleagues.

The year before Edwards identified a lack of understanding of power, L'Etang (2005) had identified the need for more ethnographic research into the practices of PRPs. Some researchers have responded, including Edwards (2009), who examined power relations in a corporate affairs department of a passenger-transport company. Yet studies that explicitly identify how power and relationships are enacted at the interpersonal level between practitioners, their clients, and other stakeholders are few.

Approaching power as a necessary, yet often indiscernible, element of public relations practice (Place, 2012) and locating it in public relations' operational or social context (Edwards, 2006) at the micro (interpersonal) level seems an appropriate approach to extending current scholarship. It provides "a fundamental constructivist starting point ranging from micro studies of individual action to macro perspectives of system theory" (Ihlen & Verhoeven, 2012, p. 168).

Power is Embedded in Processes of Meaning-Making

Power can best be described as the "ability to manage meaning" (Sias, 2009, p. 67), and is exerted through communication, and indeed language. Citing Kunda (1992), Sias (2009) identified these peer-to-peer conversations as "important sites of meaning creation" (p. 67) and the management of that meaning. Thus, it is integrally linked to relationships where the site of power lies in the space "in-between" (using Buber's terminology), where interlocutors construct meaning, and conversations between peers are not only important sites for the enactment of personal power and influence but also for organizational influence. Having power, therefore, is conceptualized in this chapter as *having the ability to exert influence over how and what meaning is constructed*. Sias (2009) explained that "the nature and quality of one's relationships with peers has important implications for both the individuals and organization as a whole" (p. 71), and specifically how meaning is constructed and decisions are made.

Integral to our construction of meaning and exerting power is the use of language. Language and its use is specific to our world (Ramsey, 2016) and is critical in constructing social reality (Holmes & Stubbe, 2015). It not only communicates how we see our world and the work we do, but it also *shapes* the world in which we live (Theunissen, 2018), and because practitioners often share an occupational outlook and culture, using similar jargon and frames, it is easy to fall into the trap of not questioning these everyday interactions. Together, practitioners make sense of situations and decisions—see, for example, Chapter 7 when the team, while planning their communication strategy, attempts to make sense of the organization's decision to switch waste disposal providers—and it is through these shared activities that power relationships are maintained (Conrad & Poole, 2005).

Thus, PRP-PRP interactions become sites where meaning and power are simultaneously enacted and contested. In our research, we found that relational power is never enacted without challenges, but like Holmes and Stubbe (2015), we found these challenges to take place in subtle and socially acceptable ways, or as Holmes and Stubbe called them: *polite* ways. Politeness is focused on displaying mutual respect and concern for the other or the other's "face needs" (Holmes & Stubbe, 2015, p. 5), and is an essential part of relationship-building and maintenance. While it is not limited to peer relationships, but is also used in relationships of unequal power through *deference*, politeness is used, among other things, to manage problematic talk in the workplace and avoid overt conflict (Holmes & Stubbe, 2015). In the email exchange discussed in Chapter 3, for instance, overt conflict is avoided through superficial acts of politeness. It would, therefore, be fair to argue that politeness is an integral part of developing personal influence.

In the first critical incident presented here, for example, the discussion between the PRPs and the architect appears innocuous, but upon further analysis, and knowing the key players and context involved, it becomes clear that power is enacted almost imperceptibly.

A Difficult Discussion

The first critical incident presented in this chapter involves Kate and Andrew, two PRPs, and Tom, the local authority's architect, discussing designs Tom's team has drawn up for a key public facility to be built on the city's waterfront.

The practitioners are sharing their opinions on the designs and how they might be perceived by the mayor, the public, and the media. The interaction is framed by the PRPs as an opportunity to give "preliminary feedback."

Just before the start of this clip, the trio had talked about the cost of the proposals that are presented in the designs, and Tom has admitted that having sought advice, the proposals would cost "a hundred over the eighty-four," that is, 100 million New Zealand dollars more than the 84 million dollars set aside for the project by the local authority from taxpayers' money—thus far exceeding the allocated budget. The discussion that ensues is an uncomfortable one, marked by politeness (Holmes & Stubbe, 2015) and power enacted through specific behaviors and actions. As Allen (2006) suggested, power is "always exercised in particular ways, it is never power in general" (p. 454).

It is obvious from the beginning that this meeting is intended to be brief, occurring as it does before Tom meets the mayor and presents his team's vision. Andrew (the mayor's media relations manager) does not take off his coat, and both he and Kate (the authority's media relations manager) pace around the table with neither sitting down.

The PRPs are aware they have to deliver some harsh news, as the authority's development manager has already made it clear he is unimpressed, especially with the estimated cost of the project. So, Andrew has framed the meeting to Tom as one that "preempts" the feedback that the mayor is likely to give. Hence, they are doing Tom a *favor* by giving him this preliminary feedback, and by doing so, preserving their relationship with him. Andrew ensures Kate is in agreement by asking her, after he has explained the purpose of the meeting to the architect, "What do you think," and she agrees it is a good idea.

In Figure 4.1, image 1, Andrew is asking Kate what she thinks the mayor's reaction will be. He leans slightly towards her, using the notes in his hand as a pointer to the drawings, and just after the "uhm," he gives a quick beat with the notes followed by two more on "do" and "think." Then he makes a repair, possibly from "going" (which could be the start of "going to say 'wow'") to a more indirect way of eliciting her opinion. As he asks whether the mayor's reaction will be "wow," he walks

A: uhm (0.7) do you think the
   mayor's g-
   I was interested (.)
   Kate when you saw this
   what do you think the mayor's going
   to say when he sees that¿
   do you think he's going to say "<u>wow</u>"?

A: no no?=
K: =no
A: (1.2) what's going to make him say "<u>wow</u>"

K: (0.7) more <u>color</u>?
   (1.5) I just think

A: (0.4) yes so [(indistinct)]
K: [uh and we're ge]tting
   now this is <u>re:al</u> sim[plistic stuff]
T: [mm no of course]
   of course

Figure 4.1 Giving preliminary feedback.

K: uhm=
A: =some colorful fla:gs?=
K: =yeah I think he'll say more color (0.5) uhm::: some <u>fla:gs</u>, some <u>shade cloths</u>, some

K: (0.9) uhm Rachel's talking about protecting it from the <u>elements</u> so:: (1.2) even:=
T: =yeah=

K: =uh:m (0.8) little <u>tents</u> dotted <u>arou:nd</u>, carn- more carnival?
T: yeah yeah
A: (0.9) uhm uhm=

T: =ys yeah an and the[se can all] be <u>done</u>
K: [yea:h]
K: yeah=
T: =and the guys <u>can</u> do it,=
K: =yeah=
T: =they just need we're just running out of time¿

Figure 4.1 (Continued)

behind Tom to the bottom of the table *distancing* himself physically from the other two as if to give Kate and Tom an opportunity to engage. However, as we have seen in Chapter 2, increasing physical distance is also used to decrease intimacy, and thereby, Andrew may have wanted to make the situation "less personal."

As soon as Andrew has passed, Tom backs away from the table towards the door, closing his left arm across his body to the crook of his right arm, the hand of which he brings to his mouth (Figure 4.1, image 2). By doing this Tom signals his unease and possibly his disagreement with what is occurring (Bousmalis, Mehu & Pantic, 2013; Givens, 1999). Throughout this, Kate is staring intently at the drawings, using her left hand to hold her hair away from her eyes. This is the first of two hair-touching actions that can be interpreted as self-adaptors used by Kate in this interaction. Hair-touching is more common among females than males, and is often associated with female courting rituals, but in the two instances here it is more likely to be the result of feeling discomfort (Goldberg & Rosenthal, 1986), or alternatively, she may be attempting to create an impression of honesty and approachability (Harrigan, 2005) thereby alleviating possible tension.

Exerting Power Through Exclusion

In Figure 4.1, image 2 Andrew is off-camera. He has left substantial distance between him and the other two but remains part of the conversation. As he asks, "do you think he's going to say 'wow'," Kate grimaces and shakes her head slightly. When Andrew says "no," she shakes her head more vigorously. As he repeats the word "no" she looks up at him and mouths "no" before looking down at the pictures again. Her body, angled towards the table, remains open to Andrew, while closed to Tom. Tom's eyes are cast down at the table, possibly focusing on the drawings, but he shifts his gaze to Kate just as she voices her "no," thereby intercepting her nonverbal communication with Andrew.

Kate then straightens up and walks towards Andrew while they both keep their gazes on the picture, avoiding eye contact with Tom, and making themselves unavailable or socially inaccessible to him at this point (Figure 4.1, image 3) (Kendon, 1967). After a pause of more than a second, Andrew asks Kate what is going to make him (the mayor) say "wow."

It becomes obvious that power is being exerted through a process of *exclusion*. Kate and Andrew, through their nonverbal language, have formed a unified front in their disagreement, thereby fusing their power in what is essentially a peer-to-peer, egalitarian relationship, tipping the balance in their favor. Because their continued working relationship with Tom is important, they are evidently reluctant to negatively affect the long-term relationship through verbal sparring or aggressive tones, and thus *politeness* is evident (Holmes & Stubbe, 2015). Arguably, then, power is enacted but it is *low key*, and, as per Allen's (2006) view, "a modest form of power" (p. 445) that lies in the *experience* of the person who is subjected to it. As a result, the experience of power *seduces*, rather than forces, Tom to want to know what must he do, what must he do to satisfy them (and the mayor) to return to the triangle of power?

Although Allen (2006) described power from an urban design perspective, it is useful when understanding influence and its enactment at the micro level. Based on Allen's description, this "modest form of power," or *ambient power*, is asserted through a process of *exclusion* and *inclusion*, rather than dominance and manipulation. In these everyday places (or sites of relational enactment—as we argue), ambient power is "felt before it is understood" (Allen, 2006, p. 446); Tom feels it. More specifically, like ambient awareness (see Chapter 3), ambient power refers to the *peripheral awareness of power.*

Kate stops after having taken three steps and just as Andrew finishes speaking. She leaves a gap between herself and Andrew that accommodates Tom (Figure 4.1, image 3)—a nonverbal act that symbolizes and acknowledges Tom's return to the triangle. She pauses for about half a second, her gaze is (as are Andrew's and Tom's) on the picture nearest to Andrew. This diverts the focus away from her action back to the object of discussion: the architect's draft of the proposed plan. However, the actions suggest Tom's vulnerability in what can only be described as a low key "dance" of power.

The Site of Relational Enactment

To understand ambient power, one must, in the first instance, understand the "space" in which the interaction takes place. In Chapter 3, we proposed social networking sites as sites of relational enactment. In this interaction, the site is *physical* and participants have a *physical social presence*. As Scollon (2001) argued, sites of (relational) enactment are created by social and mediated actions that take place within a specific space, and therefore these sites are *social spaces*. While Allen had in mind specifically constructed designs (i.e., buildings and public spaces), space can be interpreted as our surroundings or the context of our interactions. In interpersonal communication, this space communicates something; it is not free of meaning. Not everyone, for example, is allowed in our "personal" or "intimate" spaces. Moreover, when people join a group, they *create* their surroundings together, determining the context and meaning of that space.

Problematic Talk

Returning to the interaction, Kate says she believes more color is required in the picture (Figure 4.1, image 3). In this part of the interaction, she uses several linguistic devices that indicate hesitation.

Either she is uncertain of what she is saying or she is mitigating her message. The first indication of hesitation is the pause of more than half a second after Andrew's question. In talk, a silence of more than one beat (about a tenth of a second) is interactionally relevant (Liddicoat, 2011), indicating to the co-participant that there is a problem. Her following words, "more <u>color</u>?" while stressing the word "color," end in an upward inflection, signifying doubt. Her next statement, "I just think," is her *assessment*, rather than fact, and she downplays it with the modifier "just." Both hedging devices are employed in problematic talk, such as this one where the two PRPs must convey bad news to the architect; they serve as "linguistic politeness devices" (Holmes & Stubbe, 2015, p. 146).

Kate then turns to Tom, perhaps feeling it necessary to explain, or realizing how inconsequential her comments might appear (Figure 4.1, image 4). Her comment "uh and we're getting now this is re:al simplistic stuff" shows her changing tack (called a *repair*) and she sounds somewhat apologetic. The latter can be an attempt to downplay any possible confrontation (and note how she stresses the word "real"), thereby reinforcing the idea of politeness. Indeed, speakers use repair talk (Schegloff, Jefferson & Sacks, 1977) to resolve problems. In this case, it also diverts attention from direct attempts to exert power in a dominant manner. On the word "simplistic," her left-hand moves from her hair and makes two short beats to emphasize "simplistic."

Tom remains in a closed-body position even as he steps forward into the discussion (Figure 4.1, images 4 and 5). This posture communicates defensiveness, stress, and discomfort, making it evident that he is experiencing the power play although it is very low key, that is, on the peripheral of their interaction. Combined with face-saving strategies, this low-key presence of power creates ambient power in the relationship.

Drawing on Third-Party, Peripheral Power

Andrew has kept his gaze on Kate, despite hers being on Tom (Figure 4.1, images 4 and 5), as if observing. Then Kate uses the filler "uhm" (Figure 4.1, image 5), which is often an indication of reduced confidence and fluency (Hirschman, 1994; Schegloff, 2010). She reaches down with her left hand and moves the illustration towards her while keeping her gaze on it. Then she leans over the picture as she utters "uhm," and begins speaking. As she says "some <u>fla:gs</u>, some <u>shade cloths</u>," she uses a head nod to stress both "flags" and "shade cloths," and her voice takes on a slight sing-song character. This use of syntactic parallels (Schiffrin, 1987) creates a pattern that is effective in *persuasive speaking* (Tannen, 1990). It is, therefore, evident that Kate wishes to persuade Tom of the veracity of what she and Andrew are suggesting. She has taken up Andrew's suggestion of "colorful flags," by agreeing and saying "he" (the mayor) will want "more color uhm::: some fla:gs," drawing on third-party power, that is, someone who is not present to strengthen her argument and influence.

As Kate mentions Rachel, Tom and Andrew shift their gazes to her, but as the list of extras grows, Tom displays increasing discomfort. On the word "even" (Figure 4.1, image 6), he moves his hands to his trousers and hitches them slightly before placing his hands on his hips, a gesture that may appear less defensive than his previous stance, but is aimed at making himself appear bigger, thus reclaiming some of the power removed by Kate's list of suggestions.

He also attempts to show he is noting her suggestions by stepping closer to the table to observe what she is pointing at (Figure 4.1, image 7), but, though he nods once, his mouth is tightly closed and his lips pulled inwards in what is known as an orbicular clamp (Seaford, 1975). This tightening of the mouth is associated with emotions of *displeasure* (Beaudry, Roy-Charland, Perron, Cormier, & Tapp, 2013) and it is clear that his expression is somber. His "yeah" (Figure 4.1, image 6) appears to be an expression of "I understand what you are saying" rather than one of "I agree with you" (Saville-Troike, 1989), and although he further nods with each "yeah yeah" (Figure 4.1, image 7), he gives Kate only the briefest of glances.

Meanwhile, Kate has warmed to her argument, using the forefinger of her right hand to point to five different places on the design where tents might be placed (Figure 4.1, image 7). Then, as she searches for the word "carnival," she grasps it with her right hand and shifts her gaze to Tom and nods, satisfied that she has done what she needed to.

At that point, Kate seems to notice how uncomfortable Tom is and grimaces. It appears that her attempts at politeness and saving face have not been effective enough. She tucks her hair behind her ear and glances quickly at Andrew (perhaps for support). As Tom begins to speak she says "yeah," nods and shifts her gaze back to the pictures. She nods again and adds another "yeah," still leaning over and looking at the pictures. This behavior allows her to avoid eye contact with Tom without it being obvious.

Andrew has also avoided looking at Tom during this part of the interaction, although he appears to react to Kate's glance with a rapid "uhm uhm" (Figure 4.1, image 7). He is interrupted by Tom whose gestures demonstrate his concern about what is being asked. First, he brings both hands off his hips to cup them in front as if holding the suggestions—a gestural version of a *conduit metaphor* (McNeill, 1992, 2005) (Figure 4.1, image 8). Following McNeill (1992), a conduit metaphor can be seen as a gesture used to create an image of a bounded, supportable object, known as a "cup of meaning," which in fact represents an abstract concept. The gesture, in this case, is wide, illustrating Tom's perception of the scale of what is being asked. He continues, bringing his right hand forward slightly towards the drawing and making a beat gesture on the second "<u>can</u>" to stress that it is possible, but as he makes the repair from "they just need" to "they are running out of time," it is clear that this is an important point. His arms make a back and forth movement, first, the left-hand pushes forward, then the right, twice each, as if simulating running. He then drops his hands and puts his left hand in his pocket.

It is evident in this brief, seemingly innocuous, encounter between two PRPs and an architect that there is a subtle power struggle, which resonates with Allen's (2006) description of the *experience* of power. Here, the participants are at the same hierarchical level with none having more authority than the others, and at first glance, it may be mistaken for a rather hum-drum discussion about a picture that is about to be presented to the mayor. Yet, the two PRPs have consolidated their power in the subtlest of ways to get the architect to agree with changes they want to have made. Furthermore, that the picture (the message) will be presented to the mayor, a source of formal power, contributes to the *experience* of power between these peers. From our fieldwork, we know that Kate's association and standing with the mayor provide her with expert power, which she downplays in this interaction—perhaps because she knows Tom may feel threatened or defensive.

Thus, it is not about control, or formal power, in this interaction—it is about *ambient power*, that is, *power that is generated in the setting and the interactions*, and that lies on the periphery of the relationship maintenance process. In this understanding, power is neither palpable nor separate from its surroundings, which echoes Place's (2012) observation that in public relations, power "is an often *invisible*, yet essential, element" (p. 435, emphasis added).

The Briefing

In the second critical incident, Kate is briefing a colleague, James, about a meeting he was unable to attend. As the communications and marketing delivery manager, James is, among other things, responsible for the authority's marketing campaigns, and at this briefing two issues were discussed: one being the development of a waterfront site, the same site that was discussed in the first interaction in this chapter, and the second being a controversial decision by the local authority to change the waste removal contractor for a local area, an issue that is again the topic of discussion in Chapter 7.

We join the interaction seven minutes into a 12-minute conversation. Kate is discussing the second item and outlining the options they are considering for placating angry residents, or as James refers to them, albeit jokingly, the "civil unrest, insurrection."

Kate is seated at her desk; James has entered her space and is standing a few feet away. We know from our fieldwork and from other critical

K: and Zara's idea is that there must be <u>something</u> that
(0.6) CWL can <u>offer</u>
(1.4) ((name of the area))

K: so something <u>beyond</u> what's contracted <u>already</u>:
l:ike >for example< (1.0) ((lip smack))
(0.4) uh:m

K: (1.1) we would be the first opportunity
(0.5) to: look at the CVs of the current <u>w</u>orkers
(0.7) to see if they want to:
(0.6) come work for us

K: o:r uhm
we'll give you two days once the inorganic stuff's
collected we'll give wa- ((name of the area)) <u>two</u> days
to come in >pick o:ver it< nn
(0.5) pick out what they wa:nt,
coz that's what the:y (0.4) will <u>mis:s</u>,
is the opportunity to pick out uh- a-
J: (0.8) junk

Figure 4.2 Briefing a colleague.

K: (0.4) swing sets and stuff
   th[at ghhe]t thrown away
J: [yeah]
K: .hh uh:m ((lip smack))
   before we transport everything over
   [to the ((name of area)]
J: [off the ((name of area))]
   yeah

K: or
   you kno:w
   I know
   so none not necessarily contra:ctual stuff
   but ju:st compromise .hh hh

J: (clicks 1:00) yeah
   yeah we'd need to get CWL to a-agree=
K: =mm=
J: =that they're prepared
K: mmm
J: to do some stuff
K: yeah

J: there's also I think the question which Shelley raised
   quite rightly
   is there's a big question I think about casting for that
   meeting?

Figure 4.2 (Continued)

incidents that there is tension between them (Sissons, 2012). Thus, while their interactions remain civil and polite throughout, there is no evidence of *seeking affinity* (see Chapter 2), which suggests that they are in an acquaintance relationship, perhaps one that can be accurately described as *information peer* as discussed earlier.

Seven minutes into the discussion, James still has not attempted to find a seat nor has Kate offered him one. This is perhaps indicative of a lack of willingness to spend extended time in each other's presence or shows the interaction was intended to be brief.

Conveying Another's Thoughts

Kate is relating an idea put forward by Zara, Group Manager, Communications and Marketing. She must report from memory the discussion that occurred in the meeting James was unable to attend, and in the first part of this extract, she represents Zara's thoughts to James. In the second part, they discuss who should attend a meeting with the residents.

As she conveys Zara's thoughts, Kate's relatively slow, deliberate, and fluent delivery indicates that she may be repeating the words as she remembers Zara saying them. Her words, combined with the inflections, demonstratively convey her memory of what was said, especially at the beginning of this extract when she is setting out the theme. Her stressing of the words "<u>something</u>," "<u>offer</u>," and the name of the area, as well as "<u>beyond</u>" and "<u>already</u>," portray how important the team believes resolving this issue is (Figure 4.2, image 1). She pauses twice in this part of the interaction, before "CWL,"[2] the name of the contractor, and before she names the area (which has been left out for reasons of confidentiality). Normally, such pauses of more than 0.5 seconds and 1.5 seconds in the middle of a clause would indicate the speaker was in trouble, perhaps unable to recall a word, and it would be disruptive to the listener (Reich, 1980). However, in this case, the pauses appear to be for emphasis (Strangert, 2003) as they occur before the names of the two entities involved, CWL and the area. That Kate is purposefully employing this pace and inflection is reinforced by her unwavering gaze and small nods as she says "<u>offer</u>" and the name of the area.

Her hand gestures have the hallmarks of an appeal, being open-handed and open-armed, but it is unlikely she is appealing to James for his approval. The goal here is to report the events of the meeting; hence a more likely explanation is that the gestures are illustrative of an appeal or offering (Kendon, 2004) by the authority (through the contractor) to the residents. In this way, Kate takes on the role of *mediator* between Zara, the authority, and the residents.

Her gestures in this first part of the interaction are almost exclusively gestural versions of *conduit metaphors* (McNeill, 1992, 2005) and beats.

As mentioned in the previous interaction, the analyses in this book see conduit metaphor gestures as creating a *cup of meaning*, holding or representing an abstract concept. As she says "Zara's idea is," she lifts her right hand, which is cupped, holding the idea, and makes two quick beats as she says Zara's name (Figure 4.2, image 1). These beats attach importance to the name (McNeill, 1992), which is understandable as Zara is the head of their department. They also signal to James that this idea comes from someone of whom he needs to take note. By doing so, she calls on another aspect of ambient power, namely that this idea is not her own, but the wish of someone more important than either of them: their boss. Unlike "name-dropping," the reference to their boss is a natural part of the discussion, and a *low-key reminder* of where the formal power lies.

We know that Kate used this strategy in the previous critical incident to increase her own ambient power, but it is only when we compare the strategies Kate uses in various micro-interactions that we realize that she is less concerned about her long-term relationship with James than she is about her other relationships. Here, her performance is much more measured and forceful than in the previous interaction. It seems, they do not share the same view about how to communicate to the organization's publics or how to deal with "dissident" residents, as we will see in Chapter 7.

As she mentions Zara's name, Kate turns her right palm face-up and brings her left hand up at the same time, containing the idea now in her two hands, both cupped, as she says, "there must be something," and moves them back and forth, as if representing the give-and-take between the waste management company and the residents.

As she says "offer," she brings the hands together, the backs of the fingers touching and makes two beats on the two syllables of the word (Figure 4.2 image 1). Her gaze is resting on James and her head too makes two beats, further emphasizing the notion of the "offer." The residents and the waste management company are brought together by the offer, but the back-to-back fingers possibly illustrate the divide that still exists between the two (Figure 4.2, image 1). Then she pauses for nearly a second-and-a-half, possibly for effect, before saying the name of the area. Just before the word, she begins to move her hands, still with her fingers back-to-back, separating them outwards and turning the palms upwards while making three beats. On naming the area, she makes three further beats. Her gaze is still on James and she nods in emphasis, making the beats as her hands do. Spreading the hands in this way is a common image for *potentiality* (McNeill, 1992), while also possibly representing an *appeal* to the residents of the area. It seems, rather than seeing the residents and the waste management company as being at loggerheads, she sees the potential for compromise, which is reinforced by her bringing her hands together, lacing her fingers as she says, "so something," possibly to show the two sides coming together in agreement about an offer. Then on "beyond what's contracted already," she pushes her right hand out leaving the left behind and moving the boundary of one side (the authority perhaps) outwards—illustrating an offer that goes beyond what exists already in its contract with the islanders (Figure 4.2, image 2).

We can see clearly in the first part of this interaction how Kate brings together her gesture and speech to create what Kendon (2004) refers to as "semantic coherence" (p. 119). Her co-verbal gestures reinforce her speech, signifying that this interaction is also about persuading James to agree with the decision.

Once she has outlined the authority's aim to find a compromise, she then gives a couple of examples of what the authority might offer. Here she is less fluent to begin with, perhaps because the examples are harder for her to recall than the main idea, or she is thinking of fresh examples on-the-hoof. Her use of the bilabial percussive or lip smack followed by "uh:m," indicate she is searching for the right words (Ogden, 2013). She also switches from stressing the individual, whose idea this is, to using the collective first-person pronouns "we" and "us" for the remainder of the interaction. This use of the pronouns by Kate, consciously or sub-consciously, includes James as a member of the group implementing this decision, perhaps making it more likely that he will go along with the plan. It also serves the purpose of *relationship maintenance* by making him feel part of the team and thereby masking any potential negativity or opposition that may exist.

Conflicting Views

When she gives the first example, she makes only two short gestures, both using her right hand in a palm-upward cup. As she says, "first opportunity," she lowers and raises the hand quickly in two beat movements synchronous with each word (Figure 4.2, image 3). The second cup gesture is produced on the word "workers." Clearly, these are the two points to which Kate wishes to draw James's attention.

Her hands then return to her lap until part-way through her second example of what might be offered by the authority to the residents, when she lifts them to mid-chest height as she says, "inorganic stuff's collected." At this utterance, both hands are held in front of her, vertically with the palms facing towards each other as if grasping the "inorganic stuff." They make two beats together on "inorganic" and one beat on "collected." Then Kate links the fingers of the two hands together and clasps them towards her chest on "we'll give [the residents]," then thrusts them outwards hands flat and palms down on "two days."

This palms-down or "open hand prone" (Kendon, 2004) gesture, one of the largest in this interaction, is important. While the authority is looking for a compromise, this offer is limited to two days. As Kendon (2004) writes, "the context in which these [open hand prone] gestures are used can all be interpreted as involving a reference to some line of action that is being suspended, interrupted or cut off" (p. 255). This action is about getting the residents' agreement to the change by making a small but limited offer, and so the gesture is adding to the information about the scope of the compromise (Harrison, 2010) that is included in the concurrent speech.

Immediately after this part of the interaction, and as she says, ">pick o:ver it< nn pick out what they wa:nt," each of Kate's hands alternatively moves slightly backward and forward seven times as if picking at the inorganic waste (Figure 4.2, image 4). Here Kate is describing what happens verbally while at the same time demonstrating it nonverbally (Lascarides & Stone, 2009). Watching, we understand that Kate's action is representative of the *type* of action that is habitually carried out by the residents in the days after the rubbish is collected. To do this, she has taken a "character viewpoint" (McNeill, 1992, p. 118) or the *viewpoint of the publics*. Even her facial expression changes to be smiling, with eyebrows raised in an open, contented expression. Her gestures are adding content that is distinctive but related to the content of the speech. She finishes the gesture by turning her hands palm up on the word "want" of "what they wa:nt," and holds the gesture until the end of the sentence "what they will mis:s is the opportunity." The open-hand palm-up gesture suggests she is *offering* the idea to James (Kendon, 2004; Müller, 2004). James, however, does not accept the offer. She adds one forward wrist-roll on her repetition of "to pick out," suggesting continuity into the future (that will be missed) and then hesitates slightly "uh."

At this point, James interjects with "junk." Undeterred, Kate continues, seemingly ignoring him, but uses "laugh particles" or "interpolated particles of aspiration" (Potter & Hepburn, 2010, p. 1544) that are incorporated into several words that follow the interruption. According to Potter and Hepburn (2010), these laugh particles have nothing to do with humor, but rather are often used to mark one or more words as being problematic. In this case, the laughter particles are inserted into "ghhet," and "away" as in "ghhet thrown away," which suggests that there are issues with these words (Figure 4.2, image 5). Indeed, the words may represent the potential difficulties in resolving the relationship to the satisfaction of all parties involved. Regardless, Kate still uses them as they do the interactional job of supporting her use of "swing sets" and highlighting her disagreement with James's use of the word "junk." Perhaps in her estimation "stuff" is not as specific as "swing sets," and she would like to have given another concrete example, or perhaps "get thrown away" is problematic as it infers unwanted items, whereas she is trying to illustrate that the residents think of the inorganic collection as items that are pre-loved, and could be useful again.

Preserving the Peer Relationship

Here, it becomes evident that while Kate disagrees with James' dismissive utterance of the public's concerns, she does so in a subtle, non-confrontational way, preserving civility and collegiality even though, as we have established, there is tension between the two PRPs. It also highlights her ability to perceive multiple points of view and display empathy for the residents.

Kate's nonverbal actions support her spoken language throughout, and as she says "swing sets and stuff," she displays a wrist roll towards the body as if enacting a swing motion (Figure 4.2, image 5), and then holds her hands in front of her with her palms down on "that ghhet thrown away." The motion does not only emphasize her words, but creates *visual imagery* in the mind of the listener, mimicking the motion of a swing, and thereby enhances the *persuasive appeal* of what she is saying.

Following James's backchannel response, "yeah," which probably communicates he *understands* rather than actively *agrees* (Saville-Troike, 1989), Kate turns her hands palms up again, takes a breath and says "uh:m," followed by a bilabial percussive or lip smack, indicating slight trouble finding her next words (Ogden, 2013). This pause may link back to James's previous interruption, which necessitated a more detailed response from Kate than she might have been prepared for, and consequently had interrupted her train of thought.

She gathers her thoughts and says "before we transport everything" at the same time as making a deep beat of her hands and moving her left arm across her body towards the right while extending her right arm out to the right side so that both arms are pointing to her right. The movement depicts a different space for the waste—the moving to one side or transporting the waste away from the area.

She appears about to try to think of another example as she says "<u>or</u>," but then decides against it, and sums up instead by saying "not necessarily <u>contra:ctual</u> stuff but <u>ju:st</u> compromise." Through her use of two restrictors "just" and "but," Kate downplays the seriousness of any compromise. During the utterance, her gestures distinguish between "contractual stuff" and "compromise." When talking about the contract, her hands are vertical facing each other and cupped, as if holding a solid object, and she twists them back and forth perhaps representing the back and forth of negotiation (Figure 4.2, image 6). When she moves to talk of the compromise, her fingers briefly lace together and then the hands are held vertically, both palms facing inward. Then the right hand, followed by the left, is thrust forward and backward twice, appearing to depict the give and take of compromise. It seems, then, *the contract is more tangible than the idea of compromise* as it is given form as a gestural conduit metaphor.

Her gaze shifts to James on "compromise," before inhaling deeply and letting out a post-completion sigh (Hoey, 2013). This brief and almost imperceptible nonverbal utterance provides us with a rare and interesting insight into her unconscious thoughts: the post-completion sigh exhibits a weakly negative emotion along with resignation (Teigen, 2008). This attitude marker is enhanced by her facial expression, which sees her mouth tightly closed and her lips pulled inwards, which has been mentioned earlier as associated with displeasure (Beaudry et al., 2014).

Before James responds, he makes a series of rapid clicks or tuts (Ogden, 2013; Wright, 2011). The most common location for clicks is in the pre-turn position, and it would be possible to assume he is simply marking his turn at talking or perhaps is delaying speaking as he thinks of what to say. However, in this case, the clicks are not used in isolation; they are accompanied by what Ogden (2013) refers to as "response tokens." As he produces the clicking sounds, his head is tilted back, his arms are crossed in front of him, and he is holding his pen in an upright position (Figure 4.2, image 7). At the same time, he rocks back and forth, actions typically associated with feelings of disagreement or contempt (Matsumoto & Hwang, 2013). Even as he says "yeah," his head is still tilted back and his arms remain crossed, contradicting what appears to be agreement with what Kate has said. He only looks at Kate when he says, "agree that they're prepared to do some stuff." Kate gives three backchannel responses that each become progressively more emphatic "mm," "mmm," and "yeah," to signal that James is correctly surmising what needs to happen rather than encouraging him to continue talking (Saville-Troike, 1989).

Subterranean Disagreement

James then pauses and rolls his eyes upwards, also a sign of disagreement, rejection or even contempt, before speaking again. The next point he wishes to make is obviously important to him as he repeats it. First, he attributes the raising of the topic to a female colleague, Shelley, but endorses her action with the words "quite rightly," and then repeats the point again "there's a big question I think about casting for that meeting?" referring to the meeting between the authority and the dissident residents (discussed in Chapter 7).

His gesture during this extract indicates that James realizes this is a sensitive topic. As he says "the questions which Shelley raised," he lifts his left arm (the right arm remains across his body) and uses his left hand to rub his neck and around his ear (Figure 4.2, image 8). This adaptor gesture may be indicating discomfort and hence the need to soothe himself (Matsumoto & Hwang, 2013) although it can also be a sign of dominance (Goldberg & Rosenthal, 1986). He uses this gesture until he has finished stating his point of view.

The discussion moves to who should attend the meeting. Kate suggests that there needs to be a woman, with which James seems to agree. Then, as the discussion discounts several possible female attendees, James (whose left hand has moved from his neck to his face where his fingers are tapping on his mouth), asks *why* it has to be a woman. This is a closed gesture, which indicates thought, but also doubt (Mahmoud & Robinson, 2011), possibly as he knows it is a controversial question.

Kate consults her notes, but this is unlikely to be for fact checking, as she is well-versed in the detail of the issue; rather it is for support for what she is to say next. She then asserts that she believes it "makes for a nice balance." Here she is talking about balance between the authority's negotiators and the residents. She backs up her argument by pointing to the fact that residents' group have a female spokesperson whose name she finds in her notes. James responds with a "yeah," which Kate takes to be a continuer and opens her mouth to add something, but before she can respond verbally, James counters "women can be just as threatened by women though." At this point, Kate lifts her left arm which is resting on her desk and uses the forefinger to twirl her hair. This self-adaptor is likely to be the result of feeling discomfort or irritation (Goldberg & Rosenthal, 1986).

Throughout the interaction, Kate has only partly orientated her body towards James while James faces her directly, standing, and thereby remaining physically higher than she is. According to Matsumoto and Hwang (2013), the degree of orientation is associated with attitude towards the interactant. The least direct orientation is meant for those we are most disinclined to interact with. Thus, while Kate remains polite and civil throughout the discussion, it is evident from her nonverbal language that she wants to minimize contact with her colleague. It appears that in this instance they have different views of the purpose and practice of public relations. There is also a suggestion of some level of subterranean gender conflict.

Equally revealing is the fluency with which Kate relates their boss's view, and her ability to empathize with the residents, who are unhappy with the authority's decision to change provider. Through her fluent verbal and supportive nonverbal language, she displays her *specialist tacit knowledge* (Collins & Evans, 2007) about communication, relationships and interaction, a knowledge that James appears not to appreciate in this case.

Conclusion

In this chapter, we explored peer-to-peer and, specifically, PRP-to-PRP relationships with a focus on power and relationships. We highlighted two critical incidents in which the PRP, Kate, plays a key role. In the first, she is involved in "problematic talk" (Holmes & Stubbe, 2015) with the architect who has exceeded the financial brief by far. In the second, she has to relay the content of a missed meeting to her colleague and get him on board with the message. In both instances, she is the sole female in the discussions, and in both, her strategies differ in the subtlest of ways. In the first incident, she is a little more hesitant in delivering her message and her body language is controlled. In the second, she delivers her message clearly with nonverbal supportive language. Both meetings are meant to be brief, but for very different reasons.

In the first interaction, there is no evident tension between the PRPs involved. In fact, we know from our fieldwork that Kate has a good relationship with her colleague, Andrew. Although he frames the meeting and appears to take the lead, the watchful gazes of the male participants on Kate, combined with the reaction her comments invoke in Tom, show us that Kate wields much power. This micro analysis also demonstrates that the two PRPs subtly empower each other through their actions. At no point is her power undermined. In addition, the analysis highlights that power is ambient, that is, embedded in the context; it is experienced but not obviously asserted. This type of power we have labeled as *ambient power*, and it is a power that Kate enacts very well.

Suggesting that power is ambient and a low-key phenomenon in public relations that *seduces* rather than dominates holds implications for the theorizing about power and its place in public relations. It presents a more feminine notion of power that sees it *embedded in relationships* and the *enactment of these relationships*, and rejects the idea that power "is a symbolic value which is transferable only within narrow limits" (Zerfaß, 2008, p. 79). Furthermore, it infers that ambient power is, and should be, part of our understanding of *personal influence* (see Chapter 2).

In the second encounter, we see a different side to Kate as she projects the persona of her boss. In this encounter with James, she is fluent, directive and expressive, using supportive gestures to get her point across and convince her colleague to agree—even though he was at times noticeably reluctant. We reason that here, her language and gestures show a form of specialist tacit knowledge, namely, *interactional expertise* (Collins & Evans, 2007). As Collins and Evans (2007) state, "with interactional expertise, conversation about technical matters has a normal lively tone and neither party is bored" (p. 33). Yet, James does not reciprocate, and Kate's imperceptible sigh suggests that perhaps this is one of the reasons this relationship is strained. Kate knows that James does not share her interest in the technical matter of communicating with the residents and resolving the conflict between them, the local authority and the waste management provider, and appears dismissive. This does not deter her, however, from trying to persuade him otherwise and asserting influence over the meaning that is being created.

If we view these micro-interactions as sites of meaning-making about the role and place of public relations practice, as well as sites of relational enactment, then these interactions highlight some of the key challenges facing practitioners daily, including how to persuade and influence others. In the next chapter, we look at PRP-client interactions as sites of meaning-making and relational enactment.

Notes

1 Part of this chapter was presented as a conference paper at the International Communication Association Annual Conference in Fukuoka, Japan, July 2016.
2 The name of the contractor has been changed for reasons of confidentiality to CWL, which stands for Clean Waste Ltd.

References

Allen, J. (2006). Ambient power: Berlin's Potsdamer Platz and the seductive logic of public spaces. *Urban Studies, 43*(2), 441–455. doi:10.1080/004209 80500416982.

Beaudry, O., Roy-Charland, A., Perron, M., Cormier, I., & Tapp, R. (2013). Featural processing in recognition of emotional facial expressions. *Cognition and Emotion, 28*(3), 416–432. doi:10.1080/02699931.2013.833500.

Bousmalis, K., Mehu, M., & Pantic, M. (2013). Towards the automatic detection of spontaneous agreement and disagreement based on nonverbal behaviour: A survey of related cues, databases, and tools. *Image and Vision Computing, 31*(2), 203–221. doi:10.1016/j.imavis.2012.07.003.

Collins, H., & Evans, R. (2007). *Rethinking expertise.* Chicago, IL: University of Chicago Press.

Conrad, C., & Poole, M. S. (2005). *Strategic organizational communication: In a global economy* (6th ed.), Belmont, CA: Wadsworth.

Edwards, L. (2006). Rethinking power in public relations. *Public Relations Review, 32,* 229–331. doi10.1016/j.pubrev.2006.05.013.

Edwards, L. (2009). Symbolic power and public relations practice: Locating individual practitioners in their social context. *Journal of Public Relations Research, 21*(3), 251–272. doi:10.1080/1062726082640674.

Givens, D. (1999). *The nonverbal dictionary of gestures, signs, and body language cues.* Spokane, CA: Center for Nonverbal Studies.

Goldberg, S., & Rosenthal, R. (1986). Self–touching behaviour in the job interview: antecedents and consequences. *Journal of Nonverbal Behavior, 10*(3), 65–80.

Harrigan, J. (2005). Proxemics, kinesics, and gaze. In J. Harrigan, R. Rosenthal, & K. Scherer (Eds.), *The new handbook of methods in nonverbal behavior research* (pp. 137–198). Oxford: Oxford University Press.

Harrison, S. (2010). Evidence for node and scope of negation in coverbal gesture. *Gesture, 10*(1), 29–51. doi:10.1075/gest.10.1.03har.

Hirschman, L. (1994). Female–male differences in conversational interaction. *Language in Society, 23*(3), 427. doi:10.1017/s0047404500018054.

Hodges, C. (2006). "PRP culture." A framework for exploring public relations practitioners as cultural intermediaries. *Journal of Communication Management, 10*(1), 80–93. doi:10.1108/13632540610646391.

Hoey, E. (2013). Do sighs matter? Interactional perspectives on sighing. *Annual Meeting of the Berkeley Linguistics Society, 39*(1), 61. doi:10.3765/bls.v39i1.3870.

Holmes, J., & Stubbe, M. (2015). *Power and politeness in the workplace. A sociolinguistic analysis of talk at work. Routledge linguistics classics.* New York: Routledge.

Ihlen, Ø., & Verhoeven, P. (2012). A public relations identity for the 2010s. *Public Relations Inquiry, 1*(2), 159–176. doi:10.1177/2046147X11435083.

Kendon, A. (1967). Some functions of gaze in social interaction. *Acta Psychologica, 26,* 22–63.

Kendon, A. (2004). *Gesture: Visible action as utterance* (3rd ed.), Cambridge: Cambridge University Press.

Kram, K. E., & Isabella, L. A. (1985). Mentoring alternatives: the role of peer relationships in career development. *Academy of Management Journal, 28*(1), 110–132.

Lascarides, A., & Stone, M. (2009). Discourse coherence and gesture interpretation. *Gesture, 9*(2), 147–180. doi:10.1075/gest.9.2.01las.

L'Etang, J. (2005). Critical public relations: Some reflections. *Public Relations Review, 31*(4), 521–526. doi:10.1016/j.pubrev.2005.08.011.

Levordashka, A., & Utz, S. (2016). Ambient awareness: From random noise to digital closeness in online social networks. *Computers in Human Behavior, 60,* 147–154. doi:10.1016/j.chb.2016.02.037.

Liddicoat, A. J. (2011). *An introduction to conversation analysis* (2nd ed.), New York: Continuum International Publishing Group.

Macnamara, J. (2012). The global shadow of functionalism and excellence theory: An analysis of Australasian PR. *Public Relations Inquiry, 1*(3), 367–402. doi:10.1177/2046147X12448581.

Mahmoud, M., & Robinson, P. (2011). *Interpreting hand-over-face gestures.* Retrieved from www.cl.cam.ac.uk/~mmam3/pub/ACII2011-Doctoral-2011.pdf.

Matsumoto, D. R. & Hwang, H. S. (2013). Body and gestures. In H. S. Hwang, M. G. Frank, & D. R. Matsumoto (Eds.), *Nonverbal communication: Science and applications* (pp. 75–96). Thousand Oaks, CA: Sage Publications.

McNeill, D. (1992). *Hand and mind: What gestures reveal about thought.* Chicago, IL: University of Chicago Press.

McNeill, D. (2005). *Gesture and thought.* Chicago, IL: Chicago University Press.

Müller, C. (2004). Forms and uses of the palm up open hand: A case of a gesture family? In R. Posner & C. Müller (Eds.), *The semantics and pragmatics of everyday gestures* (pp. 233–256). Berlin, Germany: Weidler Buchverlag.

Ogden, R. (2013). Clicks and percussives in English conversation. *Journal of the International Phonetic Association, 13*(3), 299 320. doi:10.1017/s0025100313000224.

Place, K. R. (2012). Power–control or empowerment? How women public relations practitioners make meaning of power. *Journal of Public Relations Research, 24,* 435–450. doi:10.1080/1062726X.2012.723278.

Potter, J., & Hepburn, A. (2010). Putting aspiration into words: 'Laugh particles', managing descriptive trouble and modulating action. *Journal of Pragmatics, 42*(6), 1543–1555.

Ramsey, R. E. (2016). Ethics from the edge: A sketch of precarity from a philosophy of communication. *Atlantic Journal of Communication, 24*(1), 31–39. doi:10.1080/15456870.2016.1113964.

Reich, S. S. (1980). Significance of pauses for speech perception. *Journal of Psycholinguistic Research, 9*(4), 379–389. doi:10.1007/bf01067450.

Saville-Troike, M. (1989). *The ethnography of communication: An introduction* (2nd ed.), New York: Blackwell Publishers.

Schegloff, E. A. (2010). Some other "Uh(m)"s. *Discourse Processes*, 47(2), 130–174. doi:10.1080/01638530903223380.

Schegloff, E., Jefferson, G., & Sacks, H. (1977). The preference for self–correction in the oganisation of repair in conversation. *Language, 53*(2), 361–382.

Schiffrin, D. (1987). *Discourse markers*. Cambridge: Cambridge University Press.

Scollon, R. (2001). *Mediated discourse: The nexus of practice*. New York: Routledge.

Seaford, H. (1975). Facial expression dialect: An example. In A. Kendon, M. R. Key, & R. M. Harris (Eds.), *Organization of behavior in face-to-face interaction* (pp. 151–159). The Hague, Netherlands: Walter de Gruyter & Co.

Sias, P. M. (2009). *Organizing relationships: Traditional and emerging perspectives on workplace relationships*. Thousand Oaks, CA: Sage Publications.

Sissons, H. (2012). Multimodal exchanges and power relations in a public relations department. In S. Norris (Ed.), *Multimodality in practice: Investigating theory-in-practice-through-methodology* (pp. 35–49). New York: Routledge.

Strangert, E. (2003). Emphasis by pausing. In M. J. Solé, D. Recasens, & J. Romero (Eds.), *Proceedings of the 15th international congress of phonetic sciences, Barcelona, Spain* (pp. 2477–2480). Rundle Mall: Causal Publications.

Tannen, D. (1990). Ordinary conversation and literary discourse: Coherence and the poetics of repetition. *Annals of the New York Academy of Sciences, 583*(1 The Uses of L), 15–30. doi:10.1111/j.1749–6632.1990.tb12183.x.

Taylor, M., & Kent, M. L. (2014). Dialogic enactment: Clarifying foundational concepts. *Journal of Public Relations Research, 26*, 384–398. doi:10.1080/1 062726X.2014.956106.

Teigen, K. H. (2008). Is a sigh 'just a sigh'? Sighs as emotional signals and responses to a difficult task. *Scandinavian Journal of Psychology, 49*(1), 49–57.

Theunissen, P. (2018/in press). The philosophy and ethics of enactment. In K. A. Johnston, & M. Taylor (Eds.), *The handbook of communication enactment*. Malden, MA: Wiley-Blackwell.

Valentini, C. (2010). Personalised networks of influence in public relations. *Journal of Communication Management, 14*(2), 153–166. doi:10.1108/136 32541011034600.

Wright, M. (2011). On clicks in English talk-in-interaction. *Journal of the International Phonetic Association, 41*(2), 207–229.

Zerfaß, A. (2008). Corporate Communication revisited: Integrating business strategy and strategic communication. In A. Zerfaß, B. Van Ruler, & K. Sriramesh (Eds.), *Public relations research: European and international perspectives and innovations; [this book has been published as a Festschrift for prof. Dr. Günter Bentele, University of Leipzig, on the occasion of his 60th birthday in march 2008]* (pp. 65–96). Wiesbaden, Germany: VS Verlag fur Sozialwissenschaften.

5   The PRP–Client Relationship

The commonality between science and art is in trying to see profoundly—to develop strategies of seeing and showing.
—Edward Tufte (1942–), Educator

An Asymmetrical Relationship

While peer relationships create the workplace culture that governs a public relations practitioner's (PRP's) practice, their relationships play out in what Goffman (1959) refers to as the backstage area of their professional lives. Here they prepare their parts and rehearse their lines, as we saw in the last chapter. This current chapter sees the PRPs stepping from behind the backstage curtain to take their places on the front stage as they interact with their clients.

Client relationships are integral to the success of a business, and creating and maintaining them is both an art and a science. They require skills that are often downplayed and skimmed over in public relations courses, and yet, "Building and maintaining positive partnerships with clients may be the most important skill a consultant possesses" (Capozzi, 2015, p. 367).

Not surprisingly, popular advice on how to build long–term and "lasting" relationships with clients—ranging from improving communication to meeting deadlines—abound. In his article, Jacobs (2008), for example, provides advice on how a PRP can build better relationships with a client through listening, understanding their world and fears (empathy), using their language (rhetoric), caring about the client's success, being proactive and strategic (including going out to visit them and being "the call the client wants to take"), changing with them, articulating standards (and presumably ethics), and generally creating win–win situations. The advice is upbeat, aimed to inspire. It also suggests that if the PRP simply interacts according to the *client's* expectations by *seeking affinity* (see Chapter 2), she will be successful in building such "lasting" relationships.

But this simplistic advice is somewhat contradictory: it suggests that the PRP has the power to make and break the relationship because, after all, *she* is the one that must articulate standards and expectations, is expected to change *with* the client, use *their* language and understand *their* world; there is no mention of it being a co–constructed process, or clients having equal responsibility for the success of this relationship.

Possibly in response to the one–sided approach to PRP–client relationships, PRP and consultant, Heather Whaling (2010), set out four key requirements for being a *good client* in her blog, prTini.com, and in doing so, intimated that not all PRP–client relationships are desired nor are all clients "good" ones. A good client wants a partner, she said, not just a vendor, and added that good clients have realistic expectations, pay their bills on time, and are open to new ideas. Her statement highlights the idea of *partnership*, suggesting a *symmetrical structure* where power is shared, as opposed to "client" and "practitioner" roles, which suggest a clear distinction of roles. Yet, herein lies a dilemma. When drawing a distinction between roles, a *role relationship* is implied, and as discussed in Chapter 2, the relational structure of these relationships is *complementary* (inequality in power) and *transactional*, accompanied by a clear set of expectations. In the PRP–client relationship, for example, the one is a client that requires a service, and the other provides that required service; the one pays and the other receives the money in return for their expertise. Although it may be useful to counteract the idea of the PRP in service of the client and thus taking sole responsibility for the relationship, proposing a normative symmetrical relationship is not constructive. In our fieldwork, we found the complementary and transactional structure to be the most commonplace. Consultants are hired for their expertise and are paid for providing a service. While they may attempt to be a partner, the power structure remains *asymmetrical*. Therefore, we choose to label these relationships as *PRP–client relationships* as opposed to "partnerships."

PRP–Client Interaction as Expertise

In our research, we found PRPs skillfully managed their interactions with their clients, ensuring that the required service was delivered while strategically maintaining amicable relationships that could potentially lead to future work. Indeed, the first critical incident shows one of these PRPs contemplating how she might approach the client to ensure they received the desired outcome without affecting the relationship negatively.

Citing a study by Tom Harris, the founding partner of Golin Harris, Capozzi (2015) highlighted five *relationship principles* that drive client satisfaction: "chemistry," client service, quality of the team responsible for the account, quality of the (account) management, and the stability of staff. Capozzi also specified *technical principles* that include the overall quality of work, meeting deadlines, keeping promises, creativity, quality of writing, and attention to detail. He pointed out, however, that in the study, the relationship principles were rated higher than the technical ones, and that overall, *chemistry* was rated the highest. It would thus be fair to argue that there is more to PRP–client relationships than the idea that client relationships can begin in "simple and unexpected ways," or that follow–up projects lead to "a continuing and expanding relationship as the client draws on the full range of the firm's public relations capabilities" (Broom, 2009, p. 73).

In this chapter, we present and discuss three critical incidents that highlight the skills required to navigate complex interpersonal PRP–client relationships. These interactions involve two agency PRPs preparing for and then meeting with client representatives. It is evident from these interactions that preparing for and strategizing about the interaction and how they might approach "delicate" topics, requires a high level of diplomacy and interpersonal skills. It also requires insight into the psychology of the client, and the ability to identify, set and navigate the unique relational structure.

Furthermore, these consultants' work, much like other public relations work, is characterized by meetings, and it is therefore not surprising that all three critical incidents presented here are types of meetings. Meetings, then, become sites of meaning–creation, agenda–setting, and relational enactment; they provide us with insight into the complexities of relationship maintenance between PRPs and those for whom they work.

Maureen's Conundrum

The critical incidents presented in this chapter are centered on two Auckland–based PRPs, Gail and Maureen, as they prepare to meet with Kirsty, the client's project manager, and Pip, an independent consultant. The meeting has been called to make necessary last–minute decisions ahead of an event being held in two days' time in Sydney, Australia. The client, a local authority, hopes the event will encourage businesses to invest in New Zealand. While Gail and Maureen have good news to share at the meeting, they also must do some trouble–shooting and convey news that may potentially not please the client.

The first interaction occurs between the two PRPs just before the client meeting. The interaction shows Maureen wrestling with a conundrum. She has been in contact with the producer of an important television news program covering business in Australia, who is interested in interviewing one of her client's spokespeople. The spokesperson will be in Sydney supporting the client at the upcoming event.

Before she can set up the interview, Maureen must find out when the spokesperson will be arriving in Sydney, as well as whether he will be available to do the interview. If not, then she needs to know when he is available, so that she can negotiate a different interview slot. She is reticent to approach Kirsty because, as Maureen says, "she [Kirsty] is not a communications person," and experience of working with her leads

Maureen to believe she is unlikely to appreciate the importance of the opportunity or understand the benefits of such exposure in the media. Just before this extract, Maureen's colleague, Gail, has said about the business news program, "that's almost perfect target market for them isn't it." Despite this, Maureen is concerned that the client won't think the interview is important enough to encourage the spokesperson to prioritize it in his schedule.

We join the extract as Maureen is leaning back in her chair with her hands behind her head stroking her ponytail—an action she continues for eighteen seconds into the extract. Seemingly deep in thought, her gaze remains fixed on the computer screen. As mentioned in the previous chapter, this type of self–touching or self–adaptor is most often considered a sign of anxiety or discomfort (Meadors & Murray, 2014), and here is also likely to be a manifestation of irritation or frustration as she worries about how to ensure the spokesperson does the interview (Goldberg & Rosenthal, 1986).

She then leans forward and addresses her colleague who sits across the room to her right, but is not caught in the camera shot.

Maureen's body language displays frustration as she strategizes how to manage the situation with the client, but the tone between the two women remains relaxed, suggesting their relationship is convivial.

Maureen is keen to find out what flexibility the news program has if the interviewee is not available on Tuesday, "if he's not¿" (Figure 5.1, image 2). Gail agrees that it is a good idea to check if there is the "option" of doing the interview that Wednesday. But, if they are to negotiate a different time, they would need to know the spokesperson will be available. Finding this out is proving to be more complicated than it seems. In an ideal world, the PRP could simply approach the spokesperson directly and ask about his availability. However, in the second part of the interaction, it becomes clear that there is sensitivity around approaching the spokesperson themselves rather than going through the client's representative, Kirsty.

Contemplating Relationship Risk

Maureen's frustration and anxiety continue throughout the first part of the extract. Her arms drop to her side and she leans forward furrowing her brow with her top lip raised, letting out a long sigh as she says, "yeah::" (Figure 5.1, image 1). Her "yeah::" is unlikely to be a response to what Gail has said previously about the business program being the perfect target market as she has already acknowledged her agreement with that and a period of four seconds has passed. It is more likely to be the result of the contemplation she has been doing, and in fact, is typical of a negative emotion; in this case, possibly irritation or mild disgust at the situation (Rozin, Lowery, & Ebert, 1994).

M: hhyeah::

M: I'm tempted to think whether I <u>prompt</u> her now
    about <u>Wednesday</u>
    and say if he's <u>not</u>¿
G: (1.8) I think it'd be <u>worth</u> [(indistinct) find if we've
    got an option]
M: [(indistinct) still keen to
    talk to him just to s-]
G: yeah
M: °just to° see

G: (7.0) be tempting to give Josh a ring di<u>re:ct</u>
M: yeah=
G: =coz we've got=
M: =I don't want to step on=

G: =I <u>kno:w</u>=
M: =[I <u>kno:w</u>
G: =[I <u>kno:w</u>
M: I don't want to step on Kirsty's toes but I <u>definitely</u>
    wanna know
    (1.2) ↑why: >don't I just ring im.<
    (1.4) .hhh hhh

Figure 5.1 Wrestling with a conundrum.

M: (1.7) I ↑could just ring him couldn't I¿
   (2.3) or not.
G: (0.8) uhm

M: °do you think they'd get a bit miffed°

M: (4.0) I tell you what,
   I'll flick a note back to Kylie to sa:y
   (0.4) if he's not there tomorrow,
   if he's not in the country tomorrow morning

G: (1.0) how about=
M: =he definitely is on Wednesday (.) is that a
   possibility:=
G: =yeah
M: (sniff)

Figure 5.1 (Continued)

She shifts her gaze to Gail as she begins to outline what she is thinking, expressing a wish to explore the possibility with the news program of alternative times for the interview (Figure 5.1, image 2). This gaze–shift can be described as "back-channeling," that is, compensating for the lack of visual attention given earlier to her colleague (Sandgren, Andersson, van de Weijer, Hansson, & Sahlén, 2012). When expressing the wish, Maureen begins with the verb "tempted," which has overtones of a wish that might be attractive, but somehow is not legitimate. She even rehearses the words she would use "and say if he's not¿" which shows that she is planning her communication approach.

She is encouraged by Gail who says she thinks it would be "<u>worth</u>" it to find out if there is an option, wording that again indicates there may be some *risk*. Maureen downplays the act of finding out, using the restrictor "just," in "just to s–" as if it's not really a transgression and downplays the force of the proposal (Holmes & Stubbe, 2015). The "s–" in "just to s–" is probably a shortened "see," indicated by the later use of "see." She then repeats "°just to° see" in full when her speech is overlapped by Gail, who has begun to speak at a point that Jefferson (1984) would recognize as a state of "syntactic completeness" or a possible transition point to another speaker. Indeed, Maureen had paused after "if he's not," and appeared to be waiting for a response, but after hearing agreement from Gail in "it'd be worth," she completes her thought despite Gail not having finished her turn. Maureen's interruption of Gail speaking also falls into Jefferson's recognitional overlapping talk category where the hearer is listening not for completeness, but for *adequacy* or when the *meaning is available* to them. In this case, once Maureen has heard agreement from Gail, she feels able to finish her thought, even though Gail has not finished speaking. Gail seems unperturbed by the interruption, suggesting that the two women have developed a shared understanding that allows for idiosyncratic rules of politeness.

Maureen's need to repeat the last point "just to see" implies she is keen for it to be clear that she does not mean for there to be any serious consequences to her speaking to the television producer. "Just seeing" would not lead to decisions being made of which Kirsty might not approve. It appears as if a resolution has been made as Maureen begins typing.

There is a pause of seven seconds before Gail speaks again, admitting it would be "tempting" to go a step further, not only to call the broadcaster "just to see," but to call the spokesperson direct (using the colloquial term "ring"). Maureen stops typing but does not immediately make eye contact, as if thinking through Gail's suggestion. She then turns to Gail, saying "yeah," acknowledging that she heard but not that she agrees (Figure 5.1, image 3). Her brow remains furrowed and top lip lifted, indicating frustration or doubt with the situation (Rozin et al., 1994).

Gail then starts to explain "coz we've" (suggesting she was about to say "got to know"), but Maureen interrupts, using the same recognitional overlapping talk she exhibited earlier, saying, "I don't want to step on." She then stops and Gail, understanding, replies "I know." They both simultaneously repeat "I know," and Maureen turns back to her computer. She then appears to finish Gail's thought, "I don't want to step on Kirsty's toes but I <u>definitely</u> wanna know." *Overlapping talk* or interruptions such as happens here can be "a sign of fine–grained attention" (Jefferson, 1986, p. 153), and therefore of a close working relationship that has developed between Maureen and Gail. As a result, the two PRPs start up their next turn either where they believe an utterance has been completed or where it is ready for a transition.

As Maureen utters "I don't want to step on Kirsty's toes but I <u>definitely</u> wanna know," she lifts her left hand up to her left brow, and on each of the words "Kirsty's," "toes" and "<u>definitely</u>" she rubs her left eyebrow with the fingers of her left hand from the inside out—three times in all (Figure 5.1, image 4). This self–adaptor, as it involves repeated rubbing, is likely to be a subconscious reproduction of being comforted (Meadors & Murray, 2014). She continues looking at her computer screen until the third rub when her gaze follows her hand to the left of the computer screen where she has some paper.

The Obvious Solution Won't Work

As she collects a piece of paper, she almost blurts out the suggestion, "↑why: > don't I just ring im.<" The first word "why" is spoken in a raised pitch, indicating a marked emotional stance (Günthner, 1999; Yu, 2001), as does the faster tempo of the second part of the utterance. Raised pitch and fast tempo are indicative of a turn that is oppositional in character as if Maureen is expecting to be disagreed with (by Gail or possibly Kirsty, the client) (Yu, 2001) because she is suggesting that they give into the temptation mentioned earlier. Again, she inserts a mitigating "just" in front of the action of making a phone call to the spokesperson to make this less of sin.

After the utterance, she turns her head towards Gail for confirmation (Kendon, 1967). Her shoulders are raised and she has an expression of what appears to be delighted surprise—brows and upper eyelids are raised, and her jaw is slightly dropped (Figure 5.1, image 5). She then breaks into a broad smile and exhales noticeably as her gaze momentarily fixes on Gail before she looks away and then back at Gail before she begins speaking again.

The function of the surprise expression (raised eyebrows, open eyes, open mouth) is to allow the person displaying the reaction to take in as much information as quickly as possible about the surprising event and to process it before reacting further (Matsumoto & Hwang, 2013). In this case, Maureen's expression of delighted surprise could be communicating that this is a startling idea to them both; it changes Maureen's position from one of "not wanting to step on Kirsty's toes," to one that is prepared to do precisely that.

However, once Maureen has announced this possibility, there is a pause of nearly two seconds. It appears she is waiting for a response from Gail: either for approval or a reason why she cannot do this. Gail's lack of response could be because she does not realize she is being asked a question. While the statement begins with a "why," it seems to be rhetorical as it does not contain any request for new information nor a rising intonation, which would be common for a question (Schiffrin, 1994).

After a 1.7 second silence, Maureen repeats the question, but this time using the modal verb "could," followed by an explicit question, "couldn't I¿." She uses a lower modality that illustrates her awareness of the power asymmetry; she is not the senior PRP—Gail is—and therefore she needs Gail's approval (Machin & Mayr, 2012). "Could" has a lower modality than "will," for example, as it avoids being direct or specific. That she is unsure of the suggestion at this point is also indicated by her facial expression. Her gaze has shifted from Gail to the paper in her hands and her left–hand index finger moves to her mouth (Mahmoud & Robinson, 2011). Her head then turns towards Gail again, finger still to her mouth, and her brow furrowed with uncertainty.

As two seconds pass and Maureen has still not elicited a response from Gail, she answers her own question, saying perhaps calling him is not an option: "or not." She has realized if Gail were going to agree (despite her earlier suggestion that it was a tempting option), then the agreement would have been given with the minimum of gap after it was put to her (Pomerantz, 1984). A disagreement assessment is more likely to be delayed, as we see here. Even now Gail delays, using the filler "uhm." In a low voice, Maureen articulates what she thinks Gail is saying by her silence, "°do you think they'd get a bit miffed°" (Figure 5.1, image 6). When another four seconds of silence pass she makes a suggestion, signposting it with "I tell you what," (Figure 5.1, image 7). She then uses the high modality verb, "will," as she says she'll "flick a note" to the producer of the news program. Maureen is more confident now as she knows she is back on solid ground with Gail, and Gail responds, appearing to agree by joining in Maureen's thought and then adding a "yeah." After negotiating a result, Maureen turns back to her computer with a sniff, possibly indicating an emotional stance that is slightly irritated or even contemptuous of the situation (Figure 5.1, image 8).

Silence has been argued to be one of the ways participants in an interaction can express disagreement while avoiding loss of face or open confrontation (Schnurr & Chan, 2011). Here, Gail's response is quite marked, but perhaps more one of cold feet than strong disagreement, indicated by the fact that it was her idea in the first place to consider calling the spokesperson.

Expressing Frustration

Immediately after this extract Maureen overtly expresses her frustration with the client by telling Gail that it would be "so much easier if I could organize these things myself" to which Gail responds "true." Later, in an interview with the researcher, Maureen explained that they had already come up against problems with Kirsty when they tried to organize interviews in Sydney with a reporter from Auckland:

> ...and she was kind of like: Well, why would we need to do that? Can't he just phone them before he goes—and stuff like that. And we're kind of: Well kind of the point of actually being there is to be part of the whole thing and part of the atmosphere.

When asked why they were concerned about the PRPs calling the spokesperson, Maureen responded:

> Kirsty likes to be the person to liaise with all the internal people. Sometimes I guess I just do all of that and they [the client] are quite happy with that—and that's the way I prefer it. Others sort of, "you can do this part of it, but not quite that part of it." It would be a heck of a lot easier for me to just call Josh on his mobile and say, "where are you? Are you in the country or not—or what?" If we could sort this.

Meetings as Sites of Relational Enactment

As mentioned earlier, meetings are integral to PRP–client work, and as Holmes and Stubbe (2015) stated, communication interactions focus directly or indirectly on workplace business. Based on their research in the New Zealand workplace, Holmes and Stubbe found that these meetings range from small one–on–one meetings, either face-to-face or mediated through phones or other technologies, to large formal meetings that are directed by a chairperson and include a minute taker. By their definition, meetings can, therefore, take place anywhere, such as in a café or a boardroom, which fits our understanding of public relations work. In the first critical incident, for example, the two PRPs share an office, and their discussion can be seen as a meeting of sorts.

Meetings provide opportunities to express institutional and expert power while at the same time developing and maintaining relationships through what Holmes and Stubbe (2015) described as manifestations of politeness, respect (or disrespect), collegiality, and solidarity. They are "prime sites of doing power" (Holmes & Stubbe, 2015, p. 58), that is, where workplace power and relationships are built, developed and maintained. Paying attention to relationships while maintaining a focus on the purpose of the meeting can, therefore, be regarded as an essential skill for PRPs.

While the informal meeting between Maureen and Gail can be viewed as a *problem–solving or present–oriented meeting,* because it arose spontaneously to solve a problem, the second meeting where the PRPs meet with the client, can be seen as a hybrid of a *planning or forward–oriented meeting,* where tasks are assigned, permissions are given and action is requested, and a *reporting or backward–oriented meeting,* where feedback is given, information is requested, and participants are updated on what has been happening (Holmes & Stubbe, 2015).

The second critical incident is taken from the first part of this meeting with the client. There are four participants: Gail and Maureen, the consultant Pip and the client Kirsty. We join the interaction as the four women engage in what appears to be small talk before they move to matters of business.

Engaging in Small Talk

In the first part of this extract, the women engage in typical pre–meeting talk (Mirivel & Tracy, 2005). This kind of talk can include personal updates, information about the industry, or information needed for the meeting (agenda items, etc.). Holmes and Stubbe (2015, p. 89) refer to this as social chat or *small talk,* stating that, "In every social encounter participants are unavoidably involved in constructing, maintaining or modifying the interpersonal relationships between themselves and their addressee."

Small talk fulfills an indispensable role of building rapport, and maintaining and establishing relationships; "it reorients participants to *personal* rather than *role relationships*" (Holmes & Stubbe, 2015, p. 91, emphasis added). Very often, it can be found at the boundaries of workplace interaction, and can, therefore, be viewed as a *boundary marker* where it functions as a standard device for *politeness* or marking transitions between different phases of interaction (Holmes & Stubbe, 2015). In this case, it marks the beginning of a meeting, and functions as *shop talk* where participants discuss the health status of someone in their industry. Shop talk, according to Mirivel and Tracy (2005, p. 16), has a "gossipy quality" and helps participants keep abreast of the people, events, and issues in their industry. Thus, it serves the additional function of information–sharing and being–in–the–know. It indicates that this PRP–client relationship is like that of an *information peer relationship* where information is shared, but self–disclosure is low (see Chapter 4).

The pre–meeting talk finishes with all the participants falling silent and looking down at the table (Figure 5.2, image 1). This lasts for just over a second, although Gail's mouth is beginning to form the transition marker "right," to move the conversation to another topic, for more than half a second before she speaks. Verbal markers such as "right," "so," "anyway,"

K: has she closed up <u>shop</u>?
P: she's not well
G: mmm no
K: isn't she?
G: yeah
K: oh ↑<u>no</u>:
P: mm
K: .hhh hhh

G: (1.2) [<u>ri:</u>]<u>ght</u>
M: [(click)]
P: <u>right</u>
G: shall we t[alk abou]t the <u>good</u> news stuff¿=
M: [right]
M: =wha-
G: <u>Potent</u>
   you got my <u>email</u>?
P: yes (.) I just looked briefly

G: hhhhh °god°
K: ri[ght]
P: [it's all ok]ay=
M: =(indistinct)
G: °it's all oka:y°.
M: it's all good tha[t's the main thing]
G: [((indistinct))]
P: that's [always good]=
G: [uhm]
M: =mmm=
G: =they want to do the <u>wine</u> <u>tasting</u>

K: o:h shit
   oh
G: uhm a:nd the gifts.
P: the [gifts] (.) fa:ntastic
K: [okay]
G: (1.7) .hhh what they're just working through because
   (.) of (.) the: uh:m the the de-
   .hhh the deal with the Wine Ba:r
   it's going to become a bit of a:
   <u>housekeepi:ng</u> (1.3) issue

Figure 5.2 The client meeting.

G: so <u>what</u> they are going to <u>do</u> is
   that the wines for the tasti:ng
   (1.8) (click) (1.9) they w- hh
   the Wine Bar will <u>charge</u> you <u>guys</u> and then (0.8)
   <u>Potent</u> >will pay for all the gifts for <u>free</u> an- it wor-<
   so it will be an <u>accounti:ng</u> (0.4) <u>smoothi:ng</u> (0.5)
   >out sort of process but I'll get all the numbers<

G: but the <u>upshot</u> is
   that .hhh >it's going to be a really good deal<
   but it's the only <u>way</u> that they can make (0.5)
K: so we don't [have to]
G: [the thing ((indistinct))]
M: ((indistinct))
K: do the gifts but we pay for anything that's <u>drunk,</u>
G: at=
K: =abu- in the wine tasting
G: in the wine tasting [yeah]
K: [consumed]=

G: =that is <u>consumed</u>
   so that is the on- from an <u>accounting</u> point of view
   so that they do:n't (1.4)
   <u>muck</u> (0.3)
M: the Wine [(.) Bar b-]
G: [the Wine Bar]
   [coz the Wine Bar are being]
K: [((indistinct))]
G: we wi' we wo- they want to get everything
   that goes through their place <u>paid</u> for¿

G: so >I'll get you the <u>details</u>< but it's just a wa:y
   it's sort of like the <u>easiest</u> way (0.6)
   uhm (0.3) to <u>do</u> that so: .hhh
K: it's not like we're going through a bottle each person
   are we¿
M: [no]
P: [no]
G: [not for tasting]

Figure 5.2 (Continued)

and "okay" are deployed strategically in meetings to maintain control over the topic and keep discussions on track (Holmes & Stubbe, 2015).

Immediately, the mood changes from somber to purposeful, Gail's "ri:ght" is repeated by both Pip and Maureen. Maureen gathers her documents, bangs them on the table, before putting them down again, thrusting both her arms out while uttering a fleeting laugh, overlapping Gail's proposal "shall we talk about the good news stuff" (presumably the "bad" stuff was the sad news they had just shared) (Figure 5.2, image 2). Maureen's gesture is wide, possibly indicating her keenness to move to the "good stuff" or main business of the meeting.

The Most Senior Person is in Charge

Gail's actions and speech marker of "ri:ght" place her as the chair of the meeting, and therefore as the person influencing the meeting's agenda and structure. This may be because she is the senior PRP present and the meeting is occurring at the offices of the public relations agency. Hence it is through her role that power manifests itself in the meeting, because typically, the most senior or influential person manages interactions by setting the agenda, summarizing progress throughout, keeping the discussions on track, and reaching a decision (Holmes & Stubbe, 2015). It is also their actions that determine the consideration given to relationship and "face" maintenance. Equally, setting an alternative agenda can be a means of resisting or subverting the sanctioned power structure (Holmes & Stubbe, 2015)—something that does not appear to happen at this meeting. In fact, Maureen and Pip's echoing (Zhang, 1998) or repetition (Tannen, 1987) of Gail's "right" is used as a way of contributing to social relations, to show involvement and agreement. *Echoing* reflects the speaker's desire to seek common ground (Zhang, 1998), and we can see it between Gail, Pip, and Maureen throughout the interaction. Kirsty, on the other hand, has not joined in this initial echoing. In fact, as Gail states "shall we talk about the good news stuff," she smiles at Kirsty, who in return nods, and displays a tight–lipped smile that does not reach her eyes, which could be the result of the sad news that she has just learned or it could indicate a less than enthusiastic attitude towards the meeting (Ekman, 1992).

Solidarity is Confirmed

Gail then states the main business of the meeting, by using the name of the drinks manufacturer, Potent,[1] that is supporting their event. In doing so, she solidifies her power position in this meeting (Holmes & Stubbe, 2015). Looking straight at Pip, she says pointedly: "Potent you got my email?" When Pip responds that she had, Gail exhales audibly and mutters "°god°" under her breath, shaking her head with her eyes closed, but still smiling. Her actions infer that the situation had been problematic. Kirsty responds with a "right," acknowledging what Gail has said, but she appears not to understand fully what has gone on. Pip steps in to reassure her that "it's all okay" (Figure 5.2, image 3) and Maureen also appears to reassure her, although her words are indistinct. All participants are smiling while looking at Gail as if waiting for her to continue, reaffirming her guiding role in this meeting. Gail then echoes Pip that it is "all oka:y." She uses a falling tone, which expresses finality and certainty—she is certain that it is now okay. Maureen turns to Pip and puts her hand on the table in front of her, again echoing Gail and expanding, "it's all good that's the main thing," and Pip agrees, nodding.

Important here is that the meeting starts with *seeking common ground, consolidating points of view* and the *negotiation of peer solidarity* through acknowledging that they had dealt (successfully) with a difficult situation. This seems to provide reassurance to the client that the consulting PRPs have everything in hand, and therefore legitimizes their expertise and the client's decision to use them.

An Embarrassing Moment

Once solidarity has been established, Gail signals that she wishes to continue through uttering "uhm" (Schegloff, 2010). She then announces the substance of the "good stuff," "they want to do the wine tasting," which surprises Kirsty and she responds to this information "o:h shit." The "oh" is used to indicate the speaker, Kirsty, has received new information. She also shows surprise with a lifting of the eyebrows and widening of the eyes, along with a quick lifting of her head (Ekman, 2007). The "oh" is accompanied a very short time later by an *assessment* of the information, which commonly occurs with an "oh" (Heritage, 1984). In this case, it is "shit," which prompts Kirsty to deliver a second "oh" accompanied by wide eyes and mouth slightly open. As "ohs" are essentially *backward looking* (Heritage, 1984), we know Kirsty's second "oh" refers to her own words and she briefly glances directly at the camera before putting her hand up to her mouth to stop herself saying anything else. These gestures tell us that first she is surprised by what she has said (Ekman, 2007), then she is embarrassed at her language because it is being filmed by the researcher. Next, she laughs, with her right hand up to the left side of her face, palm towards the camera, hiding her mouth (Figure 5.2, image 4). Her initial unilateral laughter can be interpreted as displaying some of this embarrassment, but she drops her hand and leans across the table towards the others inviting them to participate, and they do so. This joint laughter, or collaborative humor, reduces the tension in what could be an embarrassing situation for Kirsty (Kangasharju & Nikko, 2009). Holmes and Stubbe (2015) proposed that *collaborative humor* is evident where there is attention to workplace relationships and the face needs of another participant. While it is used here as relieving tension, it also typically occurs when solutions are sought for a difficult problem, and when there is tension release after tough discussions.

Conveying Problematic Information

After the laughter has died down, all participants look down at their notepads, ready to continue with work-related discussions. Gail continues with "uhm a:nd the gifts." This time Kirsty is more subdued, keeping her gaze on her notebook and responding "okay," while Pip echoes Gail saying, "the gifts" followed by the assessment "fa:ntastic," which she stretches out. Here she has to inform the client that while the sponsor, Potent, will pay for the gifts of wine, the client will have to pay for the wine-tasting. This is an unplanned expense, and Gail appears to be uncertain how Kirsty will react to this, and so the meeting shows Gail's attempts to gain her acceptance.

While Gail is delivering the uncomplicated good news, she is fluent, needing no repairs to her speech and she keeps eye contact with Kirsty and Pip. Then she becomes less fluent, suggesting that she is not as confident about what she must say next. The first indication of trouble may have been signaled with her use of "uhm" before "the gifts" (Figure 5.2, image 4). Using an "uhm" in this position could be what Schegloff (2010) described as introducing a "dispreferred" (p. 141) sequence, that is, one that is in some way not preferred. Perhaps it is not what the speaker wants to say (they have to ask someone for a favor) or not what the hearer wants to hear (they are being rejected or a course of action is being blocked or interfered with in some way).

Trouble is confirmed when Gail uses a couple of short, but definite, pauses between words, coupled with the lengthening of the final syllable in "because (.) of (.) the:" (Brennan & Schober, 2001). These are all signs that she is struggling to formulate her next words. She then uses "uh:m" as a filler, which in this position also indicates imminent trouble-in-talk (Schegloff, 2010). She gives two quick repeats of "the," then uses a mid-word interruption that cuts her off, before taking a deep breath and starting again. Her gaze is on her notes until the end of the sequence when she looks up as she says, "Wine Ba:r" (Figure 5.2, image 4).

Clearly, Gail is struggling to explain "the deal" and "what they're just working through." Her use of the modifier, "just," is an attempt to downplay the significance of what is being worked through, and is likely to be an indication of her concern about how this information will be received by the client. It also might explain why she formed it as a dispreferred sequence. Even her choice of "housekeepi:ng," which is part of domestic rather than financial discourse, shows her trying to make light of what she must say.

In the next part of the interaction, Gail is momentarily fluent again. She uses a familiar, rather formulaic expression (Van Lancker-Sidtis & Rallon, 2004) "so <u>what</u> they are going to <u>do</u> is," which gives her time to formulate what she wants to say next. The use of the discourse marker "so," helps coherence by relating back to the "housekeeping issues" and forward to "what they are going to do" (Fraser, 1999; Schiffrin, 2001). It also signals that she intends moving the discussion forward (Holmes & Stubbe, 2015).

At this point, she puts down her pen, possibly so that her small hand gestures can aid her memory or help her think (Goldin-Meadow, 2003). Her hands form a cylinder in front of her to contain "what they are going to do" before she drops her fingers to the table in front and to one side delineating an area, as she says, "the wines for the tasti:ng," possibly for the tasting of the wines, as opposed to the wines as gifts. However, her gaze stays on her notes and towards the end of the utterance, she is again less fluent. We see a lengthening of a syllable in "tasti:ng," after which she closes her mouth and makes an audible click or tut sound as she opens it again. Clicks are common when a speaker is involved in a word search (Ogden, 2013), and in this case, there is a silence of nearly two seconds before she speaks again. Just after the click, and while Gail is searching for the next words, Kirsty watches her intently, smiling vaguely as if showing some discomfort at Gail's hesitation (Keltner, 2005).

Following the nearly two-second silence, Gail begins to speak again, but she carries out an instant mid-word interruption "w–," takes a breath before seemingly deciding how to proceed. It appears that she was going to say, "they will," but she then names who is charging the client, changing the "they" to "the Wine Bar," so there can be no confusion about who is charging whom. This correction may be due to the client believing Potent wants to charge them. Gail then quickly follows with the information that Potent "> will pay for all the gifts for <u>free</u> an– it wor–<." These words come as a burst of speech that she is obviously eager to say.

To Gail, it is important that the client understands how it will work. She illustrates clearly how she feels about this information. Unlike the small gestures she used to delineate the wines for the tasting, when she says that Potent will pay for the gifts, her two parallel hands are showing a large area in front of her. Hence, it is clear that to Gail, the *gain* from the free gifts outweighs the *cost* of the wine tasting.

As she explains, Gail has divided her gaze between Pip and Kirsty. She then sums up the reason for the arrangement, "so it will be an <u>accounti:ng</u> <u>smoothi:ng</u> out sort of process" (Figure 5.2, image 5). Her gesture here perfectly illustrates her meaning, that this will smooth everything out between the client, the Wine Bar, and Potent. As she says "<u>accounti:ng</u>," she brings her hands up in front of her, left palm on top of the right, facing down, she then separates them in an action that looks like the smoothing of a table top that ends with the palms facing together, shoulder width apart, as if forming the sides of the table, or perhaps the container for the problem to be smoothed out. She repeats the gesture as she says, "smoothi:ng out sort of process," reinforcing the meaning of her verbal statement.

Despite this appearing to be the end of the sentence, Gail then quickly adds (perhaps before she can be questioned), "but I'll get all the numbers but the upshot is that." She also performs the previous "smoothing out" gesture to accompany both these statements, each beginning on the "but" of the utterance although they are on a much smaller scale, less than half the size, and with her arms closer to the table (Figure 5.2, image 6).

It is noteworthy that Gail chooses the contrastive marker "but" (Schiffrin, 1987) to introduce the utterances. In the first case, it is possibly because she realizes the client may expect to be informed of how much the wine tasting will cost and she does not have those "numbers." The use of "but" indicates she understands this and is saying "I don't have the numbers yet, but I will get them." The use of "but" again in the next utterance signals a contrast or apparent contradiction between statements. Gail has just admitted that she has yet to provide an estimate of the cost of the wine tasting. Despite this, she is now claiming that what Potent is offering is a good deal, that is, the company's offer to provide the gifts if they (the client) pay for the wine tasting is one they should accept.

However, she then employs a third "but," as she has yet another contrast to acknowledge: "but it's the only way they can make" the event work, trailing off as she adds "the thing" (the event) almost a second later. So, even though the deal is a good one, it is also the only way they can make it work.

In the pause following Gail's explanation, Kirsty, who is nodding, responds, wanting to ensure she has understood correctly. Gail confirms she has, and adds, that this is "from an accounting point of view so that they do:nt" and she searches for the word "muck," which she stresses, and then pauses again (Figure 5.2, image 7). Her delay invites Maureen to fill in "the Wine Bar," which Gail overlaps slightly as she echoes "the Wine Bar." In other words, the plan for the client to pay is so that "they" don't "muck" the Wine Bar around.

It is not clear who "they" is. Earlier "they" was the bar itself who was going to charge "you guys." Here "they" is perhaps Potent, whose plan this is, or "you guys," the client, whose event this is. That it might refer to the client is given weight in the next utterance as Gail begins with "we wi–," which was possibly going to be "we will"—"we" being presumably an inclusive, collaborative framing of the client that includes Gail and Maureen. Gail then makes a repair to change this to "we wo–," possibly "we would." She makes a final repair to "they want to get everything."

This shifts the argument away from the *action* of the client paying to the *reason* for the client having to pay.

She then quickly repeats that she will get the details, before again using the contrastive marker "but," "but it's just a wa:y." Co–expressive with this utterance is a two–handed gesture that twice draws a ball–shaped container, first for the "details" and then for the "way" (Figure 5.2, image 8). The "but" in "but it's just a wa:y" is here coupled with the modifier "just," and Gail then uses the hedge "sort of" in "sort of like the <u>easiest</u> way" (Gries & David, 2007). It appears Gail is again keen to play down the significance of the client paying for the wine tasting as well as hedging her claim that it is the easiest way, which casts doubt on her confidence in the claim or in how the claim will be received by the client. This doubt is strengthened as the utterance is followed by a pause and then the filler "uhm" followed by another pause and then she finishes with a "so:" that can be taken as acting as a turn–transition device, marking Gail's willingness to allow someone else to speak (Schiffrin, 1987). Kirsty steps in, saying "it's not like we're going through a bottle each person are we¿" This acknowledgment that she accepts the arrangement leads to obvious relief around the table with everyone speaking at once.

The Sensitive Issue of Media Coverage

The third extract is taken from the same PRP–client meeting, and occurs just over 15 minutes later as Maureen updates the participants about the media coverage arranged for the event. Around one minute into the update, she brings up the media interview we saw her discussing with Gail in the first interaction.

Maureen has just been listing the reporters who will be covering the event when she announces that there is an opportunity for Josh, one of their main spokespeople. This is where we join the interaction.

At the start of the extract, Maureen is looking at the notes in front of her as she mentions the "opportunity" (Figure 5.3, image 1), adding that she could not remember if Josh was "there" in Sydney "tomorrow morning." On the word "there" she lifts her gaze to Kirsty, where it remains until "or <u>not</u>," which marks the end of the phrase (Kendon, 1967), after which she looks down at her notes again. Kendon (1967) refers to this gaze shift as a sign of the speaker checking for the response to what they have just said. As Kirsty provides no response and no indication that she wants to say anything, Maureen continues.

Her use of "but uhm" next is noteworthy as this phrasing can be used as an attempt to "exit a sequence" or hand over the floor to another speaker (Schegloff, 2010, p. 140). But here, there are other actions that contradict this interpretation. Maureen's nonverbal actions make it clear that she wishes to continue speaking. Not only has she removed a key device (eye contact) that

M: uhm and we ↑have an opportunity for <u>Josh</u> actually¿
.hhh I also wasn't sure
I couldn't remember if he was there tomorrow
morning or <u>not</u>, but (0.5) uhm (0.5)
<u>Sky</u> (.) <u>News</u> (.) <u>Business</u> has come back over the:re=
P: =h[mm]
M: [and said] they'd like to talk to JOSH
K: great

M: they want to talk to Josh tomorrow <u>morning</u>
(0.9) was he in the <u>country</u> and I said look I'm not
actually <u>sure</u> I'll find out [and get back to you]
K: [((indistinct))] doesn't it?=
M: =hhh ye:ah hhh
so I went back to her and said look (0.5) I'm not sure
if he is or <u>not</u> I'll get back to you
but if it's <u>Wednesday</u> (0.7) would you be in- still be
interested in for him for <u>Wednesday</u> coz I know
he's <u>definitely</u> [going to be] (0.5) there by <u>then</u>¿
K: [yeah]

M: uhm
and she said yeah <u>quite</u> <u>possibly</u> it may just be at a
different <u>time</u> which is probably better
because it was like 6.15 6.30 tomorrow morning¿
K: so would that be at their <u>studios</u> or something¿
M: <u>CBD</u> studios yea:h so: [we'll s- we'll see]
G: [it's a <u>great</u> opportunity]=
M: =[that we can]
P: =[awesome]
K: great
M: ((click)) make <u>that</u> one come off

M: but I don't know what if Josh has got other
<u>commitments</u> on [the <u>Wednesday</u> morning] and
things so
K: [yeah I'm not sure either]
P: I think so
K: I think he wants to try and <u>pack</u> some things in
but then he ha[s to be at the uhm]
M: [do you want to check] with him about
that or do you want me to liaise with him?
K: ((click)) uh:m

Figure 5.3 Broaching a sensitive topic.

G: (0.7) ((click)) I'm wondering whether it'd be worth
   giving him a call now if that's d[oable]
P: [yeah]
G: ju[st to say]
K: [I know he's] on holiday with his ↑family
   [((until)) this afternoon]
M: [that's right]
P: [oh is he]
K: yeah ((indistinct))
P: ahh

K: that's why uhm [I haven't been worrying too much]
   about [sending him an email]
M: [he's down south actually isn't h]e¿
P: [oh really]=
M: =mmm I don't know if he was anywhere near
   Christ[church but he was in the South Island]
K: [((indistinct))] oh yeah?
M: yeah
K: °I didn't think about that°
M: uhm=

G: =and doesn't his daughter live in Christchurch or
   something didn't he say?
M: oh [yeah] he said down there yeah
K: [Dunedin]
G: oh Dunedin
K: uhm I might:
   w- when will we need to call and ge- confirm this
M: I'll ha- j- I'll let obviously need to c-
   let her know that we definitely can't do (0.4)
   [tomorrow]
K: [tomorrow]

M: and no doubt it'll uhm evolve over (0.6) [tomorrow]
K: [tomorrow]
   yeah
M: [so]
K: [so] i- if we can go back to him with a more more
   definite ti:me coz I know that he's got he has got
   meetings o:n¿
M: [well let's]
P: [well] we could pencil in Wednesday morning
   couldn't we
K: yeah

Figure 5.3 (Continued)

allows the other participants to signal to her that they wish to take over, but also just before she says "but uhm," she does not pause.

In fact, she pauses for half a second following the contrastive marker "but" (Schiffrin, 1987) as she seemingly frames her thoughts for what she must say next, which is more complex. As we saw in the first critical incident, Maureen believes it is important that they take advantage of the publicity opportunity provided by a television interview. However, she is concerned that Kirsty does not share her conviction and therefore the next few minutes will be crucial to gain her support.

Gaining the Client's Support

Maureen follows the pause with the filler "uhm" before pausing for another half a second. She then proceeds, carefully spelling out the company name, and further emphasizing it with her pencil in a beat gesture on the first word of the name and again as she says "over there" (Figure 5.3, image 1) highlighting that the program is broadcast in Sydney, the audience that this event is trying to target.

As she says the name of the company, she raises her head to look first at Kirsty and then at Pip. Pip gives an *attention signal* (Kendon, 1967), a nod accompanied by a "hmm." At the end of the phrase, Kirsty also gives an attention signal—one that could be taken to additionally carry information of assent or agreement, "great." Following an agreement signal such as this, a speaker often looks away having received the information they need, but in this case, Maureen continues to look at Kirsty, perhaps because she remains unconvinced of Kirsty's support and is seeking explicit confirmation for what she is proposing.

Maureen explains that the program had wanted to speak to Josh "tomorrow morning." She chuckles, perhaps as acknowledgment that she realizes the improbability of Josh making it at such short notice. (As we have seen in Chapter 4, "laugh particles" indicate that the words are problematic in some way.) However, by mentioning the specifics she also indicates the seriousness of the offer. Pip smiles in response to Maureen's chuckle, but Kirsty does not. At the end of the utterance, Kirsty's response is indistinct, it is also co–expressive with her left hand adjusting the right sleeve of her top (Figure 5.3, image 2). Such clothing adjustments are identified as showing increased anxiety (Meadors & Murray, 2014). Kirsty has not answered the question, because Maureen continues, explaining there may be the possibility of him being inter-viewed the following day, Wednesday. During this utterance, Pip nods four consecutive times as Maureen looks at her when she says, "I'm not sure if he is or <u>not</u>," apparently seeking information or confirmation (Sandgren et al., 2012) from Pip.

Maureen then shifts her gaze to Kirsty on the word "Wednesday." Kirsty nods briefly and confirms with a "yeah" when Maureen reports that she has told the news program that Josh will be in the country on Wednesday. Maureen continues to explain that the program may be amenable to interviewing Josh on Wednesday, although it is likely to happen in a different time slot, which, she adds, was good news as the original interview time was "6:15 6:30 in the morning." At this, both Pip and Kirsty laugh; Pip very audibly.

That Maureen may still not have Kirsty's full support is shown when Kirsty checks whether the interview will be held at the "studios or something." At this point, she rubs her nose twice (Figure 5.2, image 3). According to Meadors and Murray (2014) this gesture, along with many face touches, can be a sign that a person does not feel comfortable and is shielding themselves from what is going on.

Gail voices her support for Maureen, pointing out what a great opportunity this is. By doing so, she increases Maureen's credibility and *influence*, a strategy we have also witnessed in the PRP–PRP interaction with the architect (Chapter 4). Pip immediately responds with "awesome," indicating her approval and possibly also her support, while Kirsty follows with "great," perhaps echoing Gail (because she is the senior person in the meeting); its meaning remaining ambiguous, however. Thus, it is evident that Kirsty and Pip are receiving and understanding Maureen's message, but whether Maureen is going to be able to secure a commitment from Kirsty for Josh to attend an interview with the program remains uncertain.

Seeking Confirmation

Seeking certainty of commitment, Maureen again tries to discover if Josh will be available for an interview on Wednesday. Kirsty admits she does not know (Figure 5.3, image 4). However, she does try to add some information, using the contrastive marker "but" to indicate that while he might want to "try and pack some things in" of his own, Josh still "has to be at the uhm." She puts her hand under her chin on the word "try" and trails off when Maureen overlaps her. It appears Kirsty was going to mention that Josh did have to be at the event they arranged. However, Maureen's interruption may have been motivated by her anticipating what Kirsty is about to say, and realizing that Josh being at the event does not secure him for the interview, which is likely to be earlier in the day.

Maureen then comes to the crux of the interaction and asks, "do you want me to check with him about that or do you want to liaise with him?." While asking this, Maureen lifts her right hand to her head and strokes her hair (Figure 5.3, image 4). As we have seen earlier, this act of self–touching can be a sign of anxiety or discomfort (Meadors & Murray, 2014) but in this case, it is more likely a sign of frustration (Goldberg & Rosenthal, 1986).

Kirsty responds by shifting her gaze from Maureen to her handbag resting on the chair to the left. As she looks at the handbag, she makes a click (tutting sound) followed by an "uh:m," and then pauses for half a second before looking back at her notes. These actions indicate her lack of certainty over how to respond or an unwillingness to disagree directly with the proposal. Turning her head away from the speaker signals discomfort or displeasure (Ogden, 2013), and, if she was in enthusiastic agreement, she would have responded positively with "yes Maureen you can contact him" almost immediately after it was put to her (Pomerantz, 1984).

When Kirsty fails to respond after more than half a second and it appears evident that she is unwilling or unable to agree to the proposal, Gail begins speaking. She also uses a click, but here its use is probably to announce herself as the next speaker (Ogden, 2013). She suggests they give Josh a call now, thus employing persuasive strategies to elicit a decision. As she says, "if that's <u>doable</u>," Kirsty reaches towards the handbag she had looked at earlier, takes out her mobile phone and explains that she knows Josh is on holiday with his family (Figure 5.3, image 5).

Maureen says, "that's right," but the use of self–adaptors by her and Gail highlight that this part of the interaction is a particularly tense one for the two PRPs. Maureen's left-hand moves to her nose and makes five long rubs from the bridge down its length before using her index and middle fingers to rub down the side of the nose. She then rests her chin on her bunched fingers. Gail is touching her cheek with the forefinger of her right hand. She makes two small strokes and then moves the finger to her chin, which she rests on her thumb, and continues to make five small strokes with her finger before it stills (Figure 5.3, image 5).

While Maureen is rubbing her nose, Kirsty appears to be operating her phone but also displays some discomfort. As she says, "I haven't been worrying <u>too</u> much about sending him an <u>email</u>," she laughs and lifts her left hand to her face and rubs her nose, then drops it again to the phone where she makes two swiping movements on the screen.

Kirsty continues like this with her phone and the others appear to be waiting for her to check if she can contact him. The next few utterances address where Josh may be traveling with mention of Christchurch, which has just suffered a serious earthquake. During this part of the discussion Maureen has her hand on her chin, but as Kirsty says she "didn't think about that" in a low voice, Maureen looks down, moving her left forefinger to support her cheek while her middle finger is across the top of her mouth, and Gail begins to chew the end of her pen (Figure 5.3, image 7).

Kirsty appears to give up. She says "I might:" (perhaps she was going to suggest she might get in touch with Josh) then makes a repair to ask when they need to confirm the interview. Maureen responds and is echoed by Kirsty, but the echo is about what can't be achieved: the interview tomorrow. Again, there are signs of tension in Maureen. As she says, "it'll uhm evolve over tomorrow" she uses a forward wrist roll with her left hand, which she then rests on her chest just below her neck in a V shape. Her thumb then strokes her collar bone three times and she pats herself three times, ending with a finger bunch lightly stroking the base of her neck in what is a *comfort gesture* (Figure 5.3, image 8).

Kirsty suggests they get a "more definite time" with which to approach Josh. She may sense the tension in the PRPs as she initially makes a false start "i– if" then makes two repetitions of "more" and "he's got" suggesting disfluency (Figure 5.3, image 8). This may be because she is unsure of how this request will be received. She is right to be concerned; her colleague Pip's response indicates she wants something more certain and would at least like to see if they can "pencil in" a Wednesday morning interview. This is agreed to and a little later in the meeting, it is decided that they should make sure that a spokesperson is interviewed on the program even if Josh cannot make it.

The meeting ends with small talk as they leave the room, shifting again back from work talk to more social talk, thus reaffirming relationships.

Conclusion

All interactions with clients take place through meetings, presentations, and other mediated forms of communication (see Chapter 3), and are aimed at solving problems, making decisions and reporting back. While the PRP's expertise is often relied on by the clients, these interactions show that one of the key difficulties faced by PRPs is explaining the value of actions taken and decisions made. A lack of understanding on the part of the clients foreseeably makes sign–off on decisions and strategic plans difficult.

Politeness, and adhering to the norms of politeness, as discussed in the previous chapter, play an important role. PRPs need to ensure that their client's face needs are taken care of by hedging and attenuating the problematic talk (Holmes & Stubbe, 2015). At times, however, the *absence of certain talk* can be equally elucidating. Telling in the interactions we observed, was the absence of *deferential language* such as "I suppose," "well," or "just" (see Holmes & Stubbe, 2015), thereby signaling the PRPs' expert power in these situations. It seems therefore that while the relationship cannot be viewed as symmetrical, various strategies are employed to "equalize" the relationship and power in that relationship without engaging in face–threatening acts, such as explicitly showing frustration, anger, contempt or other forms of negativity. Understanding and employing politeness devices are therefore integral to effective public relations work and can be seen again in the interaction between journalists and PRPs, which we discuss in the next chapter, albeit that this relationship is more controversial and has been studied more often than the preceding relationships.

Note

1 The names have been changed to protect the identities of the participants and organizations involved.

References

Brennan, S. E., & Schober, M. F. (2001). How listeners compensate for disfluencies in spontaneous speech. *Journal of Memory and Language*, *44*(2), 274–296. doi:10.1006/jmla.2000.2753.

Broom, G. M. (2009). *Cutlip and Center's effective public relations* (10th ed.), Upper Saddle River, NJ: Prentice Hall/Pearson Educational International.

Capozzi, L. (2015). Public relations consulting: Consulting and corporate communication – the nexus. In J. Doorley & H. F. Garcia (Eds.), *Reputation management: The key to successful public relations and corporate communication* (3rd ed., pp. 357–376). London: Routledge.

Ekman, P. (1992). Facial expressions of emotion: New findings, new questions. *Psychological Science*, *3*(1), 34–38. doi:10.1111/j.1467–9280.1992.tb00253.x.

Ekman, P. (2007). *Emotions revealed: Recognizing faces and feelings to improve communication and emotional life* (2nd ed.), New York: Holt, Henry & Company.

Fraser, B. (1999). What are discourse markers? *Journal of Pragmatics*, *31*(7), 931–952. doi:10.1016/s0378-2166(98)00101-5.

Goffman, E. (1959). *The presentation of self in everyday life*. New York: Anchor Books.

Goldberg, S., & Rosenthal, R. (1986). Self-touching behavior in the job interview: Antecedents and consequences. *Journal of Nonverbal Behavior*, *10*(1), 65–80. doi:10.1007/bf00987206.

Goldin-Meadow, S. (2003). *Hearing gesture: How our hands help us think.* Cambridge, MA: Belknap Press of Harvard University Press.

Gries, S., & David, C. (2007). *Studies in variation, contacts and change in English* (Volume 2—Towards Multimedia in Corpus Studies ed.). Retrieved from www.helsinki.fi/varieng/series/volumes/02/gries_david/.

Günthner, S. (1999). Polyphony and the "layering of voices" in reported dialogues: An analysis of the use of prosodic devices in everyday reported speech. *Journal of Pragmatics*, *31*(5), 685–708. doi:10.1016/s0378-2166(98)00093-9.

Heritage, J. (1984). A change–of–state token and aspects of its sequential placement. In J. M. Atkinson & J. Heritage (Eds.), *Structures of social action* (pp. 299–334). Cambridge: Cambridge University Press.

Holmes, J., & Stubbe, M. (2015). *Power and politeness in the workplace. A sociolinguistic analysis of talk at work. Routledge linguistics classics.* New York: Routledge.

Jacobs, K. (2008, September 2). The ties that bind: Building better client relationships. Retrieved December 18, 2016, from PRSA, www.prsa.org/SearchResults/view/7551/105/The_ties_that_bind_Building_better_client_relation#.WFX63oVOI2w.

Jefferson, G. (1984). Notes on some orderlinesses of overlap onset. In V. D'Urso & P. Leonardi (Eds.), *Discourse analysis and natural rhetoric* (pp. 11–38). Padua, Italy: Cleup Editore.

Jefferson, G. (1986). Notes on "Latency" in overlap onset. *Human Studies*, 9(2–3), 153–183. doi:10.1007/bf00148125.

Kangasharju, H., & Nikko, T. (2009). Emotions in organizations: Joint laughter in workplace meetings. *Journal of Business Communication*, 46(1), 100–119. doi:10.1177/0021943608325750.

Keltner, D. (2005). Signs of appeasement: Evidence for the distinct displays of embarrassment, amusement, and shame. In P. Ekman & E. L. Rosenberg (Eds.), *What the face reveals: Basic and applied studies of spontaneous expression using the facial action coding system (FACS)* (2nd ed., pp. 133–157). Oxford: Oxford University Press.

Kendon, A. (1967). Some functions of gaze–direction in social interaction. *Acta Psychologica*, 26, 22–63. doi:10.1016/0001-6918(67)90005-4.

Machin, D., & Mayr, A. (2012). *How to do critical discourse analysis: A multimodal introduction*. Los Angeles, CA: Sage Publications.

Mahmoud, M., & Robinson, P. (2011). *Interpreting hand–over–face gestures*. Retrieved from www.cl.cam.ac.uk/~mmam3/pub/ACII2011–Doctoral–2011. pdf.

Matsumoto, D. R. & Hwang, H. S. (2013). Body and gestures. In H. S Hwang, M. G. Frank, & D. R. Matsumoto (Eds.), *Nonverbal communication: Science and applications* (pp. 75–96). Thousand Oaks, CA: Sage Publications.

Meadors, J. D., & Murray, C. B. (2014). Measuring nonverbal bias through body language responses to stereotypes. *Journal of Nonverbal Behavior*, 38(2), 209–229. doi:10.1007/s10919-013-0172-y.

Mirivel, J. C., & Tracy, K. (2005). Premeeting talk: An organizationally crucial form of talk. *Research on Language & Social Interaction*, 38(1), 1–34. doi:10.1207/s15327973rlsi3801_1.

Ogden, R. (2013). Clicks and percussives in English conversation. *Journal of the International Phonetic Association*, 43(3), 299–320. doi:10.1017/s0025100313000224.

Pomerantz, A. (1984). Agreeing and disagreeing with assessments: Some features of preferred/dispreferred turn shaped. In J. H. Atkinson & J. Heritage (Eds.), *Structures of Social Action* (pp. 57–101). Cambridge: Cambridge University Press.

Rozin, P., Lowery, L., & Ebert, R. (1994). Varieties of disgust faces and the structure of disgust. *Journal of Personality and Social Psychology*, 66(5), 870–881. doi:10.1037//0022 3514.66.5.870.

Sandgren, O., Andersson, R., van de Weijer, J., Hansson, K., & Sahlén, B. (2012). Timing of gazes in child dialogues: A time–course analysis of requests and back channeling in referential communication. *International Journal of Language & Communication Disorders*, 47(4), 373–383. doi:10.1111/j.1460-6984.2012.00151.x.

Schegloff, E. A. (2010). Some other "Uh(m)"s. *Discourse Processes*, 47(2), 130–174. doi:10.1080/01638530903223380.

Schiffrin, D. (1987). *Discourse markers*. Cambridge: Cambridge University Press.

Schiffrin, D. (1994). *Approaches to discourse*. Malden, MA: Blackwell Publishing.

Schiffrin, D. (2001). Discourse markers: Language, meaning, and context. In D. Schiffrin, D. Tannen, & H. E. Hamilton (Eds.), *The handbook of discourse analysis* (pp. 54–75). Malden, MA: Blackwell Publishing.

Schnurr, S., & Chan, A. (2011). Exploring another side of co–leadership: Negotiating professional identities through face–work in disagreements. *Language in Society, 40*(2), 187–209. doi:10.1017/s0047404511000030.

Tannen, D. (1987). Repetition in conversation as spontaneous formulaicity. *Text – Interdisciplinary Journal for the Study of Discourse, 7*(3), 215–243. doi:10.1515/text.1.1987.7.3.215.

Van Lancker-Sidtis, D., & Rallon, G. (2004). Tracking the incidence of formulaic expressions in everyday speech: Methods for classification and verification. *Language & Communication, 24*(3), 207–240. doi:10.1016/j.langcom.2004.02.003.

Whaling, H. (2010, December 21). Effective PR agency–client relationships. Retrieved December 18, 2016, from http://prtini.com/effective–pr–agency–client–relationships/.

Yu, C. (2011). The display of frustration in arguments: A multimodal analysis. *Journal of Pragmatics, 43*(12), 2964–2981. doi:10.1016/j.pragma.2011.03.007.

Zhang, X. (1998). *Echoing in Real-Life English Conversation*. The Poetics and Linguistics Association. Retrieved from www.pala.ac.uk/uploads/2/5/1/0/25105678/paper09.pdf.

6 The PRP-Journalist Relationship

All things must be examined, debated, investigated without exception and without regard for anyone's feelings.
—Denis Diderot (1713–1784), French philosopher

A Case of Sibling Rivalry

Besides their clients, the most significant public with whom a public relations practitioner (PRP) must build relationships is that of journalists. Yet the PRP-journalist relationship has historically been tetchy, to say the least. Going back to the very beginning of public relations, when journalists resented PRPs' attempts to gain free publicity (DeLorme & Fedler, 2003), one could argue the relationship between journalists and PRPs has been anything but amicable. As journalists' job prospects dwindle and public relations practitioners' rise, the acrimony is taken into the 21st century with the relationship variously characterized as antagonistic, tense and negative (Macnamara, 2014; Tilley & Hollings, 2008; Wilson & Supa, 2013).

Both practices are prone to blame the other for the problems (Shin & Cameron, 2004; Tilley & Hollings, 2008), habitually labeling the other as less than ethical (Tilley, 2012; Turk, 1985, 1986). Journalists have been characterized by Julia Hobsbawm (2010, p. 8) as being so distrustful of their PRP suppliers of information as to "despair" of them.

Moreover, while some might say individual members of the other practice are allies, more often they are seen as adversaries (Bishop, 2009). Journalists describe public relations practitioners as on the "dark side," practicing the "dark arts" (Burt, 2012; Parker, 2011), and accuse them of being obstacles (sometimes dishonest ones) between them and the sources of the story (Callard, 2011; Lewis, Williams, & Franklin, 2008; Tilley & Hollings, 2008). For their part, PRPs charge journalists with being lazy, last minute, and interested only in conflict or controversy (Theaker, 2004; Tilley & Hollings, 2008).

But this relationship has endured too long and proved too useful to be purely negative. Indeed, we must be careful not to overstate the enmity. While accusations and complaints are constant—and perhaps have become integral to the relationship—the relationship itself is more nuanced than it appears from the outside (Sallot, Steinfatt, & Salwen, 1998; Sallot & Johnson, 2006).

Its tension lies in an interdependence (Reich, 2006) that both practices are unwilling to admit, and that is so ingrained that neither could function in its current form without the other (Davis, 2013; McNair, 2011). In fact, both are at their most effective when their links remain hidden, especially from the public (Davis, 2003). Hence, PRPs keeps quiet about the third-party endorsement provided by gaining (independent) editorial, and journalists stay mum about needing help to fill editorial space from public relations' pre-packaged information and provision of sources (Davis, 2000; Ericson, Baranek, & Chan, 1989; Fishman, 1980; Franklin, 2011; Gans, 1979; Matthews, 2013).

Concealing their links allows both practices to save professional face. For journalists, to admit their dependence on public relations materials would be at odds with their perceived Fourth Estate role (Louw, 2010), which demands professional autonomy to carry out their watchdog function (Davis, 2013). For public relations, confessing their influence on the news media would mean losing the advantage of the perceived independent endorsement, which is valuable to clients (Sissons, 2015).

This chapter takes a "peek under the hood" of a working relationship that has been studied and discussed at length, but is still little understood and is often enacted behind closed doors (Macnamara, 2014; Sissons, 2015).

It can be said that journalists and PRPs are interdependent to such an extent that it is fair to call them *content siblings* (Sissons, 2015). Between them, they construct the news that the public consumes and contribute to a healthy public sphere and a democratic society. They share a societal function: to support and create a communication system that leads to Öffentlichkeit or the "making public" of issues, which allows these issues to be potentially debated by all (Ihlen & Van Ruler, 2007).

However, the power relations between the two suggest that while journalists rely heavily on their public relations sources, these sources are often unwilling to provide information (or will release only partial information), and display a keen wish to control both the detail and the timing of any material released to the media, as seen in the examples in Chapters 3 and 7. This asymmetry in power within the relationship has consequences for the quality of news published and is largely contradictory to the normative idea of "symmetry" and "mutual benefit" (see the next chapter for a discussion) that has been widely upheld as the norm for "excellent public relations" (Grunig, 1992).

A Public Disagreement

We start our examination of the relationship with an example that illustrates clearly the way each practice views the other and provides some explanations for those opinions. While the example is a few years old, it marks a moment in New Zealand history when public relations flexed its muscles and moved the power pendulum a little more in its favor, beginning a new era. This act did not go unnoticed by the news media.

The Organization Changes the Rules for Interaction

In 2008, Auckland City Council decided to set up a media relations team to handle all future media inquiries to the authority. It announced this seemingly innocuous decision in a media release:

Centralized contact point for media

August 2008

Auckland City Council is streamlining media access to council information and key contacts.

To help you get quick, accurate information we have set up a new, dedicated media team that will be available to answer all media queries and requests from Tuesday, August 12.

We encourage you to call this new team on 307 7482 [number changed] with queries and requests rather than the previous system of calling your usual contact person in the organization.

This will help us get you the information you need faster and put you in touch with the right people.

We appreciate your cooperation.

Mark Fenwick
Group Manager, Communications and Marketing

The message was upbeat and positive, reinforcing the idea promoted in public relations textbooks that the role of the practitioner is to assist journalists in their job. As Broom (2009) stated, the "quickest, surest way to gain the cooperation of journalists is to provide them with newsworthy, interesting, and timely stories and pictures that they want, when they want them, and in a form, they can readily use" (p. 275). Bishop (2009) concurred, writing:

Work with the journalists to help them write their stories. Give them access, information, prompt service and accessible people.
(p. 133, original emphasis)

So, on the surface, this new development was in the journalists' best interests and aligned with public relations best practice. The overall message was simple: things will be *better* because journalists can now go to a central point where the information will be given to them *quickly and efficiently*. Thus, journalists should be happy; their job has been made easier.

Yet a deeper analysis shows that the media release is not only promotional in nature (Erjavec, 2005) but also employs what Fairclough (1989) called "synthetic personalization" (p. 52). *Synthetic personalization* is used when an organization wishes to give the impression of treating a client or consumer as an individual when in fact they are being "'handled *en masse*" (Fairclough, 1989, p. 52, original emphasis). Promotion and synthetic personalization are both aimed at creating the *illusion of inclusion*, which Pullman (2013) described as a common persuasive technique.

Indeed, the release uses promotional language when it describes Auckland City Council as "streamlining media access" to council information and key contacts, and refers to the provision of "quick accurate information." These phrases are designed to appeal to the journalists' demand for high-quality information and their need to meet deadlines (Broom, 2009). The release also refers to a new "dedicated" team, suggesting that this team will be there exclusively to serve journalists. But synthetic personalization is also evident in the ubiquitous use of "we" and "you," which is contradicted by the headline "centralized point for media," and the first line saying, "Auckland City Council is streamlining media access." It would be clear to the journalists that one set of rules was going to be applied to all, and individualization was merely an artifice.

Journalists React

While the Council wished for journalists to accept that this new, dedicated media team would make their job easier, the message that was received was a less benign one. In response to the media release, the influential newspaper, the *New Zealand Herald*, published an article with the telling headline: "Council unveils spin doctor team" (Orsman, 2008).

Council unveils spin doctor team

NZ Herald.co.nz Wednesday, Aug 13, 2008

The Auckland City Council is revamping the way it deals with the media mining it for information.

Communications and marketing group manager Mark Fenwick yesterday announced a new team to answer all media queries. "We encourage you to call this new team with queries and requests, rather than the previous system of calling your usual contact person in the organization," he said.

Acting chief executive John Duthie said the new set-up was not an attempt to stop journalists speaking to council contacts. It was his understanding the new team would provide journalists with a one-stop shop for information and assistance.

A marketing strategy, obtained by the Herald, suggests the council's media management is a failure and should be handed to a "specialist PR team." It suggests most of the communication and marketing team's 50 or so staff should concentrate on council-controlled channels such as the weekly newssheet, City Scene, the website and images such as the new council logo.

Media commentator Jim Tully said there had been a growing tendency in the past 10 years for public service organizations to increasingly manage their communications strategies. Mr. Tully said there was a long tradition of journalists being able to speak with public sector managers and they should not have to go through filters. "Anything like this is not for altruistic reasons. It is for self-interest. It is certainly not in the interests of the public or the media," he said.

Edward Rooney, chief reporter for the community newspaper the Aucklander, said reporters had encountered difficulties getting past communications and marketing staff to talk directly with council staff. He said one young reporter was told "that is not how it works" for going to a council officer after waiting for a response from a member of the communications and marketing team.

Liz Waters, who owns the Gulf News, said she knew of two occasions in the past few months where reporters were told to go through communications and marketing. The stories were about a property owner burying a septic tank in the Onetangi sand dunes and bush clearing on businessman Graeme Hart's Church Bay property. "Communications and marketing are spin and news isn't spin. News is what they don't want you to know," she said.

In a letter to the Herald in July, former city promotion committee chairman John Strevens said he set up City Scene as a better way to inform residents about council activities. He was disappointed to see it decline into an apologist for council actions. "The spin doctors have taken control," Mr. Strevens said.

Article courtesy of the *New Zealand Herald*

The headline gives the angle away immediately. In the writer's mind (and other journalists quoted in the story), the new media team is about "spin," a term that Macnamara (2009) defined as "derived from spinning thread to fabricate material and subsequently applied to spinning stories connoting factitious, fabrication, hype and misrepresentation" (p. 2). Further, in his discussion of spin and its meanings, Andrews (2006) stated the term originated in United States election campaigns in the

1980s when political handlers or campaign operatives tried to ensure reporters interpreted the meaning of a debate or event in the way the particular operative wanted, but it soon moved into everyday political communications with journalists, and eventually the word "spin" became synonymous with public relations itself.

Macnamara (2009) pointed to how the term is now accepted as a part of public relations more generally in media articles and books such Stuart Ewen's (1996) book *PR: A social history of spin* and Bob Burton's (2007) *Inside Spin: The dark underbelly of PR*. More recently, in her thesis on the representation of public relations in popular culture, Dennison (2012) stated that the "idea that public relations is related to and concerned with controlling situations and people is [...] linked to the use of spin and spin doctoring" (p. 141), adding that "people's perception of reality is itself *constructed* and *shaped* by the words and signs used, in whichever social context they occur" (p. 52, original emphasis).

In the case being examined here, what was presented by the PRPs as a "helpful" activity is seen through the lens of "spin" by the journalists as an attempt to control and manage communications with the Council. Their perception of PRPs as spin doctors encouraged the journalists to interpret the media release as an attempt to "filter" their access to publicly elected representatives and their officials, and as a result, the animosity spilled over into public debate (Broom, 2009).

A Struggle for Power

The journalists' suspicions about the Council's real motive for establishing the media relations team are evident from the way the text has been structured. It first sets up the argument put by the Council, then casts doubt on it, and finally knocks it down. The first three paragraphs put the Council's expressed plans before the public. The third paragraph of this section is a denial by the acting chief executive that this was a deliberate strategy to stop journalists speaking to "council contacts."

According to Van Dijk (1993), the reproduction of dominance in modern societies often involves the justification of actions or attitudes and the denial of alternative viewpoints. He uses the example of *privilege*.

> Thus, we have seen that the reproduction of dominance in contemporary societies often requires justification or legitimation: it is 'just,' 'necessary' or 'natural' that we have privileged access to valuable social resources. Another strategy of the reproduction of dominance is that of denial: there is no dominance, all people in our society are equal, and have equal access to social resources.
>
> (Van Dijk, 1993, p. 263)

In this case, the Council's justification for its actions and its refusal to accept that it could be seen as a control strategy conform to Van Dijk's thinking.

In public relations theory, specifically situational crisis communica-tion theory (SCCT) (Coombs, 2007), *denials* are used as a crisis re-sponse strategy where the manager asserts there is no crisis. That also appears to be what is happening here, as will be discussed a little later, it seems the Council is reacting to its "failure" to manage the media (see paragraph four) while denying its actions have anything to do with "managing" the media.

A more careful reading of the statement could even put this in the "non-denial denial" category, a term attributed to Ben Bradlee, the *Washington Post* editor during the Watergate affair (Chapman & Nuttall, 2011). The term has been used by those studying public relations tactics among climate change deniers (Hoggan & Littlemore, 2009; Washington & Cook, 2011). A *non-denial denial* can be deployed when an individual or organization is rightly accused of something that they do not wish to admit to. Thus, they respond with what sounds like a denial but actually is not. As Froomkin (2014, September 27, p. 3) wrote in *The Intercept*, "You issue a very narrowly-crafted denial involving a lot of hairsplitting while avoiding the central claim." In this case, the acting CEO correctly states this is not an attempt to stop journalists speaking to council contacts, as of course (and here comes the hair-splitting) *the media relations team members are, strictly speaking, council contacts*. They are not, however, the contacts the journalists would choose to approach, preferring to speak to the *elected* representatives.

Section two, the fourth paragraph, provides a précis of what the writer says is the Council's leaked marketing strategy. The paragraph tells the reader that the Council believes its "media management strategy is a failure." This implies to the reader that what the Council really believes is that too much negative (and probably publicly important) information is getting into the media, which only a dedicated media relations team can prevent. Its other communication staff, less specialized in this area, can then concentrate on controlling the messages to the public through "council-controlled channels." Interesting too is the use of "scare quotes" (Fairclough, 1989, p. 74). The inclusion of "specialist PR team" in quotation marks indicates this expression is problematic in some way. The inverted commas *distance* the writer from the expression, making it clear it comes from someone else that the writer disagrees with. It invites the reader to think the "specialist PR team" is perhaps a euphe-mism for something else, such as the "spin doctors" referred to in the headline—and that perhaps that such a thing as "specialist PR" does not really exist.

All three individuals quoted in this section complain about the in-creased difficulty getting access to public servants, with two explicitly referring to the Council in the months leading up to the establishment of the media team—seeming to suggest the Council was preparing for the move. All three were disapproving of the restrictions, with two clearly suggesting the move was self-interested. This section is designed to alert the reader to what the writer believes is the nub of the issue thrown up by the new media relations team.

The fourth and final section brings in a former councilor who broadens the discussion and criticism to cover council-controlled media. The former councilor complains that one of these channels, the one he set up, has become an avenue of promotion, or as he puts it, "an apologist for council actions." The source finishes the article with the quote, "The spin doctors have taken control." Thus, ending the article with the same point set out at the beginning in the headline. In addition, by finishing the article with criticism from a former councilor, the writer is setting the council against itself and saying "look, even one of them agrees there is a problem here."

From this example, it is not only clear how the *framing* of a message can be construed differently depending on the lens through which one looks, but it also highlights the lack of critical awareness among PRPs about the broader impact of their actions on a democratic society. While they may have *thought* they were being helpful and supportive—or at least tried to convince their audience that they were—their actions were seen otherwise. These actions were, of course, dictated by their client, the Council, and had little to do with what the journalists wanted or did not want. Ultimately (as seen here), a PRP's relationship with their client is more important than their relationships with journalists. Thus, in public relations practice, the journalists become a means to an end, and the relationship is therefore purely *transactional*. This undertow is also evident again in Chapter 7 when communication staff members discuss whether they should approach a media contact to do a story about recycling.

A Non-Voluntary Relationship

Sissons (2015) argued that a *web* of essentially *cooperative relationships* is at the heart of PRP-journalist interactions. Most journalists interviewed for this study admitted, for example, that they relied on PRPs and their materials. Some were more open about their dependence than others, with one confessing, "I couldn't do my job without them." In fact, in Chapter 2, we discussed the case of the beauty editor who admitted to relying on PRPs for her material.

For the journalists who participated in the research, daily contact with PRPs was the norm. However, these relationships can only be characterized as "non-voluntary" (Waymer, 2013), meaning that they are ones that both PRPs and journalists find necessary, but would prefer to avoid. They are, as we discussed in Chapters 2 and 4, *information peers*, and having this relationship is a necessary part of both parties' career advancement. But the research revealed that journalists' dependence has led to feelings of *frustration,* even resentment, of the *control* PRPs exercise over the information journalists need to write their stories. This view from one news reporter is typical:

> I was calling a police comms guy, and he's notoriously...useless. He doesn't give out any information at all...We've got to the point where we just don't call him anymore...because it's like talking to a brick wall. We were saying, he probably congratulates himself because, "yes, nobody calls me anymore, my job's really easy! And I've let nothing out to the media." And it's like, surely you must know that's not your job.

It is a frustration mirrored by senior editors, such as this one:

> It's been my experience largely that the comms people frequently are just mired in an idea of protection and they will do anything and everything to avoid putting questions to the companies that they represent, to avoid giving honest answers, to avoid giving full disclosure etc., etc.. The principal tactic they use is just delaying.

However, there is recognition that the relationship has to be *symbiotic*, as expressed by this reporter:

> Oh we both rely on each other totally, especially here. I mean if they want good PR they have to give me good info, and if I want good info, I have to run their good PR. At times it's a power struggle, definitely, at times.

Increased Dependence on PRPs

For a significant number of journalists, relationships with PRPs are proving increasingly necessary since editorial staff cutbacks began to take effect in the early to mid-2000s. More journalists now admit that public relations subsidies are useful to them (Lewis et al., 2008; Sallot & Johnson, 2006). Less staff and the introduction of multi-platform working has seen journalists' workloads on average triple (Lewis, Williams, Franklin, Thomas, & Mosdell, 2006; Starkman, 2010).

However, as is evident from the quotes, the resulting increased dependence on public relations materials has caused resentment among journalists (Jempson, 2005) and alarm among some media researchers. They argue that the pressures on journalists to produce more news copy in less time is resulting in many becoming reliant on public relations material and failing to corroborate and/or challenge much of that material (Cottle, 2003; Davies, 2008; Davis, 2003; McChesney & Nichols, 2010; Moloney, Jackson & McQueen, 2013; Motion, Leitch & Cliffe, 2009; O'Neill & O'Connor, 2008; White & Hobsbawm, 2007).

The BBC's head of news, James Harding, referred to these pressures in his 2014 WT Stead lecture at the British Library (Harding, 2014, January 14, pp. 10–12) and he was clear about the result, "fewer journalists does not mean less news, it means more PR—more corporate puffery, more canny product placements, more unchecked political spin."

While journalists interviewed for the research expressed frustration with the relationship, PRPs appeared comparatively happy, with one senior practitioner at a consultancy saying he worked "very closely with journalists on a daily basis," and another saying, "I speak to at least four or five of them [journalists] every day" and these were positive interactions. These statements proved typical of the findings of the fieldwork, with most of those spoken to saying they had pretty good relations with journalists.

Where there were frustrations, they often seemed to be triggered by the PRP spending time explaining a situation to a journalist and then finding that the printed story did not reflect any of the conversation and presented the client organization in a bad light. One PRP described being "hurt" when this happened. The same practitioner is quoted in Chapter 2 describing how they sometimes repaid journalists who, for whatever reason, found themselves off-side by swamping them with information.

A Relationship Strained

New technology had also affected the relationship, with the two practices increasingly interacting using technologies such as email, contributing to what we have labeled "mediated relationships" (Chapter 3). This has proved both a positive and a negative development. Journalists prefer receiving media releases, fact sheets and advisories via email, but, as was mentioned in Chapter 2, several complained that they did not like conducting interviews via email as there was no chance to build rapport or challenge an answer. PRPs, on the other hand, felt that email questions and answers afforded them some protection against being misunderstood or misquoted. Their accountability to their organization for what was reported in the media made them more sensitive to what they perceived as the journalistic practice of sometimes over-simplifying a situation or editing quotes or facts to fit a preconceived story.

Another development that has made PRPs cautious is a perception that there are now more, young and inexperienced journalists in newsrooms and that these are not necessarily as trustworthy as older, more experienced journalists would be. One senior PRP said that with some of these younger journalists,

> they wouldn't know what the truth was if it got up and smacked them in the face. They are just interested in their angle for the story.

If what we tell them doesn't work for their angle then we've lied to them or we didn't tell them the truth.

As a result, he was reluctant to give off-the-record briefings unless it was part of his overall strategy.

> You used to be able to trust journalists to keep a confidence, but you can't now. There's very few that you would. A lot of it is because they're so ambitious. A lot of the kids, they just want, they don't give a shit, they just want the story and to get their name on the big story, and so you can't [...] give them decent background information and you can't do anything off-the-record. I just say to my clients, 98% of the time, you don't do off-the-record, it just doesn't work anymore.

Having said that, this PRP was not averse to using off-the-record briefings in order to stop a story appearing in the media saying he had briefed a reporter to "give him a whole lot of background he can't write about, but [the briefing] also encompasses the bit he did want to write about so you shut it down."

Concern About the State of Journalism

Despite being prepared to shut a story down, this PRP expressed concern about the state of journalism asserting that it was "easier than it should be" to get public relations material into the news media because of newsrooms being under-resourced and journalists being expected to work across platforms.

> They are now expected to write for online, for the paper, some of them are being asked to do video, and they are being asked to refresh and update things far more frequently than they, most of them, are used to.

It seemed, therefore, that practicing journalists have become out-resourced and outsmarted by those working in public relations, many of whom are former, highly successful journalists. As this practitioner said:

> There's an awful lot of very good journalists sitting in PR offices, much better and smarter and know more and are paid more and paid to know more and paid to perform than there are in newsrooms. It's not just the money thing. There are some very good, highly dedicated, excellent journalists out there but I could just about name every one.

This recognition of and concern for the state of journalism was expressed by almost all the PRPs spoken to in the research and mirrored concerns among scholars internationally. Indeed, since the early 2000s, public relations scholars have unsuccessfully warned that journalists are too dependent on public relations material and that this was damaging their role as watchdogs (Gregory, 2003; Moloney, 2006). In 2004 Gregory claimed that PRPs had become the major suppliers of information to the media, and as much as 80% of what appeared in newspapers was public relations-generated. Media researchers in a study for *Guardian* journalist Nick Davies (Davies, 2008) substantiated this claim, finding 80% of newspaper content was at least partially made up of recycled news wire or public relations copy. Of this, 60% consisted wholly or mainly of wire copy and/or public relations material, and a further 20% contained clear elements of wire copy and/or public relations to which more or less other material had been added (Lewis et al., 2008).

Studies in the United States and Australia found a similar situation. In her book, *Global Spin*, Sharon Beder wrote that various studies revealed media releases as the basis for 40 to 50% of the news content of newspapers in the United States (Beder, 1997). By 2003, Robert McChesney (2003) found that surveys showed that media releases accounted for 40 to 70% of what appeared as news in the United States. A study by Australian online news site, *Crikey.com*, and University of Technology (UTS), Sydney's Australian Centre for Independent Journalism (Crikey & ACIJ, 2010) analyzed more than 2,000 news stories over six months, establishing nearly 55% of news articles "across ten hard-copy papers were driven by some form of public relations" (March 15, p. 3).

Gaining Legitimacy and Trust

Despite what is obviously overwhelming evidence that the two practices interact closely on a regular basis, a key issue between PRPs and journalists is *a lack of trust*. Essentially, this reflects a tussle for *professional legitimacy* between the two practices. Merkelsen (2011) pointed out that "ethics, trust, and legitimacy are different concepts and one does not necessarily presuppose or lead to the other" (p. 134) yet audiences tend to see organizations that are legitimate as more trustworthy. The same can be said for the two practices: the battle for the hearts and minds of the public, and who has the right to mediate between power, commerce, and the people is reflected in this relationship.

Besides not trusting journalists, there is a belief among PRPs and their clients that a *message* can be (and should be) *managed* and *controlled*, despite it leaving the practitioner's outbox and entering the journalist's inbox and hence their sphere of influence. Underpinning the PRP's wish for control of the message is a business need to *manage risk* and *reputation* (as we will see again in Chapter 7), because negative reporting may affect the organization's reputation, its legitimacy and consequently its profit-margin or political standing. As a result, many clients prefer not to speak to the media (Bishop, 2009).

This has provided an opportunity for PRPs to gain professional legitimacy by claiming expertise, acting as intermediaries and managing perceived risk. Managing risk is not only part of their role, but a requirement of being taken seriously, which is symptomatic of the battle for "managerial recognition" within other "soft" disciplines such as marketing and human resources (Merkelsen, 2011, p. 135). Thus, being able to "manage the media," and judge when to speak and when not, is one of the skills necessary for a successful PRP. Reflective of this is the practitioner's professional discourse when strategizing about managing media messaging, which will be peppered with phrases such as "risk avoidance" and references to being seen as "knowing what I'm doing."

When seen from the perspective of the PRP, the opening example of this chapter is understandable, as their loyalty to the client outweighs their need for a close relationship with journalists. But we found in our research that at every stage, PRPs were strategizing about the media's reaction to an event or announcement and *calculating the benefits versus the risks of media coverage.* For example, when deciding whether to fund a journalist to fly to Australia to cover a story about a client wanting to attract business investors to Auckland, one practitioner referred to the potential risk of paying for a junket. She considered that although it was unlikely to result in a negative story, there were no guarantees.

> I'd be surprised if they could take too much of a negative angle on it. Although people, you know foreign investment sort of thing, not everybody likes that sort of thing, but I'd be surprised if they did, but that isn't something that we control, *it's a risk that you take and I think that's it's relatively well weighed up.*

A way of reducing the risk, this practitioner pointed out, was to *handpick* which journalists to approach. Indeed, the selection of journalists was a common theme among PRPs, illustrating the importance of having "tame" journalists who would tell the story as the PRP wanted it to be told thereby maintaining de facto control. The following quote from a practitioner is indicative of the thought processes that PRPs engage in when deciding which journalists to feed a story to:

> I'd probably use one of the guys from the *Gazette*,[1] probably Simon Marks, or...Rohan Styles has been all over the story, but Rohan's a little bit...Yeah. I'd prefer Simon, but he may not want to do it. The other guy I'd look at would be someone like Kyle Sampson at Intouch Media because he feeds all the papers—and Kyle gets this stuff. So I'd use him. And the third option, or another option also might be to do [television news program] on Sunday morning, but that's with Terry Jones, which is slightly problematic. But, if it was with Brad Stanton or someone like that you'd get a sensible conversation out

of that. But we'll give it some thought anyway. But off the top of my head that would be the kind of thing I'd look at. Or possibly even Danielle, Danielle Macmillan. Yeah, Danielle gets it, but the only thing with her is that she's politically to the right of Attila the Hun sometimes. No, but you'd need to be mindful of where her politics might color this.

While selecting the "right" journalist for the "right" story is a strategic decision, these are not the only tactics used to control or manage the message. Another one is to delay the story as can be seen in the next critical incident.

Delaying the Story

The following interaction involves practitioner Craig speaking on the phone to a journalist who is enquiring about a client organization that is facing financial and structural problems. At the time of the call, the client organization's Trustee has just announced that it has launched an investigation into the firm's financial affairs.[2] Considering this, Craig wishes to distance the client—particularly the CEO who often gave interviews—from the media.

The call has come from a journalist with whom Craig had regular contact, and we can, therefore, surmise that their relationship could be labeled as an "acquaintance relationship" as discussed in Chapter 2, suggesting some level of trust has developed. The journalist has been covering the story of the client's financial difficulties, and is now following up on the Trustee's announcement.

1	0:00.0	okay they got you on that as well?
2	0:06.8	mmm hmm¿
3	0:10.4	uh:m
4	0:11.6	has he not called you?
5	0:13.3	oh okay
6	0:14.0	uhm
7	0:14.4	I'll s
8	0:15.2	I'm not s:ure
9	0:16.3	I thought he was going to give you a call but he he
10	0.19.1	he's absolutely flat out again (.) today
11	0:22.4	uhm coz they've got a bit on their plate
12	0:24.8	as you can see¿
13	0:29.3	uhm
14	0:30.1	well he he's the one that's across it all hhyeah
15	0:36.3	yeah sure I
16	0.51.3	mm yeah
17	0.51.9	if if you just want to have a uh

18 0.54.3   off-the-record chat I can probably give you some back-
            ground that will <u>help</u>¿
19 1:00.7   yeah I understand that

This phone conversation provides clear evidence that PRPs are not averse
to using techniques such as off-the-record, not putting questions to
clients (as a journalist quoted earlier in the chapter claimed) and making
non-denial denials to delay or hinder the publishing of a story.

The CEO Is Not Available

The call starts with an acknowledgment that the journalist is now
working on the story. This is followed by Craig expressing surprise
that "he" (the CEO) has not called the journalist. He then explains that
it must be because the CEO is "flat out again today." Craig tells the
journalist that it is the CEO who is familiar with the details surrounding
events as he is "across it all," but offers to give her a background or "off-
the-record" briefing. She appears to complain about this as he answers,
"I understand that," but then she seems to reluctantly agree. In this
part of the conversation, which lasts about a minute, Craig is at his
most hesitant, which is evident by the use of "uh" and "uhm" (Clark &
Foxtree, 2002; Schegloff, 2010). These *repair operations* (Schegloff,
2010) can be a sign of *problems in speech planning* (what to say next),
finding the right word or can be about correcting speech. Clark and
Foxtree (2002) claim that speakers use "uh" and "uhm" to announce
what they expect to be a minor (uh), or major (uhm), delay in speaking.
The first example comes in line 3. The journalist has announced who she
is and why she is calling. She has received an "mmm hmm," which tells
her that Craig understands what she is saying and acts as an invitation
to continue speaking. Then, on his turn to speak, Craig uses "uhm:"
followed by a short silence before asking the question (line 4),

> "has he not called yet?"

According to Clark and Foxtree (2002), "uhm" is followed by a delay
far more often than "uh." Craig's pause of more than a second would
be considered such a delay. Craig also prolongs the syllables in "uh:m"
for more than half a second. The journalist obviously responds in the
negative, which Craig acknowledges with an "oh okay." Then there is
another "uhm" followed by a repair, "I'll s I'm not s:ure" indicating
what Clark and Foxtree (2002) refer to as a delay at the message level,
of what to say next. Craig *appears* not to be sure how to respond and his
explanation as to why Adam, the CEO, may not have rung the journalist
illustrates this, as he uses "uhm" four times (lines 3, 6, 10 and 13) and
makes two repairs (lines 7 and 9).

At lines 14/15, it appears the journalist is explaining that she needs a quote for her story. At that point, Craig seems to have decided he would step in as the source, but only as background, not for direct quoting. He starts "yeah <u>sure</u> I," but the journalist continues her turn and it is another 15 seconds and an interrupting "mm yeah" (line 16) from Craig before he can approach that compromise tentatively again. It is, therefore, evident that the conversation is not only about answering the journalist's question, but is also a process of negotiating the interpersonal relationship—while the PRP wants to delay, or even better *divert*, the story, he also wants to preserve a working relationship. To do that, he needs to *reciprocate* (see Chapter 2) with information, or in this case, an off-the-record briefing.

Briefing Off-The-Record

Once the journalist has agreed to the off-the-record briefing, Craig becomes much more fluent. The "uhm" (line 20) that had started this section acts to mark the start of his message, about which he is confident, as he has discussed it in detail earlier with the client (see Sissons, 2015).

20 1:02.5   uhm
21 1.04.5   °good°
22 1:05.1   to be <u>honest</u> they're a bit <u>surprised</u> that the Trustee's <u>done</u> this because
23 1:08.4   the
24 1:09.3   as you know the <u>audit's</u> still going
25 1:11.1   uhm in terms of getting their <u>numbers</u> out
26 1:13.6   so there's some <u>concerns</u> (.) around
27 1:17.7   >our understanding of it is the Trustee has some concerns around<
28 1:20.9   the <u>covenants</u>
29 1:22.5   but they can't answer the <u>questions</u> because they're still finalizing the <u>audio</u>
30 1:26.5   the <u>audit</u> and the <u>impact</u> of [name of subsidiary which was put into receivership]
31 1:29.4   and in the <u>interim</u>
32 1:30.4   an and this is part of the problem
33 1:32.7   the <u>Trustee</u> won't be <u>aware</u> of
34 1:35.2   some of t the <u>background</u> stuff that's <u>happening</u>
35 1:37.6   probably in the next <u>week</u> or so
36 1:40.0   and you saw we got <u>three</u> million in
37 1:42.4   and there's more <u>coming</u>¿
38 1:44.7   uhm and but
39 1:48.3   yeah
40 1:49.1   yeah so there's the

41	1:49.9	you know three and a half million being tipped into the account this <u>week</u>
42	1:52.6	a:nd and more <u>coming</u>
43	1:54.2	uhm but the Trustee ws
44	1:56.5	sort of made the decision without
45	1:58.5	asking and >you know<.
46	2:01.3	no they don't <u>have</u> to but if they <u>had</u> we wou
47	2:03.5	they could have told them that of course (name of company) doesn't spend
48	2:06.4	>you know<
49	2:07.1	isn't in touch with the Trustee >on a daily basis unless it kind of <u>has</u> to be<
50	2:10.3	so I think it's probably uh a
51	2:13.1	yeah and then they didn't get the answers they wanted from the <u>auditor</u>
52	2:15.8	because the <u>auditor</u> can't <u>answer</u> them because they are still doing the <u>audit</u>
53	2:18.9	because of the [name of the subsidiary] stuff
54	2:19.9	so it it's <u>just</u> that
55	2:21.5	>you know< that
56	2:22.8	chain of circumstances I think that's caused the <u>problems</u> so

From line 29 to line 37, Craig uses the conjunctions "but" and "and" six times. In line 29, "but" is prefacing an "idea unit" and realizing an action (Schiffrin, 2001, p. 57) of giving a *reason* why the Trustee was misguided in launching the investigation. He is also using "and" to ensure the continuation of his turn (Schiffrin, 2001), and ensure he gets his message across.

Craig concludes this part of his message with the words "and there's more <u>coming</u>" (line 37), which have a rising intonation indicating he has not finished. However, his next words (line 38) are prefaced by a pause and the discourse marker "uhm." Therefore, despite then using both "and" and "but," the journalist reads this as an opportunity to interject with a quick question to which Craig responds with a "yeah."

Controlling the Message

The next installment of his message, explaining the "background stuff," is delivered from line 40 to line 45. He uses "so" to link the three-and-a-half million (New Zealand) dollars to the "background stuff" he was talking about in his last turn and wants to make sure the reporter knows there is more coming. He then employs "uhm" in line 43 as a filler to signal that although there may be a delay, he still wishes to continue his turn, and the "but" is used again to preface an idea unit that illustrates the mistake of the Trustee. He then uses "and" as if he is about to continue before employing the discourse marker, "you know" with a falling intonation, and he tails off.

The journalist obviously takes a turn here and challenges him that the Trustee is not obligated to talk to the company before instituting an investigation. This leads him into his next message—that the company is not in touch with the Trustee on a daily basis, which he ends with the conjunction "so" (line 50), showing he could be about to sum up, but instead he trails off perhaps thinking it is unnecessary, using the discourse marker "uh" and the indefinite article "a." The two words here are used as a *finisher* telling the journalist that Craig is ready for her to take over. She makes a quick comment before Craig states his fourth point that he links to the previous one with an "and" in line 51, namely that the audit is still going on and so the Trustee is not going to get answers about the state of the finances until that is completed. He then sums up, beginning with the conjunction "so" (line 54), which has the global function of linking all his arguments together to illustrate that this is a "chain of circumstances" that has led to the current situation. And, as we have seen in the previous chapter, by doing so, it becomes apparent that he is *setting the agenda* for the phone conversation with the journalist.

Although we could only hear Craig's side of the conversation, it is clear that he wishes to maintain his relationship with the journalist, which is why he offers to give an off-the-record briefing. However, after the call, he admitted to the researcher that he was trying to buy time and delay the journalist speaking to anyone or getting any independent information. He knew that the CEO was not going to call the journalist as he had not asked him to. Hence, no questions from this reporter had been put to the CEO, giving a clear example of a PRP acting as a *gatekeeper* and preventing "the story" from being published.

Craig also admitted that, despite his insistence on the conversation being off the record, he only gave the reporter information that was in a media release he had in front of him. His aim in this interaction was to *appear* to be helping the reporter out of a tight spot by giving her material for her story (non-attributable material), and hence *preserve his relationship* with her while ensuring the client stayed out of the media spotlight. To do this, he was unable to be frank with either the journalist or the client. His expression of mild surprise in the question, "I thought he was going to give you a call" (line 9) could arguably be in the *non-denial denial category*. It implies the CEO has been told about the journalist's wish to speak to him, and that he has not been prevented from speaking to her. The PRP could argue he believed the CEO would call her (he probably would have if he had known she wanted to speak to him, as was his habit). So, while not actually saying it, he does not deny his interference either, and by doing so, employs typical strategies of *deception* by omitting, evading and withholding information (see Chapter 2).

Client Relationships Triumph Every Time

Relationships with journalists are crucial for most PRPs to succeed, and have in fact been identified in Sriramesh's 1996-study as integral to the *personal influence model*. But we found that in the end, *loyalty to the client* is even more important. Merkelsen (2011) highlighted this balancing act as one of the main challenges facing the public relations industry, and one that lacks sincerity as PRPs cannot represent all sides equally. He wrote that the idea that the PRP is a *boundary spanner* for the organization, acting as an intermediary through "two-way symmetrical communication," while bearing both the client's and the publics' interests in mind, is simply hypocritical. In reality, a key function is to ensure the organization's (the client's) legitimacy "in the court of public opinion" (Merkelsen, 2011, p. 129) even when the organization's objectives are not compatible with those of its publics. He added that public relations serves "the client's interests best by making itself invisible to the public" (p. 132). This has serious consequences for the transparency of relationships and the efficacy and reliability of the information coming from PRPs as they work to persuade, delay, or hinder the media to protect or promote their clients. Younger journalists are often not trained or experienced enough to recognize the invisible practitioner and therefore accept messages uncritically (Sissons, 2015). Further, PRP offices are often filled with former senior journalists well-versed in the tricks of the trade.

Relationships with journalists (and perhaps clients and publics), therefore, become a means to an end, rather than an end in themselves, and one could conclude that public relations is primarily about developing and maintaining relationships with the purpose of *using* these relationships on behalf of a client. Relationships are therefore *transactional* in nature (see also Chapter 7 for further discussions). The next interaction presents an example of how PRPs attempt to "manage" the news, ultimately putting their clients' interests before those of the journalist or the public sphere.

Strategizing with the Client

This critical incident involves the same PRP and client as the previous interaction. In this exchange, Craig is on the phone to the CEO, Adam. They are discussing the messaging around the recent resignation of the chief financial officer, Bob, who has stepped down in the light of the company's financial problems. Just over a minute into this conversation, Craig responds to Adam's mention of the resignation and his request for advice about how the news should be released.

Craig's "yeah" (figure 6.1, image 1) acknowledges Adam's concerns about the news with the "let's" suggesting *collaboration* and *alignment*.

C: yeah well le- let's do something on <u>Bo:b</u>¿
uhm
just a a note to <u>sta:ff</u> and and out of that I'll just
I'll have a little <u>holding</u> statement for <u>media</u>
if we get <u>approached</u>

C: but I I <u>think</u> the reality is with the <u>r:esult</u> coming
(0.3) what Thursday Friday¿
<u>Bob'll</u> get <u>buried</u> anyway?

C: th-
the the media'll be more interested in what <u>you're</u>
doing <u>so</u> i- if we if we hold the sta:ff <u>note</u>¿
until the <u>same</u> <u>time</u> as we put the

C: uhm
the <u>result</u> out there¿
a- any news about <u>Bob's</u> very likely to either
not get picked up or just <u>buried</u>
as one line somewhere?

Figure 6.1 Strategizing with the client.

He is saying "we" will deal with this together. This is in line with West (1995), who examined existing research into females and males in conversation. She discovered that women tended to use "let's" to maximize collaboration and maintain accord. As building rapport and consensus is one of the skills of a PRP, it would be expected that Craig uses the techniques skillfully.

The discourse marker "well" (figure 6.1, image 1) points to his solution, which is to down-play the news by releasing it with the more important "financial result" media release. In fact, as he says, "holding statement," he appears to draw a paragraph in front of him. Then, when he comes to his main point about preventing the resignation of the chief financial officer becoming headline news, his gestures closely reflect what he is saying. As he says, "but I I think the reality is" (figure 6.1, image 2), he has his palm-down and fingers spread in front of him and makes three beats each one slightly lower in the air on "but," "I," and "think." His hand pushes down to the desk on "the reality is," lifts, and makes a beat on "with the r:esult" before resting them palm down until the end of the sentence on the words "buried anyway," as if he were constraining the spread of the news under his hand. This is in line with Kendon (2004) who wrote that the "open hand prone" palm down family all appear to share the semantic theme of *stopping* or *interrupting* a physical action, idea, or communicative action.

Craig then lifts his hand, palm now facing away from him on "what you're doing." Again, the palm facing out is a form of rejection (Kendon, 2004), which must relate to the interest of the media in what Adam is doing. Craig wants to *prevent* the news about the resignation of the chief financial officer being reported with any prominence.

He then makes a hand roll away from him on "if we," which refers to something occurring or rolling into the future and appears to grasp the words as he says, "hold the sta:ff note" (Figure 6.1, image 3). He then makes a further hand roll for the result (Figure 6.1, image 4), which is again something that will happen in the future. His hand then rests in his lap for the rest of the utterance.

It becomes evident from this critical incident that the PRP is attempting to influence the media messages, but the *agency* is not necessarily with him, but with the client. Craig must persuade the client of a desired course of action while strategizing how it might be done. Whatever a PRP such as Craig suggests must be approved by the client before it can be implemented.

Conclusion

What is revealed in these critical incidents is that, unlike textbooks that portray PRPs as "making journalists' work easy for them," the reality is that in many instances PRPs act as *gatekeepers* and are *less than transparent.* As Merkelsen (2011) pointed out, the practitioner's work is most effective when it can be done invisibly on behalf of the organization. But invisibility may prevent scrutiny, which can, potentially allow unethical practices to flourish. Ethical practice, Messina (2007) argued, has at its core *respect*, and this respect manifests itself through providing appropriate information so the organization's publics can make informed, rational, and thoughtful choices and decisions. When gate-keeping results in important information being strategically "buried" or "delayed," respect for the public sphere and the function of democracy is lost. Thus, the PRP-journalist relationship has wider implications than being merely an "expert skill" or advancing personal influence.

PRPs are only boundary spanners in that they are the first port of call for a journalist looking for commentary. While they may be genuinely willing to act as intermediaries between the organization and its various publics (including the media), their primary loyalties lie with their client or the organization. Balancing the interest of the client with that of the publics, as has been promoted through the systems theory (L'Etang, 2013) or the idea of "mutual benefit" (see Chapter 7), is therefore simply not a reality. Still, practitioners are strategic enough to realize the importance of maintaining good relationships with journalists, as a *means to an end.*

These critical incidents point towards *persuasion* remaining at the core of public relations practice (Messina, 2007) even though "persuasion is still viewed with distaste" (Fawkes, 2007, p. 315). If we take Watkins' (2001, p. 116) five core persuasive tasks, namely mapping the influence landscape, shaping perceptions of interests and of alternatives, gaining acceptance for tough decisions, and persuading at a distance, we see that all these were achieved to a greater or lesser degree in the incidents highlighted in this chapter. For example, the influence landscape was mapped through strategizing and identifying who needed to be included and influenced when shaping a message for the media. Perceptions of interest were shaped by influencing others' beliefs about what they wanted, such as when Craig convinced a reluctant journalist to receive an off-the-record brief. Alternatives were shaped in a similar fashion by influencing what the journalist thought were her options. Gaining acceptance for tough decisions was evident in Craig's phone discussion with the client about how to "manage the story." Persuading at a distance where a broader impact is attained through mass persuasion is achieved through PRPs' ongoing work with the journalists. If we take all these together, it is clear that persuasion is alive and well in public relations practice, and at the heart of PRP's interactions with journalists is a wish to manage and control the messages being released to media, revealing at times a worrying lack of transparency. This, then, brings us to the next chapter where we discuss organization-public relationships.

Notes

1 To protect the privacy of individuals and organizations, all names have been changed.
2 At the time of the study, the client company was millions of dollars in debt and its share price had dropped dramatically. Names and some details have been changed or omitted to protect the identity of those involved.

References

Andrews, L. (2006). Spin: From tactic to tabloid. *Journal of Public Affairs*, 6(1), 31–45. doi:10.1002/pa.37.
Beder, S. (1997). *Global spin: The corporate assault on environmentalism.* Melbourne, Australia: Scribe.
Bishop, J. (2009). Media relations techniques and analysis. In G. Mersham, P. Theunissen, & J. Peart (Eds.), *Public relations and communication management: An Aotearoa/New Zealand perspective* (pp. 131–145). North Shore, New Zealand: Pearson Education Australia.
Broom, G. M. (2009). *Cutlip and Center's effective public relations* (10th ed.), Upper Saddle River, NJ: Prentice Hall/Pearson Educational International.
Burt, T. (2012). *Dark art: The changing face of public relations.* London: Elliot & Thompson.
Callard, H. (2011). *Attitudes and perceptions of newspaper journalists towards public relations practitioners in New Zealand* (Master of Communication Studies). Auckland University of Technology, Auckland.
Chapman, J., & Nuttall, N. (2011). *Journalism Today: A themed history.* Oxford: Wiley Blackwell.
Clark, H., & Foxtree, J. (2002). Using uh and um in spontaneous speaking. *Cognition*, 84(1), 73–111. doi:10.1016/s0010-0277(02)00017-3.
Coombs, W. T. (2007). Protecting organization reputations during a crisis: The development and application of Situational crisis communication theory. *Corporate Reputation Review*, 10(3), 163–176. doi:10.1057/palgrave.crr.1550049.
Cottle, S. (2003). News, public relations and power: Mapping the field [Literature review]. In S. Cottle (Ed.), *News, public relations and power* (pp. 3–24). London: Sage Publications.
Crikey, & ACIJ. (2010, March 15). *Spinning the media*: Crikey.com. Available at: http://www.crikey.com.au/spinning–the–media/.
Davies, N. (2008). *Flat earth news.* London: Chatto & Windus.
Davis, A. (2000). Public relations, news production and changing patterns of source access in the British national media. *Media, Culture & Society*, 22(1), 39–59. doi:10.1177/016344300022001003.
Davis, A. (2003). Public relations and news sources. In S. Cottle (Ed.), *News, public relations and power* (pp. 27–42). London: Sage Publications.
Davis, A. (2013). *Promotional cultures: The rise and spread of advertising, public relations, marketing and branding.* Cambridge: Polity Press.
DeLorme, D. E., & Fedler, F. (2003). Journalists' hostility toward public relations: An historical analysis. *Public Relations Review*, 29(2), 99–124. doi:10.1016/s0363-8111(03)00019-5.

Dennison, M. (2012). *An analysis of public relations discourse and its representations in popular culture.* (Master of Communication Studies). Auckland University of Technology, Auckland.

Ericson, R. V., Baranek, P. M., & Chan, J. B. L. (1989). *Negotiating control: A study of news sources.* Toronto: University of Toronto Press.

Erjavec, K. (2005). Hybrid public relations news discourse. *European Journal of Communication, 20*(2), 155–179. doi:10.1177/0267323105052295.

Fairclough, N. (1989). *Language and power.* London: Longman.

Fawkes, J. (2007). Public relations models and persuasion ethics: a new approach. *Journal of Communication, 11*(4), 313–331. doi: 10.1108/13632540 710843922.

Fishman, M. (1980). *Manufacturing the news.* Austin, TX: University of Texas Press.

Franklin, B. (2011). Sources, credibility and the continuing crisis of UK journalism. In B. Franklin, & M. Carlson (Eds.), *Journalists, sources and credibility: New perspectives* (pp. 90–106). New York: Routledge.

Froomkin, D. (2014, September 27). Anatomy of a non-denial denial. Retrieved December 29, 2016, from The Intercept, https://theintercept.com/2014/09/26/deception-heart-john-brennans-non-denial-denial/.

Gans, H. J. (1979). *Deciding what's news: A study of CBS Evening News, NBC Nightly News, Newsweek, and Time.* New York: Pantheon.

Golan, G., & Wanta, W. (2001). Second-Level agenda setting in the New Hampshire primary: A comparison of coverage in three newspapers and public perceptions of candidates. *Journalism & Mass Communication Quarterly, 78*(2), 247–259. doi:10.1177/107769900107800203.

Goldin–Meadow, S. (2003). *Hearing gesture: How our hands help us think.* Cambridge, MA: Belknap Press of Harvard University Press.

Gregory, A. (2003, September 1). *The press, public relations and the implications for democracy Symposium conducted at the meeting of the The Global Alliance for Public Relations and Communication Management.* Retrieved from http://www.globalpr.org/news/features/gregory-1-9-03.asp.

Gregory, A. (2004, November 9). *Powerful PR: a force for the future Symposium conducted at the meeting of the Chartered Institute of Public Relations.* Retrieved from http://www.ipr.org.uk/news/speeches/old/Anne_Gregory-rep-IPR_Conf_09_11_04.htm.

Grunig, J. E. (1992). Communication, public relations and effective organizations: An overview of the book. In J. E. Grunig, D. M. Dozier, W. P. Ehling, L. Grunig, F. Repper & J. White (Eds.), *Excellence in public relations and communication management* (9th ed., pp. 1–28). United States: Lawrence Erlbaum Associates.

Harding, J. (2014, January 14). *Why BBC head of news James Harding is 'extremely optimistic about the future of journalism.'* Retrieved from http://www.pressgazette.co.uk/.../why-bbc-head-news-james-harding-extremely-optimistic-about-future-journalism.

Hobsbawm, J. (2010). Introduction. In J. Hobsbawm (Ed.), *Where the truth lies: Trust and morality in the business of PR, journalism and communications* (2nd ed.), London: Atlantic Books.

Hoggan, J., & Littlemore, R. (2009). *Climate cover-up: The crusade to deny global warming.* Vancouver: Douglas & McIntyre Publishing Group.

Ihlen, Ø. & van Ruler, B. (2007). How public relations works: Theoretical roots and public relations perspectives. *Public Relations Review, 33*, 243–248. doi:10.1016/j.pubrev.2007.05.001.

Jempson, M. (2005). Spinners or sinners? PR, journalists and public trust. *Journal of Communication Management, 9*(3), 267–276. doi:10.1108/13632540510621542.

Kendon, A. (2004). *Gesture: Visible action as utterance.* Cambridge: Cambridge University Press.

L'Etang, J. (2013). Public Relations: A discipline in transformation. *Sociology Compass, 7*(10), 799–817. doi:10.1111/soc4.12072.

Lewis, J., Williams, A., & Franklin, B. (2008). A compromised fourth estate? *Journalism Studies, 9*(1), 1–20. doi:10.1080/14616700701767974.

Lewis, J., Williams, A., Franklin, B., Thomas, J., & Mosdell, N. (2006). *The quality and independence of British journalism.* Cardiff: Cardiff School of Journalism, Media and Cultural Studies. Retrieved from http://www.mediawise.org.uk/www.mediawise.org.uk/display_page2afa.html?id=999.

Louw, E. P. (2010). *The media and political process* (2nd ed.), London: Sage Publications.

Macnamara, J. (2009) *Journalism and PR: Beyond the myths and stereotypes to transparency and management in the public interest.* Unpublished paper. Retrieved from https://www.academia.edu/830291/Journalism_and_PR_Beyond_Myths_and_Stereotypes_to_Transparency_and_Management_in_the_Public_Interest.

Macnamara, J. (2014). Journalism–PR relations revisited: The good news, the bad news, and insights into tomorrow's news. *Public Relations Review, 40*(5), 739–750. doi:10.1016/j.pubrev.2014.07.002.

Matthews, J. (2013). Journalists and their sources. In K. Fowler-Watt & S. Allen (Eds.), *Journalism: New challenges* (pp. 242–259). Bournemouth: Centre for Journalism & Communication Research, Bournemouth University.

McChesney, R. W. (2003). The problem of journalism: A political economic contribution to an explanation of the crisis in contemporary US journalism. *Journalism Studies, 4*(3), 299–329. doi:10.1080/14616700306492.

McChesney, R., & Nichols, J. (2010). *The death and life of American journalism: The media revolution that will begin the world again.* New York: Nation Books.

McNair, B. (2011). *An introduction to political communication* (5th ed.), London: Routledge.

Merkelsen, H. (2011). The double-edged sword of legitimacy in public relations. *Journal of Communication Management, 15*(2), 125–143. doi:10.1108/13632541111126355.

Messina, A. (2007). Public relations, the public interest and persuasion: an ethical approach. *Journal of Communication Management, 11*(1), 29–52. doi:10.1108/13632540710725978.

Moloney, K. (2006). *Rethinking public relations.* Abingdon: Routledge.

Moloney, K., Jackson, D., & McQueen, D. (2013). News and public relations: A dangerous relationship. In K. Fowler-Watt & S. Allen (Eds.), *Journalism: New challenges* (pp. 259–282). Bournemouth: Centre for Journalism & Communication Research, Bournemouth University.

Motion, J., Leitch, S., & Cliffe, S. (2009). Public relations in Australasia: friendly rivalry, cultural diversity, and global focus. In K. Sriramesh & D. Vercic (Eds.), *The global public relations handbook, revised and expanded edition: Theory, research, and practice* (2nd ed., pp. 107–129). New York: Routledge.

O'Neill, D., & O'Connor, C. (2008). The passive journalist. *Journalism Practice*, 2(3), 487–500. doi:10.1080/17512780802281248.

Orsman, B. (2008, August 13). Council unveils spin doctor team. *New Zealand Herald.* Retrieved from: http://www.nzherald.co.nz/nz/news/article.cfm?c_id=1&objectid=10526744.

Parker, J. (2011, May 15). *The dark side inside.* Retrieved December 28, 2016, from http://failedestate.com/the-dark-side-inside/.

Pullman, G. (2013). *Persuasion: History, theory, practice.* Indianapolis, IN: Hackett Publishing Co.

Reich, Z. (2006). The process model of news initiative: sources lead first, reporters thereafter. *Journalism Studies*, 7(4), 497–514. doi:10.1080/14616700600757928.

Sallot, L. M., & Johnson, E. A. (2006). Investigating relationships between journalists and public relations practitioners: Working together to set, frame and build the public agenda, 1991–2004. *Public Relations Review*, 32(2), 151–159. doi:10.1016/j.pubrev.2006.02.008.

Sallot, L. M., Steinfatt, T. M., & Salwen, M. B. (1998). Journalists' and public relations practitioners' news values: Perceptions and cross–perceptions. *Journalism & Mass Communication Quarterly*, 75(2), 366–377. doi:10.1177/107769909807500211.

Schegloff, E. A. (2010). Some other "Uh(m)"s. *Discourse Processes*, 47(2), 130–174. doi:10.1080/01638530903223380.

Schiffrin, D. (1987). *Discourse markers.* Cambridge: Cambridge University Press.

Schiffrin, D. (2001). Discourse markers: Language, meaning, and context. In D. Schiffrin, D. Tannen, & H. E. Hamilton (Eds.), *The handbook of discourse analysis* (pp. 54–75). Malden, MA: Blackwell Publishing.

Shin, J. H., & Cameron, G. T. (2004). Conflict measurements: Analysis of simultaneous inclusion in roles, values, independence, attitudes, and dyadic adjustment. *Public Relations Review*, 30(4), 401–410. doi:10.1016/j.pubrev.2004.08.001.

Sissons, H. (2015). *Whose news? Investigating power relations between journalists and public relations practitioners.* Unpublished Doctoral thesis: Auckland University of Technology, Auckland.

Sriramesh, K. (1996/2009). Power distance and public relations: an ethnographic study of Southern Indian organizations. In H. M. Culbertson & N. Chen (Eds.), *International public relations: A comparative analysis* (pp. 171–190). New York: Lawrence Erlbaum Associates.

Starkman, D. (2010, October). *The Hamster wheel.* Retrieved December 29, 2016, from Columbia Journalism Review, http://www.cjr.org/cover_story/the_hamster_wheel.php.

Theaker, A. (2004) *The public relations handbook* (2nd ed.). Abingdon: Routledge.

Tilley, E. (2012). *The blame game: Professional stance and ethical self–examination in public relations.* ANZCA Conference, Adelaide, South Australia.

Tilley, E., & Hollings, J. (2008). *Still stuck in "A love–hate relationship": Understanding journalists' enduring and impassioned duality towards public relations.* ANZCA Conference, Wellington, New Zealand.

Turk, J. V. (1985). Information subsidies and influence. *Public Relations Review, 11*(3), 10–25. doi:10.1016/s0363-8111(85)80078-3.

Turk, J. V. (1986). Public relations' influence on the news. *Newspaper Research Journal, 7*(4), 15–27.

van Dijk, T. A. (1993). Principles of critical discourse analysis. *Discourse & Society, 4*(2), 249–283. doi:10.1177/0957926593004002006.

Washington, H., & Cook, J. (2011). *Climate change denial: Heads in the sand.* London: Taylor & Francis.

Watkins, M. (2001). In practice. Principles of persuasion. *Negotiation Journal, 17*(2), 115–137.

Waymer, D. (2013). Democracy and government public relations: Expanding the scope of "Relationship" in public relations research. *Public Relations Review, 39*, 320–331. doi:10.1016/j.pubrev.2013.07.015.

West, C. (1995). Women's competence in conversation. *Discourse and Society, 6*(1), 209–224.

Wilson, D., & Supa, D. W. (2013). Examining modern media relations: An exploratory study of the effect of Twitter on the public relations-journalist relationship. *Public Relations Journal, 7*(3), 1–20.

White, J., & Hobsbawm, J. (2007). Public relations and journalism. *Journalism Practice, 1*(2), 283–292. doi:10.1080/17512780701275606.

7 The Organization–Public Relationship (OPR)

A reputation once broken may possibly be repaired, but the world will always keep their eyes on the spot where the crack was.
—Joseph Hall (1574–1656), English clergyman

A Sticky Relationship

The three relationships considered so far in this book are all clearly between individuals. This last relationship is undoubtedly the most controversial precisely because it is not clear on this point. In fact, the concept of organization–public relationships, which seems to have taken hold in public relations scholarship and is currently talked about by many in the field, appears to accept that *entities* can form relationships. Having said that, there is no clear definition or consensus what "organization–public relationship" means (Ki & Shin, 2015). As Broom, Casey, and Ritchey pointed out years ago, scholars simply "assume that readers know and agree on the meaning and measurement of the important concept of *relationships*" (Broom, Casey, & Ritchey, 1997, p. 83, original emphasis). We would therefore be remiss not to interrogate the current approaches to organization–public relationships.

To understand the "relationship" an organization has with its publics, scholars have drawn from a range of disciplines, including interpersonal and inter–organizational relationships, psychology, and marketing (Ki & Shin, 2015). This chapter is no exception: we too have drawn our insights from disciplines ranging from linguistics to organizational psychology and critical discourse analysis. In particular, we present a case where the practitioners of a local authority meet to discuss how they will communicate a crucial decision to the organization's public and how they would deal with an unhappy activist public, the residents' group, which was—at a certain point—labeled by one of the public relations practitioners as "the rebels."

Organization–public relationship theory is problematic for many reasons, not the least that it is based on interpersonal communication theory (Coombs & Holladay, 2015; Heath, 2013), but also because we do not have a clear definition or description of what these relationships involve. Nor do we have a clear view of what these relationships look like *in practice*. And, in the absence of an explicated definition, we are unable to "describe and compare organization–public relationships with any validity or reliability" (Broom et al., 1997, p. 86). Neither do we have agreed–upon boundaries or distinguishing terminology (Ki & Shin, 2015). As Coombs and Holladay (2015) stated, "researchers have appropriated the *language* of relationships without the commitment *to* relationships" (p. 694, original emphasis). Willis (2015) agreed, pointing out that definitions of organization–public relationships exclude references to potentially negative relationships with publics and that there is a limit to an organization's willingness and capability to listen to its publics.

Perhaps one of the most pressing issues with the concept of "relationships" in public relations is the underlying assumptions that are infused in understanding the term. As Zaharna (2015) highlighted, much of the organization–public relationship work has been carried out in the United States where individualism is not only a defining and enduring cultural ideal but also "a *distinguishing* one" (p. 5, original emphasis). Relationships, Zaharna (2015) stated, are "a social condition" (p. 13), and the idea of the "autonomous individual separate from other individuals and society" (p. 14) shifts the focus to the process of *messaging* rather than seeking more suitable relational strategies or considering the context in which relationships are built—an aspect we emphasized in Chapter 3 when discussing the idea of "mediated relationships." As we have pointed out, relationships are not separate from those who are engaged in that relationship, and Broom et al.'s (1997) assertion that relationships can and should be studied as independent constructs because they "have unique and measurable properties that are not shared with the participants in the relationships and that define relationships as being something separate from the participants" (p. 96) becomes a sticky issue for scholarship that considers the management of organization–public relationships as integral to the discipline.

Public Relations as Relationship Management

The idea that public relations is not just about media relations and publicity, was first introduced in 1984 when Mary Ann Ferguson proposed that relationships, and not communication, should be the focus of public relations scholarship (Coombs & Holladay, 2015; Ledingham, 2015; Sallot, 2013) thereby pre–empting the excellence study's conclusion that "the value of public relations [...] could be found in the relationships that publics have with organizations" (Grunig, 2015, p. xxv). Even so, the majority of articles on organization–public relationships were published only after 2000 (Ki & Shin, 2015), and indeed, very little research on organization–public relationships was conducted in the 16 years after Ferguson first presented her paper (Grunig, 2015). Yet, scholars and practitioners agree that little can be achieved without relationships, although they disagree about the shape of such relationships. Indeed, Willis (2015) described thinking around these organization–public relationships as "contested territory" (p. 682).

Relationships and the Legitimacy Gap

Conventional relationship management scholarship proposes that relationships with various people and publics are necessary to legitimize the organization's goal and role within a specific community and context. Ineffective organizations "cannot achieve their goals, at least in part because their publics do not support and typically oppose management efforts to achieve what publics consider *illegitimate* goals" (Grunig & Hung-Baesecke, 2015, p. 71, emphasis added).

Legitimacy here can be described as the organization's "license to operate." It describes how an organization loses, meets, or reclaims society's or a public's sanction to continue to operate, and it is therefore directly linked to its actions (Stokes, 2013). Very often, in establishing an organization–public relationship, the organization will declare its values (the basis for its decision–making processes) either *directly*, through its messages, or *indirectly*, through its behavior. Gregory and Willis (2013) described the breach between the organization's espoused values and the publics' "lived experiences" as the *legitimacy gap*. If this gap is too great, the relationship is put at risk.

The underlying assumption, then, of relationship–building and the management of that relationship is that constructive relationships with key publics are likely to make this process of gaining, regaining, or meeting societal approval much easier. However, herein lies a dilemma. As Stoker (2014, p. 352) argued,

> It is absurd to think practitioners can manage publics in the same way they manage their bank accounts. Attempting to manage publics suggests some control over public values, opinions, and behaviors.

He went on to note that the idea of relationship management "ascribes to public relations a power only available through controlling or manipulating the choice of other parties in the relationship" (Stoker, 2014, p. 345). Willis (2015, p. 686) added that,

> scholars highlight the complex nature of relationships but then disregard the uncertainty inherent in complexity to engage in research underpinned by the belief that stakeholder relationships can be predicted and managed.

The Paradox of Mutually Beneficial Relationships

These challenges have not prevented scholars embracing *relationship management theory* as a viable and general theory of public relations, having become the second most cited theory after the excellence theory (Coombs & Holladay, 2015). Stoker (2014) traced this back to the development of public relations as a management function, followed by the introduction of the concept of *mutually beneficial relationships*, which he described as being inherently paradoxical.

> Practitioners cannot manage the relationship without abridging on the freedom of the other person or parties to define and manage their activities in the relationship. Thus, public relations' desire for mutually beneficial relationships with publics, especially if strategically planned and managed, undermines the very mutuality desired.
> (Stoker, 2014, p. 353)

Ignoring the inherent contradiction between what is desired and what can be achieved, public relations scholars and practitioners alike have embraced the idea that the "relationship" between an organization and its publics is (and can be) equally beneficial to both.

And so, the concept has been widely adopted and integrated into numerous practical definitions of public relations. As a result, the belief that PRPs should develop such relationships on behalf of the organization has become an unquestioned goal and desired outcome of practitioner activity (Coombs & Holladay, 2015). For example, the Public Relations Society of America (PRSA) describes public relations as "a strategic communication process that builds *mutually beneficial relationships* between organizations and their publics" (Yann, 2015, emphasis added). Accordingly, relationship management can, therefore, be best described as "the process of managing organization–public relationships in such a way as to benefit organizations and publics alike" (Ledingham, 2013, p. 781).

Indeed, borrowing from interorganizational relationships (IORs) Broom et al. (1997) proposed organizations enter relationships for specific reasons. In the first instance, they engage in a relationship with publics where these relationships are *required* by law and are therefore necessary and non–voluntary. Second, they enter them for *legitimacy* reasons, that is, to maintain the appearance of agreement with the current norms, rules, and expectations. Third, where scarce resources prompt unequal relationships through which power and control are exercised, relationships are required as a result of that *asymmetry*. Fourth, relationships are entered for *reciprocity* reasons, where parties cooperate, collaborate and coordinate their efforts, and the ultimate benefits outweigh the costs. Last, they enter relationships for reasons of *efficiency*, that is, to reduce the costs of transactions, and to maintain *stability* in order to reduce uncertainty and ensure order.

In the case presented in this chapter, the organization has entered a "relationship" with its publics because it is required to do so. What becomes evident through the discussions among the practitioners is that the authority has no interest in developing a "mutually beneficial" relationship. Indeed, the communication plan is focused on framing the message to justify the decision the authority has made, and the meeting with the residents' group is seen as a "risk" that needs to be "managed."

Managing risk is about making decisions in the face of uncertainty; it is about deciding which action is the most appropriate without knowing what the outcome will be. As Palenchar (2010) stated, "The challenge when addressing risk is *uncertainty*" (p. 447, emphasis added), and as our example shows, practitioners have to manage an array of uncertainty, such as not knowing when meetings will take place, what will be discussed in these meetings, or how publics might react to the way a message is framed. Ultimately, how risk is managed (through relationships) will impact on the organization's reputation.

Adopting the Interpersonal Perspective

As mentioned earlier, in order to understand the organization–public relationship and its implications better, scholars have applied various perspectives with the most commonly applied one being the interpersonal relationship perspective (Ki & Shin, 2015).

Although Ki and Shin (2015) recognized that the levels of difference between various organization–public relationships still need to be addressed, they believed that "theorizing about or researching public relations through the lens of interpersonal communication crystallizes important indicators of OPRs" (p. 37).

But Coombs and Holladay (2015) questioned whether the appropriation of interpersonal relationship dimensions has contributed significantly to theory building. In part, adopting terminologies (or "language" as Coombs and Holladay suggested) that are borne from interpersonal relationship theory may not be suited to organization–public relationships, and may, in fact, disguise the actual practice of public relations. In particular, Coombs and Holladay were concerned that scholars' "linguistic choice seems to mask public relations' true intention of strategically 'influencing the conversation'," that is in persuading the organization's publics to its point of view thereby failing to reflect the authentic two–way communication that is integral to interpersonal relationships (Coombs & Holladay, 2015, p. 691).

Willis (2015) also pointed out the original definition presented by Ledingham and Bruning in 1998 did not consider the potential for *negative relationships* to develop. Equally, Heath (2013) warned against scholars' "predisposition to adopt a rosy view of relationships" (p. 428).

Regardless, Ledingham's work, in particular, was instrumental in applying interpersonal relationship theory to organization–public relationships. He reasoned that the dimensions that affect the quality of an interpersonal relationship also impact an organization–public relationship, and by doing so, the latter relationship emulates an interpersonal relationship with dimensions that include "trust, openness, credibility, mutual control, emotion, intimacy, similarity, immediacy, agreement, issue perception, shared interests, relational history, and in certain cultures, face and favor" (Ledingham, 2013, p. 782). Thus, a valuable relationship can be judged by its *control mutuality* (the amount of control each party has over the relationship), the levels of *trust* (confidence in the other and willingness to disclose themselves), *commitment* (extent to which each party feels the relationship is worth the effort), and *satisfaction* (the extent to which each party feels favorable about the other) (Grunig & Hung-Baesecke, 2015). Presumably, a good relationship will rate high on all four dimensions.

The idea of managing relationships, however, is "driven by the imperative to create value during the consumption of goods and services" (Bourne, 2016, p. 125), which poses concerns when importing the dimensions of interpersonal relationships because the same monetary value simply does not apply to interpersonal relationships (see Coombs & Holladay, 2015). In fact, unlike interpersonal relationships, which have both an emotional and cognitive dimension (see Chapter 2), organization–public relationships are *transactional* and *functional* in nature. As Grunig (2015) suggested, these relationships become "intangible assets that, over time, reduce costs and risks for organizations, and increase revenue" (p. xxv). Managing relationships for and on behalf of organizations implies control—control we do not have (Stoker, 2014).

Besides the usual issues that have to be overcome when applying a theory from one discipline to another, there are additional questions that are raised when applying interpersonal relationship theories to organization–public relationships. For example, it is assumed that publics *want* to have relationships with the organization and that this relationship must necessarily be close to be beneficial (Coombs & Holladay, 2015; Stoker, 2014). Stoker (2014) likened this situation to that of a mother *wanting* her child to read when she has no control over the child's understanding. The adage that one can bring a horse to the water but cannot make it drink applies here.

The suggestion that a public desires "closeness" in a relationship with the organization has also been questioned by Waymer (2013), who proposed the idea of *non–voluntary relationships*. He argued that not all relationships have the potential to be positive ones, no matter how much time and effort is put into them by the PRP. He advised that practitioners should understand (and respect) *distancing behaviors* of non–voluntary publics—those who are forced by circumstance to maintain a relationship with the organization.

Stages in Organization–Public Relationships

Similar to the dimensions of interpersonal relationships, Ledingham (2015) also proposed that the stages of organization–public relationships mimic those of interpersonal ones (see Chapter 2). Accordingly, the relationship is *initiated* by parties showing interest in each other, which is then followed by *experimenting* to determine what each party wants out of the relationship, and *intensifying* as parties express their feelings openly. Organizations and their publics then *integrate* by forming a *shared identity*, culminating in public gestures about the relationship or *bonding*.

Behaviors that mimic the integration and bonding stages are not dissimilar to the behaviors associated with *parasocial relationships* (Coombs & Holladay, 2015), that is, relationships that fans have with a celebrity. Coombs and Holladay (2015) described the parasocial relationship as one–sided and illusory: although they may have never actually met the celebrity *in person*, these publics may feel they *know* him or her. Granted, organizations such as Apple have a strong brand following, but few organizations ever reach such a stage in their "relationship" with their publics—particularly if one considers that when a relationship reaches the bonded stage, it is inferred that the participants have a shared and co–constructed identity. While it is possible that there are publics who purposefully seek relationships with organizations whose identity matches their own, Coombs and Holladay (2015) argued that it is somewhat unrealistic to expect organizations to co–create and share an identity with their publics.

Though relationship management is mainly focused on developing and maintaining relationships and *remedial action* is taken to prevent the termination of a relationship, Ledingham (2015) acknowledged that organization–public relationships can come apart. He described these phases as: differentiation, circumscription, stagnation, avoidance, and termination. These stages mimic those of interpersonal relationships (see Chapter 2). When parties see themselves as "individuals" or separate from the other rather than part of a whole, *differentiation* takes place. This is followed by *circumscription* as communication decreases, *stagnation* when nothing more happens between the parties, *avoidance* as the parties attempt to put distance between themselves and, finally, *termination* where the end of the relationship is signaled. The penultimate stage is of particular interest in light of Waymer's (2013) call for acknowledging and respecting distancing behaviors as a necessary part of organization–public relationships. This seems to suggest that avoidance is not necessarily a signal that the relationship is ending nor that correc-tive actions are required to "restore" the relationship.

Theoretical Frameworks

Analyzing the articles published on organization–public relationships from 1985 to 2013, Ki and Shin (2015) found that four key theoretical frameworks were used to describe the nature of these relationships: the excellence theory, systems theory, dialogic theory, and social exchange theory. Their findings concurred with Macnamara's (2012) that the ex-cellence theory and the systems theory were the two main theories dis-cussed in textbooks.

The *excellence theory* is most commonly used to illustrate relationship management in public relations (Ki & Shin, 2015). The theory originates from a study conducted from 1985 to about 2000 and can be viewed as an overarching or umbrella theory (Bowen, 2013). It incorporates ten principles perceived to be important for effective public relations, thereby explaining "how public relations as a management function can contribute to the planning and response processes necessary for orga-nizational effectiveness" (Bowen, 2013, p. 323). Principles include, for example, emphasizing the importance of relationships, participating in strategic management decisions, and maintaining diversity. Notably, the excellence theory has been influential in promoting the idea of two–way symmetry, but without considering whether the commitment to symme-try solves "relational tension" (Heath, 2013, p. 430).

Closely related to the excellence theory is the *systems theory* which proposes that for an organization to survive, it must interact with other organizations and its publics (Plowman, 2013) and subsequently there must be mutual adaptation (Broom et al., 1997). Balanced or "symmet-rical" organizations are neither fully open nor fully closed; they endlessly *contract* (restrict funding, explore their own processes and systems) and *expand* (innovate, explore, network) (Stoker, 2014). According to Stoker, "Structure, habits, and routines help regulate this process of restricting and expanding" (2014, p. 347), and it is through structure and routines that practitioners can develop trust, confidence and thus, *relating*, which he proposed as the preferred focus of public relations work. According to him, relationships are inferred from the act of relating, and through such action, practitioners and organizations can control how they interact without affecting publics' rights to respond, enabling them to develop relationships that are *potentially* built on mutuality and trust.

Seen from the systems perspective, relationships "reflect the conjoint, *purposive* behaviors of the actors in the relationships" (Broom et al., 1997, p. 94, emphasis added), suggesting that organizations and publics are interdependent and need to adapt conjointly. Broom et al. (1997) stated that information, energy, and resources are all transferred within the relationship, and it is the qualities of these exchanges that "represent and define the relationship" (p. 94). They added that within this perspective, *antecedents* (histories) are change pressures that motivate the parties to form the relationship, and include—but are not limited to—perceptions, motives, needs, and behaviors while *consequences* (effects or results) are the outputs that result in changes in the environment or a change of goal state. All relationships have antecedents and consequences that need to be considered when analyzing them.

Like the excellence theory, *social exchange theory* encompasses "several theories that describe the emergent properties of social interaction" and specifically how social relationships, or in this case organization–public relationships, "form, expand, and deteriorate" (Leitchy, 2013, p. 842). In interpersonal relationships, social exchange is guided by *the rule of distributive justice*, which demands that each party's relational reward (outcome of the relationship) should be proportional to their costs (input into the relationship) thereby achieving a state of *equity* or fairness (Solomon & Theiss, 2013).

Dialogic theory has been core to public relations theory for more than 30 years, and the theologian and philosopher Martin Buber is generally viewed as the father of contemporary dialogic theory (Pieczka, 2011). He defined three types of dialogue: *genuine dialogue,* which sees the other person as a human being (a "you"); *technical dialogue,* which has as its main purpose to gain objective understanding; and *monologue* disguised as dialogue (de Bussy, 2010). In addition to the three key attributes that define dialogue, namely *listening, positive regard*, and a *willingness to change* (de Bussy, 2010), Kent and Taylor (2002) identified five further features of dialogue in public relations:

> *Mutuality*, or the recognition of organization–public relationships; *propinquity*, or the temporality and spontaneity of interactions with publics; *empathy*, or the supportiveness and confirmation of public goals and interests; *risk*, or the willingness to interact with individuals and publics on their own terms; and...*commitment*, or the extent to which an organization gives itself over to dialogue, interpretation, and understanding in its interactions with publics.
>
> (pp. 24–25, original emphasis)

Although some scholars such as Theunissen and Wan Noordin (2012) cautioned against hailing dialogue as the solution to the ills of the world and highlighted that the use of dialogue is likely to have broader implications than currently acknowledged (see, for example, Theunissen, 2014), it is generally perceived as "good" because it respects publics' dignity and independence (Bowen, 2010). Dialogue can, therefore, be regarded as an effective mode of communication and integral to relationship formation and maintenance. As Brønn (2010) reasoned, organizations that communicate effectively with their publics develop *better relationships*, and consequently *better reputations*.

Reputation and Organization–Public Relationships

Integral to an organization's reputation is the notion of *trust*. "It is possible to assert that it is not reputation that is damaged when organizations fail to live up to expectations; it is rather our trust in them" (Brønn, 2010, p. 310). Relationships, therefore, benefit organizations as they allow trust to develop, and consequently, improve reputation. Of course, trust is required to build "close" relationships (see Chapter 2), and where there is no trust, distancing behaviors are likely to occur, as Waymer (2013) suggested.

According to Yang and Cha (2015), there are two types of organizational reputations that are important for explicating the link between relationship and reputation management: the organization's primary and secondary reputation. These are linked to the type of organization–public relationship, which can be either reputational, experiential (Yang & Cha, 2015), communal, transactional, or exchange relationships (Grunig & Hung-Baesecke, 2015).

Reputational relationships are symbolic, superficial and abstract, while *experiential relationships* are based on publics' direct experience with the organization (Yang & Cha, 2015). *Communal relationships* are described as occurring when each party is willing to provide benefits to the other "not because they want something in return but because they care about the other's welfare" (Grunig & Hung-Baesecke, 2015, p. 86). In *exchange relationships*, one party provides benefits to the other based on past experiences or future expectations, which is akin to a *transactional relationship* where there is spurious trust and loyalty (Grunig & Hung-Baesecke, 2015). According to Grunig and Hung-Baesecke, PRPs aim to develop communal relationships, and the latter is, therefore, more desired than exchange relationships.

Primary reputation is based on direct or personal experience (Yang & Cha, 2015) and is therefore an outcome of the experiential relationship (Grunig & Hung-Baesecke, 2015). It carries more weight and is more likely to lead to accommodating behaviors with a greater potential to affect management performance. *Secondary reputation*, on the other hand, is relatively artificial and simple, being mainly the result of rumor and mediated sources, such as journalistic reports (Yang & Cha, 2015). Grunig and Hung-Baesecke (2015) described these two reputations as *first order reputational cognitions* (primary reputations) and *second order reputational cognitions* (secondary reputations).

First order reputational cognitions are held by *active publics* who have experiential relationships with the organization, while second order reputational cognitions are mostly held by *passive publics* who have no first–hand experience with the organization, but who have learned about the organization's (usually poor) behaviors through the media—a process called *megaphoning* (Grunig & Hung-Baesecke, 2015). In fact, publics without any first–hand experience with the organization will evaluate the state and quality of their current or future relationships based on what they hear or read about the organization. This second-hand evaluation may result in, for example, *shunning* or *stigmatizing* the organization (Grunig & Hung-Baesecke, 2015) and thus poses potential risk. Secondary reputation is therefore as important as primary reputation and integral to risk management.

Enacting Organization–Public Relationships

While there has been much theorizing about organization–public relationships as to their role in public relations, there has been less exploration of *how*, in practice, these relationships might be enacted (or not). In our fieldwork, we found little evidence that practitioners knowingly considered the relationship between their organizations and the publics in any way other than as a risk management exercise—that is, requiring the management of issues to minimize risk. As shown in Chapters 4, 5, and 6, the PRPs' focus was on the interpersonal relationships with their colleagues, their clients, and the journalists. So, we returned to the micro level to explore how practitioners *talked* about engaging with their publics and what they might *do* in building or maintaining relationships.

Consequently, the critical incidents presented here involve a local authority's actions following the announcement of its intention to end the refuse and recycling contract with a locally owned company with charitable status in one of its districts, and award it to a multinational company. The announcement angered residents who were supportive of the status quo and a group was set up to resist the change.

The authority's argument was that the new contractor, which was already operating in the wider region, would provide a good—if not better—service at a cheaper rate. However, residents were not convinced; they were angry by what they believed to be a lack of consultation. As one PRP explained,

> People [in the area] aren't happy with it. They think it's a decision they haven't had enough involvement in so now we are moving into the phase of having that contract signed off and the provider into the job. There is a likelihood they will mobilize and protest, so we want to make sure they have enough information to be protesting on the correct basis so they have at least all the facts, and so that those other people know when to put their rubbish out. We had a talk about whether we do that via the media, or direct mail or have a meeting with the people.

The authority, which was planning to announce the final decision about the contractor in the following week, held a series of internal meetings about how to address local opposition. The requirement to come up with a plan was made more urgent because the previous weekend residents had met to denounce the change. Hence in the meetings, there was a focus on how to represent the decision to the public and, later, how to manage the "dissidents."

The Executive Team Meets

The first critical incident presented here involves an executive team meeting of the local authority's communications and marketing department, comprising members of the internal and external communications teams. The meeting is chaired by the group manager of the communications and marketing team, Zara.

The meeting, held on Monday morning, discusses how they should prepare for the public announcement of the decision expected in the next few days. Among the items discussed are how to target two different key publics: those in the area affected by the change and those in the wider region, who are already served by the multinational waste disposal company.

One of the most important issues for both key publics is the effectiveness of the recycling system, and so another point of discussion centered on linking the proposed change of service provider into the overall "recycling story." The problem for the communications team is that in the area previously covered by the locally owned company, recycling initiatives are considered very effective, while, in the wider region, the first year of a new recycling system has not been a total success. As one practitioner put it,

> The last time we had a [name of recycling company] story in [the authority newsletter], I got like three calls from irate residents saying, 'that article was so like pro–authority, it's not even the truth, blah blah blah'.

The meeting agreed that this round of publicity should include an honest assessment of the recycling plant's first year which could be pegged to its one year anniversary. Communications manager, James, said,

> We won't have got it right first time, you know, absolutely perfect in the first year. Let's not try and say that we did. Say that, you know, we got to this point and we want to make it better.

Zara, the group manager, suggests they do a "proper journalistic report" that draws on the idea of balance and honest assessment. However, when one of her team responds that it may be more credible to approach the regional newspaper about writing such an article, that suggestion is politely dismissed:

> I personally think we should do it anyway. We should know internally what our full story is, right? That we've chosen this option because it is the right one and when you wash it all up it's the right thing for [city] even if stuff goes offshore, the carbon footprint is still better than, and there must be some science around that, that's been in previous reports for example. So, someone who's got the bandwidth, you know, needs to almost do a piece of reportage around that.

When asked how this story should be presented—perhaps as a Q&A— Zara responds that she was thinking of a feature, which is longer than a standard news story and includes more detail and background material. She makes it clear what she hopes the feature would include:

> Why did the authority choose this originally? The authority chose it because all the evidence suggests that it reduces landfill and when you wash up the whole recycling side of it, the carbon footprint is far better than, than the landfill.

The proposed piece is clearly intended as a publicity piece (rather than a piece of reportage) to legitimize the authority's decision by presenting what the practitioners have concluded are "the facts." The piece is scheduled to be published the following month to coincide with the anniversary of the city's recycling plant, in the authority's own newsletter, and then given to the news media. Even though it is a targeted publicity piece, the manager is keen for it to appear journalistic rather than promotional.

> It's a plain English straight–talking view of, you know, when we washed it all up we believe this is the best recycling solution and why. And if we can get from [recycling company] from whoever are the experts around the carbon footprint and how it all ultimately is better.

A more pressing issue for the team, however, is announcing the change of contractor to the residents. As Zara says,

> there is an imperative this week, which is more around focusing on the [local area] decision and reinforcing the reason why [the authority] made its original decisions on this.

In her view, it is crucial that when the decision is announced, some of the history and reasons for the decision accompany the announcement, particularly so that journalists have the details to include in their reports. For that reason, she suggests that some of the facts are unearthed for the feature and are presented as a fact sheet to accompany the announcement. These facts provide justification for the decision (which was made for financial reasons) and thus legitimize the authority's decision to switch contractors.

Dealing with a Dissident Public

Another important agenda item addressed by the meeting is how to deal with the group of residents that are unhappy with the decision; a group labeled by one of the PRPs as "the rebels."

The group manager, Zara, is concerned that nothing has yet been arranged by the contractor (which we refer to as CWL) to meet with the group or in any way address their concerns. In this excerpt from the meeting, it is evident how important it is in her opinion to ensure CWL takes the initiative in its relationship with residents.

In the discussion leading up to this excerpt, there has been some confusion about what has been arranged to address and manage the issue of the "rebel" group. At the beginning of the excerpt, Zara makes a request, which effectively serves as a directive with no right of refusal (Bax, 1986; Vine, 2004), "so can we just get the facts straight." The statement sets the scene for what she wishes to achieve in this part of the meeting. She then uses a direct question to discover what has been decided, while at the same time, she makes clear what she expects to be the communication team's position,

> so we are going to talk to them ((the contractor)) and give our advice?

The way the words in the question are ordered suggests another directive, despite the rising intonation signifying a query. Her utterance "we are going to talk" therefore does not require discussion, although she does require an answer as indicated by the following "yes:?."

The discourse marker "so" is used twice in this first utterance, signaling a transition to the next topic (Schiffrin, 1987), and as we have seen in Chapter 5, is used to maintain control over meeting topics and confirms that she is the most senior person in this meeting (Holmes & Stubbe, 2005). Thus, she sets the direction of what will be discussed, and what they (the team) will do to manage the issue. She also indirectly overrules one of the practitioner's attempts to diminish the actions of the dissatisfied publics by labeling them as "the rebels" by refusing to use the label. Her system of thought, or ideology, shapes the strategic communication decisions made about how to legitimize the organization's decisions and what shape the organization's relationship with its publics

Z: so can we just get the <u>facts</u> straight so we are going to
 talk to them ((the contractor))
 and give our <u>advice</u>?
 <u>yes</u>:?
J: (0.3) °yeah°

Z: that we think (.) that (.) without <u>engagement</u> (1.2)
 that the group are likely to be <u>dangerous</u> and we
 [think it's better to <u>be</u>]
S: [yep with CWL]
Z: and everybody <u>agrees</u> with that [<u>internally</u>]?
S: [yep]

S: yeah but I just don't know <u>when</u> that that meeting's
 taking [place]
Z: [and so Martin] etc are very aware that they're
 quite an <u>organized</u> group that could well go off and do
 <u>stuff</u>
S: oh=
Z: =yep=
S: =they're <u>very</u> aware of that yeah=

Z: =uhm did they have uh any of their <u>own</u> ↑thoughts
 about what <u>they</u> were going to ↑do to handle it?
 so w- we obviously had <u>our</u> discussion had <u>they</u> had
 a <u>similar</u> discussion that was¿

Figure 7.1 Strategizing about meeting with dissident publics.

S: uhm I'm not sure because it was Jim East who talked
   to Martin and Rh[onda]
Z: [right]
S: (°about that°)

J: I think what ((cough))
   (0.7) what we don't want to do is for Martin and
   Rhonda just to decide that meeting the rebels is not a
   good idea full stop end of conversation
S: mmm (0.8) I'll ((indistinct))
J: so=

Z: =SO ONCE WE've f:ollowed up (.) this morning
   can we just c- get
   even just get a brief email telling everybody what was
   what the [deal] is and what we think we're going
J: [yeah]
Z: to do on the ((local area)) about that and whether we
   are going to meet and.hh
S: (2.1) yep I'll sort that out

J: is the [film on]
Z: [AN AND FROM] the perspective of
   I think we should make it really clear and write it
   down if necessary that our view is that a successful
   roll out is depe:ndent (0.6) on ensuring that there's no
   huge groundswell of: anti: (0.4) recycling sentiment
   (0.7) so they're going °in to handle it°
S: (1.4) nods mmm

Figure 7.1 (Continued)

will take. This role is particularly relevant if we consider Motion and Leitch's (2016) assertion that,

> All public relations work is undertaken within broader organizational, social, economic and political contexts. These contexts are infused with systems of thought, which are termed "ideologies."
>
> (p. 147)

Zara's body language supports her role as chair, indicating that she is focusing on the issue. During this first part of the utterance, she covers her face with her hands (elbows resting on the table) and uses the fingers of both hands to rub her eyes once and then sweep them up over her brows before interlocking them in front of her (Figure 7.1, image 1). These gestures appear to be used to block out external stimuli in order to focus on understanding the situation as it stands (Ekman & Friesen, 1972). It may also be showing some avoidance behavior (Kahlbaugh & Haviland, 1994), possibly indicating a more negative emotion such as frustration.

Zara's opening query is directed at a specific staff member, Shelley. When she does not receive a response, she checks that her message has been received by following it with a "<u>yes</u>:?" that also carries a rising intonation. Questions by people in positions of power (such as Zara) are designed to force the other participants to respond (Fairclough, 1989). As she says, "yes:?" her gaze shifts momentarily to the communications manager, James, who immediately responds with a barely audible "°yeah°." He does not have the information to answer the question and is likely to be responding only because Zara has looked in his direction. By doing so, he displays what Saville-Troike (1989) calls "passive acknowledgment" (p. 149), which is a form of "backchannel" response designed to acknowledge what has been said, but not to take over the turn.

The Risks of Non–enactment

Zara still has not received an acknowledgment from Shelley who is looking down at her notebook, apparently taking notes, and she (Zara) continues by spelling out what that advice should be:

> that we think (.) that (.) without <u>enactment</u> (1.2) that the group are likely to be <u>dangerous</u> and we think it's better to <u>be</u>

This advice is crucial for our understanding of how organization–public relationships are perceived and enacted in public relations work. Zara's delivery shows a clear emphasis through pauses on and the stressing of two keywords: *enactment* and *dangerous*. As she starts the utterance, she slows down, giving micro pauses between "think" and "that," which are likely to do with giving her time to formulate her next words.

Speakers can use pauses to ensure their message is clear as well as using them as a means for emphasis or to signal contrasts. Pausing often occurs before "semantically heavy words, thereby giving them extra emphasis" (Strangert, 2003, p. 2477).

After the micro pauses, Zara comes to her main message, stressing the semantically heavy words: the noun immediately before the pause, "enactment," and the adjective associated with the group, "dangerous," that comes after the pause.

without <u>enactment</u> (1.2) that the group are likely to be <u>dangerous</u>

Here she is using contrast to deliver her message: without enactment, there is danger. It appears, then, that Zara believes in enactment with publics even though, perhaps, that enactment is to *minimize risk* (danger). Characterizing the group as potentially "dangerous," however, also serves an additional function: it minimizes the organization's responsibility for potential negative consequences of its decision. This kind of action is what White, Bandura, and Bero (2009) called *moral disengagement*, that is, legitimizing an action or decision (by the organization) that could potentially be detrimental, by reframing it. Minimizing consequences is one of eight mechanisms identified by White et al. (2009) for morally disengaging. The others include moral justification, disparaging the critics or victims (such as labeling the troublesome group as "rebels"), euphemistic labeling, attributing blame, advantageous comparison, displacement of responsibility, and diffusion of responsibility (such as one cannot expect good results in the first year).

The choice of the adjective "dangerous" is a conscious one, clearly shown by the pause before Zara deploys it. It is a significant one when we consider that "dangerous" in this context has connotations of extreme antisocial actions, perhaps even terrorism. Further, in this context, "enactment" could be seen as a military term as much if not more than a relational one. This group needs to be engaged and in this way neutralized.

Zara's use of such extreme terms for a domestic (civilian) situation illustrates just how concerned she is that her colleagues, and the contractor, take the group's potential to disrupt the authority's plans seriously. It is also a *persuasive strategy* if we consider that painting the potential of danger and invoking fear may prompt others into action.

At this point, Shelley looks up from her notebook and returns Zara's gaze in the pause after "enactment" (Figure 7.1, image 2). Listeners often understand pauses as happening at places in talk where it would be possible for another speaker to take over, and as a signal that the current speaker is willing to hand over the turn (Sacks, Schegloff, & Jefferson, 1974). This is the case here; Shelley prepares to respond, moving her head and mouth to indicate speech, but Zara ignores this and continues to speak after the pause.

Shelley waits until just after the word "dangerous," when Zara appears to have completed the thought, and then, even though she uses the continuer "and" (Schiffrin, 1987), Shelley overlaps the group manager, to say "yep with CWL." This response causes Zara to change tack, and she does not finish the utterance "it's better to <u>be</u>"—perhaps because she has now received confirmation about meeting the contractor. Instead, she checks that there is agreement that enactment with the residents' group is important.

Shelley nods three times as Zara finishes the question. After responding in the affirmative twice (each accompanied by a head nod), Shelley uses the contrastive marker "but" (Schiffrin, 1987) to admit that she does not know when the meeting between the contractor and the authority is taking place, although she tries to minimize the significance of her not knowing with the restrictor "just." Nonverbally, though, Shelley indicates that perhaps she is aware that this is a problem as she diverts her gaze from Zara to her notebook as she utters the first "yep," and it remains there until she has said "but I just don't know," when she looks up at Zara again. Her answer leads Zara—even before she (Shelley) has finished—to ask again about the attitude of the contractor, although the question is formed as a concluding statement, with no rising intonation and the "so" used again to sum up:

> and so Martin etc. are very aware that they're quite an <u>organized</u> group that could well go off and do <u>stuff</u>

Again, the residents are framed as "an <u>organized</u> group" as opposed to an "unorganized" one, with "<u>organized</u>" here having a meaning of systematic, efficient and structured; one that is capable of "going off," outside the control of the authority, and "doing" possibly dangerous "<u>stuff</u>". The description "<u>organized</u> group" appears to have connotations in this context of "organized crime" or posing extreme risk—again, reinforcing the persuasive strategy of fear and a common "enemy."

Shelley states that the contractor is "<u>very</u> aware" of the capability of the group. Her *echoing* (Zhang, 1998) or *repetition* (Tannen, 1987a,b) of the group manager's "very aware" signals her desire to seek common ground and show listenership (Tannen, 1987a,b; Zhang, 1998). However, Shelley's gaze has drifted to her notebook as Zara asks the question (Figure 7.1, image 3), where she appears to be writing notes, and it remains there as she answers until the final word, "yeah," when she looks up again to indicate she has finished speaking.

Zara immediately asks a more detailed question about what planning the contractor has done to "handle" the problem of the residents. As she finishes the first question, Shelley prepares to answer, but again Zara continues, seemingly wanting to illustrate what she means, referring first to how "we" (the authority) addressed the issue, summing it up with "so w– we obviously had <u>our</u> discussion." Here, the "obviously" could refer to it being a self–evident way to address an issue that should be followed by all organizations or that "obviously" everyone in this room is aware that they we had a discussion.

Next, Zara asks what the contractor has done in its turn. She uses gestures to differentiate the authority from the contractor. As she says, "we obviously had our discussion," she thrusts her hands out in front of her, slightly to the right, palms facing inward and about shoulder–width apart, holding what probably represents the authority (Figure 7.1, image 4). This is what McNeill (1992) refers to as a *conduit metaphor*, whereby meaning is a substance that can be packed into a container and presented to others. As she asks, "had they had a similar discussion," her hands move to the left, now showing a smaller container that probably represents the contractor (McNeil, 1992). In that way, she reaffirms that the authority has greater power and status than the contractor, who is, to some extent, at the beck and call of the authority.

From the point when she was ready to answer, Shelley has kept her gaze fixed on her notebook without seemingly writing anything, and it remains there as she starts to answer. Her first word "uhm," unlike Zara's "uhm" at the start of her previous utterance, which was probably about preparing her talk, this "uhm" is likely to indicate that Shelley knows that her response is one the manager does not want to hear and therefore marking a delay (Schegloff, 2010). At this point, Zara wants to hear that the contractor has a plan to deal with the residents' group but Shelley cannot confirm this. However, she does inform the meeting that a conversation has taken place between the authority and the contractor. She says, "Jim East" has spoken to them and adds emphasis to this fact with a gesture of the past (Kendon, 2004): as she looks at the group manager and says, "Jim East", she appears to grasp something with both hands (probably the conversation), and throws it over her right shoulder on the word "talked." Her gaze remains fixed on Zara until the end of the utterance, and as she says, "talked," Zara looks down, responding with a brief "right" (Figure 7.1, image 5). Shelley's voice trails off and she too looks down.

The meeting is about to lapse into silence with Zara looking down, and no one else being an obvious next speaker. At that moment, the communication manager, James, steps in, but his first utterance ends in a cough, showing disfluency, "I think what ((cough))." It displays the signs of someone starting to talk without a clear idea of what they are going to say. Indeed, the cough is a common *masking behavior* and is often used to cover gaps in discourse such as the one here (Zhang, 1998).

However, possibly because no definitive answer has been received about what the contractor is planning, James now tries to clarify what behavior would not be accepted. As he speaks, Shelley looks at him and nods slowly twice and mutters "mmm" as he finishes (Figure 7.1, image 6). She then looks down, nods rapidly five times, and murmurs something that cannot be clearly heard on the tape. There appears to be uncertainty in the meeting, perhaps because no–one can say what the dissident resident group will do, or perhaps there is ambiguity about how to deal with them. Should they be given an opportunity to voice their demands (even though they are unlikely to be met as the decision has been made) or should there be a concerted effort to convince them of the appropriateness of the organization's decision?

Zara then responds, interrupting James with a slightly raised voice, to reiterate what she wishes to know is being done to address the issue. She uses "SO" here to mark a topic transition (from what they do not wish to happen to what they do wish to happen) combined with a summation of what needs to be achieved (Schiffrin, 1987), again reasserting her role as senior manager in the meeting (Holmes & Stubbe, 2015). She makes clear that she wants to know—that day—specific written details of actions, to know "what the <u>deal</u> is," "what we <u>think</u> we're going to <u>do</u> on the ((local area)) about that," and "whether we are going to <u>meet</u>." Her gestures support her demands, showing that she expects to have some meaningful information about real actions. When she states, "a brief <u>email</u>" telling everyone what "the <u>deal</u>" is her hands appear to be holding something, perhaps "the <u>deal</u>" (Figure 7.1, image 7). Both Shelley and James nod in agreement, and James utters a "yeah."

While again this utterance is worded as a request, "can we," it has characteristics of a directive (Bax, 1986; Ervin-Tripp, 1976; Vine, 2004). Although it sounds like a request, because the speaker is of higher status, the hearer has no right of refusal (Vine, 2004). Hence, what appears to be a "request" is, in fact, an order. It is, however, what is known as a "later" directive (Vine, 2004), and consequently, it is not easy for Zara to monitor if it has been complied with, which may explain the subsequent requirement for email confirmation. She wants the contractor to be followed up that morning and details of the proposed actions noted. To check this has occurred, an email is to be sent out.

When Zara stops talking, there is a lapse of more than two seconds before Shelley responds. This is likely because of Zara having used the speaker–continuer "and" (Schiffrin, 1987) combined with an audible in–breath that indicates that she has more to say. Shelley is again looking down, making notes in her notebook, and possibly has not noticed that Zara is still looking at her. When Shelley does finally respond, it is to agree to sort it out.

Zara, however, has not finished, and once she has Shelley's agreement, she continues, talking over James, who is asking whether a video produced by the residents' group is online. Her voice is again slightly raised as she speaks, possibly to interrupt James. It appears she wants to drive home the importance of ensuring the residents' group is not able to build support within the community.

Again, the words she stresses highlight that she wants clarity and certainty about what is going to be done, in writing if necessary. Her stressing and lengthening of the word "depe:ndent" along with the pauses during the remaining part of the utterance illustrate what she believes is crucial in managing the issue (and minimizing risk for their organization). As mentioned, speakers use pauses for emphasis and to make certain that the listeners understand, pausing before the parts of speech that carry the most important information (Strangert, 2003). Here, Zara pauses in three key places:

> successful roll out is depe:ndent (i) (0.6) on ensuring that there's no huge groundswell of: anti: (ii) (0.4) recycling sentiment (iii) (0.7) so they're going °in to handle it°

Lengthening a word is also a means of stressing the importance of that word. Here the fact that "anti" is stressed is noteworthy. Plus, Zara's statement shows she believes that any build–up of opinion will be a "groundswell of anti–recycling sentiment," which is not entirely accurate. The residents are against the new contract in part because they believe the current recycling process is more effective. Reframing of the issue in order to legitimize the decision of the authority is therefore evident.

Zara then concludes that the contractor is "going in to handle it." There is an element of compulsion in this last statement. The use of "so" is the preface to a conclusion (Schiffrin, 1987)—the conclusion being the contractor will be going in to handle the issue.

Zara has very specific views about the importance of enactment with the publics, and as the most senior person in the meeting guides the discussion around this enactment, setting the tone for the relationship with the resident group and determining the power they hold in that relationship. As Heath, Motion, and Leitch (2010, p. 198) pointed out, "What individuals think about societal relationships fosters empowerment/marginalization as power resources."

However, while she is the most senior person and therefore has the power to influence the discussions taking place and the decisions being made, decisions of this nature are not made solely by individuals but are made collectively. As discussed in Chapter 5, meetings are sites of relational enactment and meaning–making, and here meanings are created around the validity and impact of the authority's decision to change contractors—regardless of the original reasons for that decision—as well as the way dissenting publics are engaged. As White et al. (2009) pointed out, *collectively* the members obscure their (personal) accountability by "diffusion and displacement of responsibility" (p. 42), which can, as we have seen, include labeling the residents' group as "rebels" for disagreeing with the local authority's decision and the lack of consultation having taken place.

In this meeting, there appears to be concern about the potential risks of *not engaging* and a focus on the message that will be given to the publics about the decision, but there is no significant evidence of a willingness to listen to the publics' point of view or have a "mutually beneficial" relationship with the publics.

Managing the Issue: Having a Plan for the Meeting

The following day, the group manager, Zara, meets with the head of the media relations team, Kate, and two members of the communications and marketing team, James and Shelley, to follow up on whether a meeting with the residents' group has been organized. Zara also wants to be sure that the practitioners and the contractor understand what should be achieved from the meeting with the residents' group:

> If we are going to have a meeting there needs to be a clear purpose and intent for it that uhm it needs to be something like, not just all get together and have a chin wag, but potentially it's a chance for CWL to meet the people and to talk through their solution.

Zara suggests that this may involve the contractor being prepared to make some concessions. She stresses that in order to manage the issue it is crucial to have a well–prepared brief covering all aspects of the messaging. In response, the communications and marketing team members admit that there is not "one piece of paper" that outlined the whole plan although they are aware that the proposed feature on recycling needs to marry up with the messaging around the change of contractor. Zara is still keen for them to prepare a brief:

> I think in terms of us going forward it is more important to follow that issues management process. Even if it's just a one–page saying three things we're doing within those, all this, and if that ends up being a brief of some kind, coz you need a brief because first and foremost we're managing the issue at the moment.

Preparing for the Meeting with the Residents' Group

Having an Agenda

A day later, Shelley has secured an agreement from CWL to meet the residents' group. She gets together with Zara, head of media relations

Kate, and another senior communication officer (who does not speak and is out of the camera's view) to discuss how to manage the meeting and the messaging around it.

Shelley's first worry is that the group will use the request for a meeting to claim that its campaign has been successful in forcing the authority and the contractor to accommodate its concerns. In an attempt to limit this possibility, it is decided the residents' group should be approached only *after* the local newspaper's weekly deadline. It is not thought the regional newspaper or other media organizations would be interested in covering the meeting, and arranging to meet after the newspaper deadline (possibly on Friday), will give the authority time to prepare a message outlining how it sees the outcome of that meeting.

Zara again stresses the importance of attending the meeting with a clear purpose and well-prepared messages. The second extract is taken from this part of the meeting. At this point, the discussion has turned to preparations for the encounter with the residents' group.

Just before this extract begins, Shelley informed Zara that later in the day she was seeing the local authority spokesperson who would be leading the meeting with the contractor. She asks Zara if there is anything she would like Shelley to say to him. In this way, Shelley acknowledges her place as the subordinate and Zara's legitimate position of expertise in this matter (Vine, 2004). It also explains much of the tone and content of the conversation that follows.

At the start of the excerpt, Zara appears to be responding to Shelley's question with some advice indicated by the words, "what I would do." Traditionally, however, advice does not have to be taken, but it is evident that Zara requires hers to be followed. The latter becomes clear after the repair midway through the utterance "c–"; the substance of which is clearly a directive to "go in with your agenda?." The utterance ends with a rising intonation, but it is not a question—more likely it is aimed at eliciting an acknowledgment or is an indication that she wishes to continue speaking.

Zara's next words flesh out what she means by "go in with your agenda." She uses a form of expression, a "need statement," that is considered as reasonably forceful and often has the meaning of "must" (Vine, 2004): "we need to understand that." In other words, Shelley "needs" to ensure that the authority's officer she is meeting "understands" that the contractor can (and it is implied "must") go in with an agenda. Zara proceeds to give a high level of detail about what that agenda might contain. This sort of detail shows the manager is concerned that without precise instructions the other person (Shelley) may not be clear about what is expected (Vine, 2004); it is an overt expression of Zara's authority and expertise. Shelley writes in her notebook (Figure 7.2, image 1). Zara's instructions go as far as rehearsing the

Z: what I would do though is have a is have a c-
   go in with your agenda?
   we need to understand that CWL can actually
   go in with anything already that says
   .hhh look this is what we think t-
   what we think we can do on the employment front
   and here's a couple of things that we can tick off that
   list that y- that's already been
   .hhh ↑provided we think we can do:
   (0.8) green waste or
K: yeah (.) yeah

Z: you know what I mean?
   so make sure that you go in
   and see if y- uhm .hhh with something
S: mmm
Z: (1.1) and agree up front what that looks like
   so that's what Jason ((authority's spokesperson)) is
   going to (get a one) page on¿
S: mmm

Z: I mean I know it's up to CWL so y- we're
   going to have to work with them as well
K: (1.4) act-=
Z: =SO can Matthew Williams ((authority's head of
   environmental and utility management)) sort of broker
   that type of discussion¿

K: yeah coz from what Jason was saying CWL's line
   will be .hhh uhm ((click)) we've met with (.) with
   ((the existing provider))
   already with Josh Ambler ((its director)),

Figure 7.2 Having an agenda ready.

K: we've <u>noticed</u> that some of the <u>things</u> that he's been
doing, are <u>very</u> <u>similar</u> to some of the <u>things</u> that
we're planning to do, so (.) <u>actually</u> we're not that far
apart <u>already</u>:, here are a cou- here are th- three or
four more things that we thin[k we]
Z: [yeah]
K: can meet <u>meet</u> you guy[s on]
Z: [maybe] just have a <u>page</u> of
<u>key</u> messages g-going into the Frida:y¿

S: (1.7) yep
Z: I really <u>like</u> that <u>approach</u> just <u>saying</u> (0.7) we're not
that far apart=
K: =yeah=
Z: =<u>here's</u> the <u>here's</u> the <u>things</u> that we would=

S: =[.hhh] hhh
K: =[that was] what <u>he</u> sugges[ted]
S: [ye:ah] I <u>guess</u> so we're
not that far apart so then the <u>response</u> is so <u>why</u> bother
<u>changing</u> it
Z: (1.1) sorry?

K: coz it's <u>cheaper</u>
S: (1.1) °mmm°
Z: (2.9) °alright?°
S: (0.9) °yeah alright°
Z: yeah and th- the additional the <u>additional</u> few <u>things</u>
are so <u>minor</u> that we can do that <u>too</u>

Figure 7.2 (Continued)

sort of wording that could be used by the contractor when addressing the residents' group.

What is evident here is that the "enactment " planned with the residents' group will not be one where dialogue is likely to take place. Providing a list and entering a discussion with a specific outcome in mind or an "agenda" counteracts the expectations of dialogic communication, which, as we have seen earlier, comprises listening, positive regard, a willingness to change (de Bussy, 2010), mutuality, propinquity, empathy, risk, and commitment (Kent & Taylor, 2002).

Making Compromises

Zara continues to speak and, after the verb "says," takes an audible in–breath and introduces the possible wording with the perception verb (Schiffrin, 1987) "look," which is often used as a discourse management device (Vine, 2004). Here it is both marking the start of Zara speaking as if she were the contractor and also orientating the subsequent hearer (it's not clear if Zara has Shelley or the residents' group in mind) to the possible compromises.

Her suggestions begin with CWL making an offer of jobs to residents. This is at the forefront of Zara's mind, as earlier in the meeting it had been mentioned that the contractor was considering making such an offer. She next refers to a list, "that list," that the authority has received from a well–placed resident that highlights requirements that would make the contractor more acceptable to the people. But, when she tries to give specific examples that could be negotiated, "we think we can do:," she becomes less confident. After nearly a second's pause, she says, "green waste or," looks towards Kate as if for inspiration and laughs as she trails off. Kate responds with a quick "yeah (.) yeah" in backchannel agreement.

Zara then shifts her gaze from Kate to Shelley for confirmation that she has been understood, despite the lack of examples, and while Zara's "you know what I mean" carries a rising intonation, she does not wait for immediate acknowledgment. Instead, she begins to conclude "so make sure that you go in," and then she changes tack from, "and see if y–," which might refer to "see if you can get an agreement" to "with something." Perhaps Zara remembers that an agreement cannot happen unless they have something to offer the residents' group. She pauses, takes a breath and finishes "with something." Interestingly, Zara has used the pronoun "you," which puts the onus squarely on Shelley's shoulders to ensure this happens, creating again a forceful directive. Without looking up from writing in her notebook, Shelley responds with "mmm" (Figure 7.2, image 2). It is not clear whether she agrees or disagrees with Zara's instructions and a silence that lasts just over a second ensues.

Zara then continues with another directive, building on the previous one, this time the second person pronoun is implied, but not stated. She tells Shelley that the "something" (referring to the agenda) they go in with (to the meeting) must be agreed "up front," presumably this means *before* meeting with the residents. She also appears to be saying (although some of this utterance cannot be clearly heard) that the authority representative Shelley will be meeting later that morning should have a one-page memo outlining "that" (meaning "the something").

Zara's last utterance is worded as a straight statement, although it has a slightly rising intonation, which prompts Shelley to look up at Zara, responding with another "mmm" (Figures 7.2, image 2).

Zara immediately continues, "I mean," which prefaces an expansion and slight modification of her previous statements (Schiffrin, 1987), acknowledging that the agenda must be accepted by the contractor. She finishes, "so y– we're going to have to work <u>with</u> them as well." This summing up of the situation shows Zara repairing her initial y–, which was probably "you," to the more inclusive "we," which allows her to appear more participative in her leadership style. By "work <u>with</u> them as well" she is likely to mean an agenda must be prepared with "them as well." "Them" in this case is likely to mean "the contractor," "as well" as the authority's officers, suggesting some level of consultation will take place to prepare the message for the residents' group.

Shelley responds in the affirmative (a nod), after which there is another pause lasting nearly a second. At this point, Kate attempts to say something, but Zara, with her head slightly turned towards Kate while keeping her gaze on Shelley, continues her turn. This time, she uses an interrogative form, "SO can Matthew Williams sort of <u>broker</u> that type of discussion¿." Her gesture appears to hold the discussion in her hand, however, the final rising intonation is not very marked (Figure 7.2, image 3). She turns to Kate who responds "yeah," and then quickly takes over the turn. The "yeah" is not a response to Zara's question, but applies to what the contractor has planned, referring to Zara's talk about having to "work with them," and even earlier to what the "agenda" might be. In this way, she brings the discussion back to what she would probably have said had she not been interrupted.

Presenting the Contractor's View

Kate introduces her point "from what <u>Jason</u> was saying," but when she gets to the meat of the message, what the contractor's "line" will be, she pauses. The pause allows her to prepare her talk, which also requires memory on her part, recalling what she has been told, and she fills it with an audible in–breath, an "uhm," and a click or tut (Clark & Foxtree, 2002). This introduction prefaces four subsequent utterances representing how CWL will approach the residents' group.

In outlining the contractor's strategy, Kate's speech has a rhythmic character; each utterance ending on a slightly higher pitch as would be used when reciting a list (Figure 7.2, images 4 and 5). The rhythm is aided by repetition throughout, specifically of the words "we've", "we're" and "that," and the phrase "some of the things that," which itself is echoed or nearly repeated in the words "more things that."

> we've <u>met</u> with (.) with ((the existing provider))
> <u>already</u> with Josh Ambler ((its director)),
> we've <u>noticed</u> that some of the <u>things</u> that he's been doing,
> are <u>very similar</u> to some of the <u>things</u> that we're planning to do,
> so (.) <u>actually</u> we're not that far apart <u>already:</u>,
> <u>here</u> are a cou– <u>here</u> are th– three or four more things that we
> think we can meet <u>meet</u> you guys on

Kate starts and finishes her turn with the verb "to meet." Her speech moves from the past "we've <u>met</u>" into the future "we can meet <u>meet</u> you guys on." However, the two instances of the verb have different meanings. In the first instance, it represents a physical meeting with the existing provider and in the second instance it is a figurative "meeting of minds" with the residents' group, showing willingness on Kate's (on behalf of the contractor) part to engage with the residents' group and meet (some of) their demands. Thus, while no overt disagreement is evident in the meeting, Kate and the group manager, Zara, appear to have somewhat differing views of how to engage with the residents' group.

This concept of the contractor moving from what has happened in the past (what is "old hat") to what can happen in the future (new possibilities) is also how Kate arranges the two utterances following "we've met":

> we've <u>noticed</u> that some of the <u>things</u> that he's been doing,
> are <u>very</u> <u>similar</u> to some of the <u>things</u> that we're planning to do,

Repetition of parts of an utterance helps a speaker produce fluent speech at the same time as allowing time to formulate the next words. In this way, a speaker can produce entire sentences with new ideas while needing to add the minimum of fresh information, as can be seen above (Tannen, 1987b). Repetition is also useful in drawing attention to words that are new (Tannen, 1990). In this case, the words and phrases "we're," "we've," "that," and "some of the things" are repeated and serve to highlight those that are not: "been doing" and "planning to do," "actually...not...far apart already," "three or four more."

Further, repetition helps listeners' comprehension. Hearers respond favorably to familiar patterns because they aid understanding, but also because they appeal aesthetically (Tannen, 1990). By appealing to the listeners in this way, speakers encourage rapport and make themselves more believable. Therefore, repetition is one of the most effective patterns in persuasive speaking, and we can see from Zara's response that she is persuaded. Thus, Kate employs effective persuasive and relational approaches to build *personal influence* in this meeting (see Chapter 2).

Zara has been sitting with folded arms through most of this encounter until Kate begins speaking. Kate's speech is directed towards Shelley and so as she says, "we've met with," Zara begins rifling through a stack of papers in front of her (Figure 7.2, image 5). She looks up only once at Kate, until almost the end of her speech. When Kate says, "here are… three or four things," Zara looks at her nodding and voicing her agreement simultaneously. She then turns to Shelley.

Though at this point, her utterance is functioning as a directive, she has softened it with "maybe" (a hedge) and "just" (a minimizer). She emphasizes the word "page," making it clear that the modifiers refer to her expectation that only a single page of key messages needs to be prepared. She then repeats some of Kate's words to show agreement with what has been said (Figure 7.2, image 6).

At this point, it becomes evident that Shelley is not sharing Zara's enthusiasm. As Zara declares, "we're not that far apart," Shelley scratches her nose, briefly tilting her head to the left and back again (Figure 7.2, image 6). She seems to take a breath and opens her mouth as if she is going to speak, but instead lets out a loud breath while Kate is still explaining that the idea she likes is not hers (Kate's), but the contractor's.

As Shelley starts speaking, her speech marginally overlaps Kate's. It appears that she is concerned that the message "we're not that far apart" is not strong enough to justify changing the provider. Addressing Kate, she asks, "why bother changing it." As she starts speaking, Zara glances up briefly (Figure 7.2, image 7) before flicking again through the papers on her desk. Only when Shelley pauses—her gaze on Zara—does Zara look up, asking "sorry?."

Shelley seems about to respond; her mouth shapes the words and she extends her left hand, palm up in the shape of a cup as if holding an idea (McNeill, 1992). But as she does this, Kate answers the question: "coz it's cheaper."

At this point, it is patently clear that while the authority's message is tied into the idea of sustainability and recycling, the real reason for the decision to switch providers is purely a financial one. The practitioners' role is simply to justify the decision by framing it to fit in with the current trend of being seen as sustainable and environmentally friendly—in other words, to reframe the decision so it can be legitimized and the legitimacy gap minimized (Stokes, 2013).

In response to Kate's blunt retort, Shelley then nods four times, muttering "mmm," and rests her hand flat on her chest for a moment before grasping the length of her scarf (Figure 7.2, image 8). Her gaze remains fixed on Kate for more than a second and she nods imperceptibly. Then Zara, who was still rifling through pages of a document, looks up at Shelley and asks if she is "alright." In response, Shelley shifts her gaze to Zara and mutters something inaudible, by which time Zara is looking down at her papers again.

After this brief interlude, Zara takes the helm again in the discussion although Kate laughs, putting her momentarily off her stride. It may have been that Kate's laugh in response to her own answer "coz it's cheaper" signaled her slight discomfort with the situation. Regardless, Zara presses on and finishes the final point made by Kate that the "additional few things are so minor we can do that too."

In her previous utterances, Zara stated that she "really" likes the approach outlined by Kate as well as the messages "we're not that far apart," "here's the things that we would," and "the additional few things are so minor we can do that too." It is evident that she has not listened to, or accepted, Shelley's misgivings about the situation, and it is Kate's proposed messages that she believes should be on the page of key messages going forward.

Conclusion

It is clear from the fieldwork that theorizing about organization–public relationships is essentially normative, and built on premises that may not reflect practice. This alone supports assertions by, for example, Heath (2013), that we need to do much more work in order to understand how these relationships function if we believe that they can be a viable part of public relations practice.

By returning to the micro level, we have interrogated the talk around an organization's enactment with its key publics. What has ensued here is an obvious need to control the message and to minimize potential risk through issues management. "Relationships" are therefore functional and transactional in nature, and are used for purposes of legitimizing the organization's decisions and actions. These relationships appear to be characterized by persuasion and not dialogue, because the antecedents for dialogue appear to be missing.

Of particular interest is that while decisions are made collectively and actions by the organization are justified and legitimized collectively in meetings, the ideological perspective of a senior person sets the tone for the strategies that follow. It is, therefore, likely that in a dissimilar setting, where a leader has a different view of the risks that dissident groups pose, a different result may follow—perhaps even a more dialogic approach. Such a possibility is, however, merely speculative; in the cases we observed, dialogue was overshadowed by persuasion. Thus, it stands to reason that persuasion is part and parcel of not only "relationships" organizations have with their publics, but of public relations work in general.

References

Bax, I. P. (1986). How to assign work in an office: A comparison of spoken and written directives in American English. *Journal of Pragmatics*, *10*(6), 673–692. doi:10.1016/0378-2166(86)90146-3.

Bourne, C. D. (2016). Extending PR's critical conversations with advertising and marketing. In J. L'Etang, D. McKie, & N. Snow (Eds.), *The Routledge handbook of critical public relations* (pp. 119–129). London: Taylor & Francis.

Bowen, S. A. (2010). The nature of good in public relations: What should be its normative ethic? In R. L. Heath (Ed.), *The Sage handbook of public relations* (2nd ed., pp. 569–584). Thousand Oaks, CA: Sage Publications.

Bowen, S. A. (2013). Excellence theory. In R. L. Heath (Ed.), *Encyclopedia of public relations* (2nd ed., pp. 323–326). Thousand Oaks, CA: Sage Publications.

Brønn, P. S. (2010). Reputation, communication and the corporate brand. In R. L. Heath (Ed.), *The Sage handbook of public relations* (2nd ed., pp. 307–320). Thousand Oaks, CA: Sage Publications.

Broom, G. M., Casey, S., & Ritchey, J. (1997). Toward a concept and theory of organization–public relationships. *Journal of Public Relations Research*, *9*(2), 83–98. doi:10.1207/s1532754xjprr0902_01.

Clark, H., & Foxtree, J. (2002). Using uh and um in spontaneous speaking. *Cognition*, *84*(1), 73–111. doi:10.1016/s0010-0277(02)00017-3.

Coombs, W. T., & Holladay, S. J. (2015). Public relations' "relationship identity" in research: Enlightenment or illusion. *Public Relations Review*, *41*(5), 689–695. doi:10.1016/j.pubrev.2013.12.008.

de Bussy, N. M. (2010). Dialogue as a basis for stakeholder enactment: Defining and measuring the core competencies. In R. L. Heath (Ed.), *The Sage handbook of public relations* (2nd ed., pp. 127–144). Thousand Oaks, CA: Sage Publications.

Ekman, P., & Friesen, W. V. (1972). Hand movements. *Journal of Communication*, *22*(4), 353–374. doi:10.1111/j.1460-2466.1972.tb00163.x.

Ervin-Tripp, S. (1976). Is Sybil there? The structure of some American English directives. *Language in Society*, *5*(01), 25. doi:10.1017/s0047404500006849.

Fairclough, N. (1989). *Language and power* (2nd ed.). New York: Longman.

Gregory, A., & Willis, P. (2013). *Strategic public relations leadership*. London: Routledge.

Grunig, J. E. (2015). Foreword. In E.-J. Ki, J.-N. Kim, & J. A. Ledingham (Eds.), *Public relations as relationship management: A relational approach to the study and practice of public relations* (2nd ed., pp. xxiii–xxvii). London: Routledge.

Grunig, J. E., & Hung-Baesecke, C.-J. F. (2015). The effect of relationships on reputation and reputation on relationships. A cognitive, behavioral study. In E.-J. Ki, J.-N. Kim, & J. A. Ledingham (Eds.), *Public relations as relationship management: A relational approach to the study and practice of public relations* (2nd ed., pp. 63–113). London: Routledge.

Heath, R. L. (2013). The journey to understand and champion OPR takes many roads, some not yet well traveled. *Public Relations Review*, *39*(5), 426–431. doi:10.1016/j.pubrev.2013.05.002.

Heath, R. L., Motion, J., & Leitch, S. (2010). Power and public relations: Paradoxes and programmatic thoughts. In R. L. Heath (Ed.), *The Sage handbook of public relations* (2nd ed., pp. 191–204). Thousand Oaks, CA: Sage Publications.

Holmes, J., & Stubbe, M. (2015). *Power and politeness in the workplace: A Sociolinguistic analysis of talk at work*. Abingdon: Routledge.

Kahlbaugh, P. E., & Haviland, J. M. (1994). Nonverbal communication between parents and adolescents: A study of approach and avoidance behaviors. *Journal of Nonverbal Behavior*, *18*(1), 91–113. doi:10.1007/bf02169080.

Kendon, A. (2004). *Gesture: Visible action as utterance* (3rd ed.). Cambridge: Cambridge University Press.

Kent, M. L., & Taylor, M. (2002). Toward a dialogic theory of public relations. *Public Relations Review*, *28*(1), 21–37. doi:10.1016/s0363-8111(02)00108-x.

Ki, E.-J., & Shin, J.-H. (2015). The status of organization–public relationship research through an analysis of published articles between 1985–2013. An appeal for further research. In E.-J. Ki, J.-N. Kim, & J. A. Ledingham (Eds.), *Public relations as relationship management: A relational approach to the study and practice of public relations* (2nd ed., pp. 28–45). London: Routledge.

Ledingham, J. A. (2013). Relationship managing theory. In R. L. Heath (Ed.), *Encyclopedia of public relations* (2nd ed., pp. 781–783). Thousand Oaks, CA: Sage Publications.

Ledingham, J. A. (2015). Managing relationship management. In E.-J. Ki, J.-N. Kim, & J. A. Ledingham (Eds.), *Public relations as relationship management: A relational approach to the study and practice of public relations* (2nd ed., pp. 46–60). London: Routledge.

Ledingham, J. A., & Bruning, S. D. (1998). Relationship management in public relations: Dimensions of an organization–public relationship. *Public Relations Review*, *24*(1), 55–65. doi:10.1016/s0363-8111(98)80020-9.

Leitchy, G. (2013). Social exchange theory. In R. L. Heath (Ed.), *Encyclopedia of public relations* (2nd ed., pp. 842–844). Thousand Oaks, CA: Sage Publications.

Macnamara, J. (2012). The global shadow of functionalism and excellence theory: An analysis of Australasian PR. *Public Relations Inquiry*, *1*(3), 367–402. doi:10.1177/2046147x12448581.

McNeill, D. (1992). *Hand and mind: What gestures reveal about thought*. Chicago, IL: University of Chicago Press.

Motion, J., & Leitch, S. (2016). Critical discourse analysis: A search for meaning and power. In J. L'Etang, D. McKie, & N. Snow (Eds.), *The Routledge handbook of critical public relations* (pp. 142–150). London: Routledge.

Palenchar, M. J. (2010). Risk communication. In R. L. Heath (Ed.), *The Sage handbook of public relations* (2nd ed., pp. 447–460). Thousand Oaks, CA: Sage Publications.

Pieczka, M. (2011). Public relations as dialogic expertise? *Journal of Communication Management*, *15*(2), 108–124. doi:10.1108/13632541111126346.

Plowman, K. D. (2013). Systems theory. In R. L. Heath (Ed.), *Encyclopedia of public relations* (2nd ed., pp. 905–908). Thousand Oaks, CA: Sage Publications.

Sacks, H., Schegloff, E. A., & Jefferson, G. (1974). A simplest systematics for the organization of turn–taking for conversation. *Language, 50*(4), 696. doi:10.2307/412243.

Sallot, L. M. (2013). Interpersonal communication theory. In R. L. Heath (Ed.), *Encyclopedia of public relations* (2nd ed., pp. 476–479). Thousand Oaks, CA: Sage Publications.

Saville-Troike, M. (1989). *The ethnography of communication: An introduction* (2nd ed.). New York: Blackwell Publishers.

Schegloff, E. A. (2010). Some other "Uh(m)"s. *Discourse Processes, 47*(2), 130–174. doi:10.1080/01638530903223380.

Schiffrin, D. (1987). *Discourse markers.* Cambridge: Cambridge University Press.

Solomon, D., & Theiss, J. (2013). *Interpersonal communication: Putting theory into practice.* New York: Taylor & Francis.

Stoker, K. (2014). Paradox in public relations: Why managing relating makes more sense than managing relationships. *Journal of Public Relations Research.* doi:10.1080/1062726X.2014.908723.

Stokes, A. Q. (2013). Legitimacy and the legitimacy gap. In R. L. Heath (Ed.), *Encyclopedia of public relations* (2nd ed., pp. 516–519). Thousand Oaks, CA: Sage Publications.

Strangert, E. (2003). Emphasis by pausing. In M. J. Solé, D. Recasens & J. Romero (Eds.), *Proceedings of the 15th international congress of phonetic sciences, Barcelona, Spain* (pp. 2477–2480). Rundle Mall: Causal Publications.

Tannen, D. (1987a). Repetition in conversation as spontaneous formulaicity. *Text – Interdisciplinary Journal for the Study of Discourse, 7*(3), 215–243. doi:10.1515/text.1.1987.7.3.215.

Tannen, D. (1987b). Repetition in conversation: Toward a poetics of talk. *Language, 63*(3), 574. doi:10.2307/415006.

Tannen, D. (1990). Ordinary conversation and literary discourse: Coherence and the poetics of repetition. *Annals of the New York Academy of Sciences, 583*(1), 15–30. doi:10.1111/j.1749-6632.1990.tb12183.x.

Theunissen, P. (2014). Co–creating corporate identity through dialogue: A pilot study. *Public Relations Review, 40*(3), 612–614. doi:10.1016/j.pubrev.2014.02.026.

Theunissen, P., & Wan Noordin, W. N. (2012). Revisiting the concept "dialogue" in public relations. *Public Relations Review, 38*(1), 5–13. doi:10.1016/j.pubrev.2011.09.006.

Vine, B. (2004). *Getting things done at work: The discourse of power in workplace interaction.* Amsterdam: Benjamins (John) North America Inc.

Waymer, D. (2013). Democracy and government public relations: Expanding the scope of "Relationship" in public relations research. *Public Relations Review, 39*(4), 320–331. doi:10.1016/j.pubrev.2013.07.015.

White, J., Bandura, A., & Bero, L. A. (2009). Moral disengagement in the corporate world. *Accountability in Research, 16*(1), 41–74. doi:10.1080/08989620802689847.

Willis, P. (2015). Preach wine and serve vinegar: Public relations, relationships and doublethink. *Public Relations Review, 41*(5), 681–688. doi:10.1016/j.pubrev.2014.02.004.

Yang, S.-U., & Cha, H. (2015). A framework linking organization–public relationships and organizational reputation in public relations management. In E.-J. Ki, J.-N. Kim, & J. A. Ledingham (Eds.), *Public relations as relationship management: A relational approach to the study and practice of public relations* (2nd ed., pp. 114–129). London: Routledge.

Yann, A. (2015, November 30). What is public relations? PR definition: PRSA official statement. Retrieved December 17 2016, from www.prsa.org/AboutPRSA/PublicRelationsDefined/index.html#.WFStquZ942x.

Zaharna, R. S. (2015). Beyond the individualism–collectivism divide to relationalism: Explicating cultural assumptions in the concept of "Relationships." *Communication Theory, 26*(2), 190–211. doi:10.1111/comt.12058.

Zhang, X. (1998). Echoing in real–life English conversation. *The Poetics and Linguistics Association.* Retrieved from www.pala.ac.uk/uploads/2/5/1/0/25105678/paper09.pdf.

8 Conclusions, Observations and Key Principles in Building Relationships

A leader is best when people barely know he exists, when his work is done, his aim fulfilled, they will say: we did it ourselves.
—Laozi (circa 6th century BC), Chinese philosopher

Four Key Relationships

In this research book, we explored four key relationships public relations practitioners (PRPs) develop during the course of their work: their relationships with their colleagues or peers, with their clients, with journalists, and the relationships they develop on behalf of the organization with its publics. In doing so, we explored and analyzed the every-day, ordinary interactions between PRPs, extracting meaning from these interactions, and thereby discovering the practice of public relations in context. We highlighted the practice as is, rather than how it is purported to be, and presented these relationships in an ever-increasing level of public enactment.

Identifying communication skills and personal influence as key, we elaborate in this chapter on aspects we believe should form part of the personal influence model, and discuss sites of relational enactment. In addition, we explore findings relating to mutually beneficial relationships, two-way symmetry, and organization-public relationships, and conclude that each relationship is unique. We also suggest that more (innovative) research is needed to further investigate the type of relationships and relationship-building in public relations.

Public Relations as Communication

Communication is, and has always been, regarded as integral to public relations work. Indeed, public relations practice is often referred to as "communication management," and public relations texts include copious references to "communication." L'Etang (2008), for example, referred to public relations as involving communication and argument to enable change to take place. She added that this process required more than merely familiarizing oneself with communication techniques, but comprised "*interpersonal communication, intra-group communication* (within groups), *intergroup communication* (between groups) and *mass communication*" (L'Etang, 2008, p. 18, original emphasis). Even so, theoretical knowledge of interpersonal communication remains undervalued in public relations, and as we discussed in Chapter 1, less than 1% of textbook pages address theories of interpersonal communication (Macnamara, 2012).

Few textbooks, if any, explain how these forms of communication apply to public relations practice or where they might be used. The reasons for this lack of acknowledgment require more research, but one potential explanation might be public relations' roots, which are closely related to publicity. These roots remain. As Wakefield (2013) put it,

> When searching for the roots of public relations in the U.S., it is easy to wander across the notion that public relations was *what most people still think it is*: publicity or persuasion.
>
> (p. 133, emphasis added)

The most visible aspects of public relations are its techniques (Mersham, Theunissen, & Peart, 2009), and publicity as an outcome of these techniques can be regarded as a very visible aspect. This, combined with its origins, has resulted in the conflation of public relations and publicity in the mind of the layperson. Publicity has traditionally been achieved through mass communication and, thus, textbooks usually address theories of mass media communication rather than interpersonal communication.

Of course, the misperception that communication involves little more than speaking with or writing to people lingers. Because we all learn to speak and write early on, many believe that we are inevitably capable communicators, and no further training is required. If the latter were true, there would be no conflict and no relationship break-up. Harmony would reign. As Doorley, Garcia, and Hauser (2015, p. 115) pointed out, "true communication skill requires more than just speaking, reading, and writing. It involves those behaviors to influence the attitudes and behaviors of others."

Our research highlights that effective public relations practitioners are exceptional interpersonal communicators. Their daily work comprises various modes of communication, from spoken to written to nonverbal communication, which supports the assertion that effective professional communicators are fluent in all modes of communication (Theunissen, 2015). This involves "a theory base that informs us about how communication operates in both personal and organizational settings and, more usefully, what public relations practitioners can learn from these theories" (Smith, 2013, p. 184). Indeed, effective communicators should continue updating their skills as these skills can become disused (Doorley et al., 2015).

This view contrasts with that of Tench, Zerfaß, Verhoeven, Verčič, Moreno, and Okay (2013) who, upon mapping the competencies of communication practitioners in Europe using online surveys and interviews, concluded that the only area where "supply meets the demand" was in the realm "traditional communication skills," namely written and oral communication and message production. Unlike the requirement for management skills (decision-making, organizing, and leading), where Tench et al.'s research identified a significant gap in practitioners' self-identified need for and the availability of training, practitioners felt they did not need to improve their communication skills.

While this suggests a lack of consensus among PRPs over the necessity of continuing to hone traditional communication skills, it acknowledges that being fluent in *all modes of communication is an expert skill* that can be learned and improved. Hence, it follows that it should be part of a new entrant's training. Indeed, our research found that PRPs adapted well to various communication situations, adjusted their speech and behavior to match the expectations of the situation, sought clarification, and displayed empathy even in difficult interactions.

Symmetry and Mutually Beneficial Relationships

Symmetrical vs. Asymmetrical Communication

Since their introduction in 1984, Grunig and Hunt's four models of public relations (press agentry, public information, two-way asymmetrical communication and two-way symmetrical communication) have dominated scholarship. It has become, as Halff and Gregory (2014, p. 399) stated, the "dominant historiography of public relations globally."

The models were presented in a linear fashion (Holtzhausen, Peterson, & Tindall, 2003), inferring a trajectory of development in practice from press agentry to two-way asymmetrical communication (persuasion) and on to two-way symmetrical communication (dialogue), or as Wakefield (2013) stated, a type of "evolutionary ascension" (p. 131). The implication was that dialogue was superior to persuasion (Theunissen & Wan Noordin, 2012), and indeed, two-way symmetrical communication was regarded as the next, or fourth, step in evolution (Culbertson, 1989/2016). The latter model was subsequently included as part of the excellence theory of public relations, which suggested that in order to be excellent, public relations should be practiced as two-way symmetrical communication.

Indeed, J. E. Grunig, L. A. Grunig, Sriramesh, Huang, and Lyra (1995) proposed the two-way models to be epitome of professional public relations, stating that,

> Press agentry and public information form a continuum of *craft public relations,* which ranges from propaganda (press agentry) on one end to journalism (public information) on the other. The two-way models make up a continuum of *professional public relations*, which ranges from persuasion on one end (two-way asymmetrical) to conflict management (two-way symmetrical) on the other.
>
> (p. 164, original emphasis)

While the models, and especially the two-way symmetrical model, appealed to many scholars, they also attracted their share of criticism. Holtzhausen et al. (2003), for example, challenged the applicability of the models in a Southern African—and international—context. They rejected the inherent dichotomy of symmetrical/asymmetrical communication and argued that practitioners in South Africa did not practice public relations with symmetry in mind.

Interrogating the notion of two-way symmetry as being the "most ethical" model of public relations practice, Browning (2015) pointed out that it is not always the most ethical and that the same results can be achieved with different intents and processes. Or, to put this into a practical context: mutual understanding as an integral part of public relations can be achieved through dialogue (two-way symmetrical communication) *or* persuasion (two-way asymmetrical communication) *or* both.

Reacting to criticism of the model, a *mixed motive* approach was proposed, whereby PRPs who practice two-way symmetrical communication engage in all forms of communications, including debate, persuasion, listening, dialogue, and relationship building (L. A. Grunig, J. E. Grunig, & Dozier, 2002). As L. A. Grunig et al. explained, "Symmetry does not reject the idea of persuasion" (2002, p. 316), and indeed, our research showed that PRPs employed various persuasive strategies in the course of their day-to-day practice.

The distinguishing factor, L. A. Grunig et al. (2002) said, was that PRPs who practiced the normative framework of public relations attempted to balance the interests of their organization and the publics by doing research and using communication to manage conflict. Bowen (2013) stated that "symmetry means balance and implies a moving equilibrium between an organization and a public" (p. 903), where they are *normative* equal partners and in an interdependent or symbiotic relationship. Symmetry does not mean "harmony" or "accommodation," L. A. Grunig et al. added, lamenting the naïve interpretation of symmetry by both proponents and critics of the model. They added that at all times, an organization will strive to be autonomous from its publics, and therefore there will always be tensions between the organization and its publics. Thus, we could argue that there is a continuous dialectic between independence and interdependence in any relationship the PRP develops during their work, whether it is with each other, with the client, with a journalist, or with the public(s) on behalf of the organization. These tensions were present in all micro interactions analyzed during this research.

What is significant for this book on relationship-building in public relations is how the tension was enacted and how it was managed in the course of the PRP's every-day work. Of particular interest was the enactment of symmetry in organization-public relationships. According to L. A. Grunig et al. (2002), public relations requires accommodation, meaning that *"both* the organization and a public must be willing to accommodate the interests of the other" (p. 315, original emphasis). It is, as Bowen (2013) advised, a "give-and-take" where there is a long-term view of the relationship. Compromise and negotiation are par for the course in the relationship. Our research showed that PRPs employed various asymmetrical strategies designed to manage communications on behalf of a client, and in some cases purposefully used them to shut down discussion rather than facilitate it in order to benefit the client.

In Chapter 7, we explored how PRPs talked and strategized about managing a dissatisfied public, which, at one stage was labeled as "the rebels." We concluded that there was insufficient evidence of dialogue taking place, and instead found evidence of persuasion, message planning and production, and manifest focus on minimizing risk for the organization (a local authority). We also found some evidence of diminishing the ethical responsibility of the organization for the decision that had been made to change service provider.

In one of the critical incidents highlighted in Chapter 4, the media relations manager attempted to persuasively represent the view of the public affected by a change of waste disposal provider using verbal and non-verbal communication. This suggests that she was aware of her role as boundary spanner (Plowman, 2013) and was attempting to manage the relationship between her organization and the affected public. By doing so, it appears that the PRP, on behalf of the organization, was attempting to accommodate the wishes of the public. The question then arises, is the communication symmetrical or not?

Bowen (2013) stated that both the two-way symmetrical and asymmetrical model make use of scientific persuasion. The key difference, she said, lies in the symmetrical model using research to *understand* the publics, while asymmetrical communication uses it to *persuade* the publics, leaving the organization itself to remain unchanged. Using this understanding as a basis for determining whether the communication was symmetrical or asymmetrical leads us to believe that the communication was asymmetrical. Indeed, most of the communication was in favor of the organization with message production being either to maintain or enhance its reputation or in service of communicating the organization's point of view without inviting feedback that might change its perspective. Echoing Holtzhausen et al. (2003), we would suggest that in their day-to-day practice, PRPs do not consciously consider whether their practice is symmetrical or asymmetrical. Rather, we would assert that PRPs' focus remains on strategic *message production* and *minimizing risk* to the organization. After all, as mentioned earlier, mutual understanding can be achieved through various modes of communication, ranging from providing the facts to employing verbal and non-verbal persuasive strategies, to justifying decisions made on behalf of the organization.

Mutually Beneficial Relationships

Linked to the normative framework of symmetry, and particularly, two-way symmetrical communication, is the idea that PRPs create mutually beneficial relationships (MBRs) on behalf of an organization. While both desirable and normative (Heath, 2013), it is an idea that is not free of self-interest. "Good relationships make organizations more effective because they allow the organizations more freedom to achieve their missions" (Grunig et al., 2002, p. 10). Thus, by accommodating, and making the relationship beneficial for their publics, the organization is provided with more freedom. We would speculate that the reason for the increase in freedom lies in the higher levels of trust that exist between parties in strong relationships (see Chapter 2). Indeed, Heath (2013, p. 589) described the key tenets for MBRs as: "openness and transparency, trustworthiness, cooperativeness, aligned interests, compatible views and opinions, and commitment to fostering communication by being involved in it, investing in it, and supporting it to earn its support."

Like symmetry, the idea of MBRs has its roots in systems theory (Heath, 2013), and is based on the premise that no organization—no matter how autonomous—can survive without maintaining balance with the environment. If this balance means that the organization must build quality, long-lasting relationships with its publics, then there must be some measure to demonstrate why and how this occurs. One measure is to suggest that the quality of a relationship is contingent on how each party benefits from that relationship (Heath, 2013).

From this perspective, a relationship can be seen as *mutually beneficial* if the organization's publics believe that both they and the organization "benefit appropriately, fairly, and proportionately on some matter of mutual interest" (Heath, 2013, pp. 587–588).

While this is not a new idea (Heath, 2013), it is one that has been embraced in public relations, and as we discussed in Chapter 7, also one that is fraught with paradox. Stoker (2014) argued that by managing relationships, the freedom of the organization's publics is curbed, thereby undermining the very mutuality that PRPs desire. On the other hand, Wakefield (2013) pointed out that relationships are by definition mutually beneficial, and one should always seek win-win situations for the sake of relationships.

This sentiment has been echoed by various other scholars. As Smith (2013) stated,

> Public relations operates on the principle of *mutual benefits*; that is, it seeks not only to assist the sponsoring organization but also to advantage its publics. It is committed to the *public interest* and betterment of society.
>
> (p. 29, original emphasis)

In their seminal work on dialogue in public relations, Kent and Taylor (2002, p. 26) stated that "From a public relations standpoint, mutuality is already an accepted practice." In fact, they argued, "mutuality" was one of the key tenets of dialogue which was, and should be, part of the practice of public relations.

While it is a noteworthy epitome of good practice, in none of the critical incidents or interactions we studied, or the practices we observed, did we find any evidence that there was a deliberate and strategic attempt to create or maintain "mutually beneficial relationships" or, for that matter, any evidence of "two-way symmetrical communication." Rather, we found evidence to the contrary: relationships were beneficial to the *organization*, and the practitioners' work was centered on strategizing how to best optimize those benefits while minimizing potential risk to the organization in the form of negative publicity or reputational damage. Indeed, *risk management* was evident throughout the critical incidents analyzed for this research. *Mutuality*, on the other hand, did not manifest itself to the extent discussed in the literature.

The notion of "mutuality," as discussed in Chapter 7, is not only normative, but also problematic in the context of public relations work. It was clear from our analyses of interactions between practitioners strategizing about message production and control, that "mutuality" was not on the table. Rather, their concern was how best to convey their client organization's message to its publics in a way that would minimize risk and counter negative feedback.

The ideas of mutuality and mutual benefits are based on the tenets of interpersonal relationships, which serve as a guide for how organizations might have "relationships" with publics. These ideas have enabled the reframing of public relations practice in ways that increase its legitimacy, but our research suggests they may well lack practical foundation. Continuing to press the idea of "mutual benefits" without interrogating practice and how this "mutual benefit" might materialize in reality, causes the gap between normative theory and practice to be broadened. This may result in a lack of fidelity of academic research and public relations education.

Personal Influence as Expertise

While we found limited evidence of two-way symmetrical communication and no evidence of MBRs, we found the *personal influence model* (see Chapter 2) to be highly relevant to New Zealand practice. Indeed, the findings of our research support calls from scholars such as Valentini (2010) that the personal influence model should be recognized as public relations expertise as well as Jo and Kim's (2004) assertion that the model is a "justifiable and valuable asset for effective public relations" (p. 299).

Personal influence can best be described as a process whereby PRPs "use their personal networks to solve organizational problems" (Jo & Kim, 2004, p. 294), although *how* it might be used or how it might be developed at a micro level has not been explicated. Nevertheless, Jo and Kim (2004) regarded the model as important for successful public relations in South Korea where there is a focus on harmony and collectivism, and consequently, they argued, a greater reliance on personal networks to achieve success.

Identified in 1995 by J. E. Grunig et al. as one of two possible "variations within the four known models" (p. 164), and later acknowledged as a practice model in India by Sriramesh (1996/2009), personal influence has often been touted as the "fifth model" of public relations (Wakefield, 2013). Subsuming the personal influence model into symmetrical communication, J. E. Grunig et al. (1995) proposed that it would provide a valuable addition to excellent public relations, adding that the model shows the theoretical link between interpersonal relations and personal influence—although this link has never been explored. In fact, there has been little development of the concept since nor has there been in-depth research into its relevance and applicability for practice. In one of the handful of attempts to elucidate the concept, Schriner (2008) applied a multidisciplinary approach to provide theoretical possibilities to explain the public relations spokesperson's personal influence in the public arena. She proposed, among other approaches, that personal influence is *triadic* in nature, that is, it incorporates personal, behavioral and environmental factors, which are interlinked and dependent on the specific situation. How the model is enacted, then, would be determined to an extent by culture, political climate, professional roles and social status of the PRPs (Schriner, 2008). Our research suggests that the relational structure (see Chapter 2) is influenced by politeness and face-saving strategies, positioning oneself as an expert through micro-level interactions, and exerting low key or ambient power. These will be discussed later in the chapter.

Most often the model has been presented as being relevant only in international settings, that is, outside the United States (Jo & Kim, 2004; Kiambi & Nadler, 2012; Sriramesh & Enxi, 2005; Sriramesh, Rhee, &

Sung, 2013; Taylor, 2004) and specifically, East Asia (Huang & Zhang, 2015). This, despite a growing number of scholars having high-lighted its global relevance and importance for public relations prac-tice (Falconi, 2011; García, 2014; Valentini, 2010; Wakefield, 2013). Equally, because it was identified in the context of media relations (Jo & Kim, 2004; Sriramesh, 1996/2009; Taylor, 2004), it is often linked to publicity. Jo and Kim (2004), for example, discussed rela-tionships and personal influence as a relational strategy used by PRPs to "manage" what is published in the media, preventing unfavorable information surfacing and pushing favorable information into the pub-lic domain. For their part, Sriramesh et al. (2013) inferred that the personal influence model is a uniquely cultural condition that differs from the (Western) two-way symmetrical model. Taylor (2004) linked the strategic use of personal influence to cultural dimensions, and spe-cifically, to (high) power distance.

The framing of the personal influence model in scholarship and research as being applicable mainly to an international (non-United States-based) context, as well as its being juxtaposed against the four models has hindered, we believe, its development as a strong and rele-vant theoretical construct.

Moreover, the framing of the model as one that epitomizes "non-Western" public relations practices has unintentionally reinforced the dichotomy between "Western" and "non-Western" practices, and could have contributed to what Halff and Gregory (2014) described as an in-correct assumption that "non-Western" public relations is "catching up" with their Western counterparts—an assumption they contested.

Indeed, our research shatters some of the preconceived assumptions about the practice of public relations outside the United States or in Anglo countries. By returning to the micro level interactions of PRP's day-to-day, mundane interactions, we found evidence that personal in-fluence is used across all public relations functions: from interactions between peers to those with clients and journalists. This suggests that the model is not limited to media relations work nor is it culture-specific or used only in non-Anglo countries. Indeed, integral to public relations work is the ability to develop and maintain significant relationships with key players ranging from colleagues to clients and journalists. These relationships are not only required to gain publicity through the mass media but also to ensure that an organization's reputation is maintained.

Politeness as a Relationship-Building Strategy

Much of the PRP's interaction style is influenced by the communication style favored by their key stakeholders or, as we would call them, relational partners (Schriner, 2008), and this was evident in their com-munication at the micro level.

For example, it was telling throughout the analysis that PRPs often made use of *repairs* in their speech, indicating that there was an issue with speech planning, finding the right word(s) or correcting speech. The use of these repairs indicated that all the PRPs were acutely aware of the impact of their speech in interpersonal situations and on their relational partner, adapting to the situation and the other party to ensure that they were able to maintain the relationship and subsequently be effective in their practice.

Equally telling was that they obviously strategized about how to approach difficult discussions and situations, or how they might best convey ideas and issues. Sometimes this strategizing occurred prior to the interaction, and sometimes it happened in an impromptu manner, as we saw in the PRP-client interaction (see Chapter 5), hence the use of repairs in the PRP's speech.

Importantly, they adhered to the *norms of politeness* set by the relational structure, thereby maintaining personal influence. These norms are usually based on general standards of politeness (Hargie, 2017), such as treating the other person with respect and dignity (Holmes & Stubbe, 2015). As discussed in Chapter 2, *politeness theory* is based on the principle that we base our behavior and interaction on a so-called "model person" who is a competent and rational member of society and who attempts to maintain their own, and others', face needs (Schnurr, 2013). This suggests that socio-political and cultural expectations are likely to dictate what is "polite" and what is not. It may not be polite, for example, to challenge a colleague's knowledge or authority in a public meeting, nor to argue with a client about a decision they have made. Yet, disagreement and conflict are present in all relationships.

Thus, politeness should not be mistaken for agreement, conflict avoidance, or "not rocking the boat." Rather, it provides a blueprint for addressing disagreement and conflict in a strategic, non-threatening way, and ensuring that "things get done" without compromising relationships, as shown in the email interaction in Chapter 3. Indeed, in the practice of public relations, politeness strategies are used to increase power and build relationships.

In a warning against confusing ethics with etiquette (politeness), Doorley and Garcia (2015) stated that "some people consider it impolite to criticize others" (p. 51), and subsequently succumb to *not* telling the truth. While there is value in saying it "as it is," politeness is not about avoiding criticizing others, but rather doing it in a way that preserves the other party's dignity. Criticism can be mitigated, for example, by using devices such as hedging, hesitations, modal verbs, suggestions, summarizing, and humor (Holmes & Stubbe, 2015). Experienced PRPs use the devices skillfully and to great effect to get their point across.

Politeness is also a device that can be used to increase and challenge power—and critical discourse analysis of interactions (see Chapter 1) allows us to identify how "people habitually enact, reproduce and some-times resist institutional power relationships in the ways they talk and write" (Holmes & Stubbe, 2015, p. 100). For example, small talk as a po-liteness strategy and the setting of the agenda at meetings (see Chapter 5) assist in building power relationships (Holmes & Stubbe, 2015) and as-serting personal influence.

According to Holmes and Stubbe (2015, p. 41), "attention to politeness concerns tends to increase as the 'right' of one person to give directives to another decreases." This suggests (and our data supports) that PRPs in PRP-PRP relationships (see Chapter 4) or in relationships with clients (Chapter 5) or journalists (Chapter 6), where they lack the power to issue directives, pay greater attention to their behavior and strategize more over ensuring compliance in order to deliver the best possible public re-lations outcome while maintaining relationships.

Not only should new entrants, therefore, be taught politeness theory and how to enact politeness in the workplace by including Interpersonal Communication as a foundation subject in public relations education, but politeness should be studied as a vital part of the development of personal influence. How is politeness enacted in public relations work between professionals and with clients, journalists, and others, and how does it affect relationship building across various contexts?

Saving Face in a "Western" Context

As discussed in Chapter 2, maintenance of face is a relational strategy and one that increases personal influence. Maintenance of "face" or "face saving" can best be described as a relational approach that aims at not diminishing the other party's standing in society (Adler, Rosenfeld, & Proctor, 2007), and is achieved through strategies of politeness (Schnurr, 2013).

Face saving or *face-work* is often associated with non-western prac-tices and, as with the model of personal influence, is presented as mainly occurring in "other" cultural realms. Indeed, Ledingham (2013) indi-cated that "saving face" is a practice limited to specific cultures. Such an understanding is disputed through this research. By "face-work" we mean "the construction and communication of face" where *face* can be seen as "a metaphor for the self-image" the party wishes to project to other people (Samovar, Porter, & McDaniel, 2007, p. 160) or as Goffman (1967, p. 5) suggested, "the positive value a person effectively claims for himself by the line others assume he has taken during a partic-ular contact." Goffman here sees "line" as a set of verbal and non-verbal actions in a particular setting.

Face in this context, then, is *socially constructed*, and one that we can lose or gain (Samovar et al., 2007), depending on the communi-cation strategies used. While these strategies can be influenced by culture—as can the emphasis placed on either "self-face" or the "face of another"—face-work or face maintenance has been identified in this research as integral to public relations work and personal influence. For example, very rarely did PRPs openly express their feelings of frustration or irritation with a colleague (Chapter 4) or a client (Chapter 5). Even when responding to an email, the organization's representative avoided responding to the expression of frustration by the journalist who wanted, quite rightly, access to information (Chapter 3), remaining neutral and polite in her response.

Face-work is vital to developing personal influence and maintaining relationships. Using Brown and Levinson's theory as a basis, Holtgraves (2002) stated that in every social interaction there is an ever-present tension between *negative face* (the wish to be independent) and *positive face* (the need to connect), and thus the inherent risk of face-threatening actions. To minimize such threats, politeness strategies (as discussed earlier) are employed.

This dialectic tension is not unlike an organization's desire to remain autonomous while building relationships with its key stakeholders or publics (see Chapter 7 and earlier in this chapter), and one could, therefore, argue that *if* we were to suggest organizations could potentially have genuine relationships with publics (see the discussion further in the chapter), then perhaps, we should consider what *politeness strategies* should be employed on behalf of the organization. Given that, "To *perform an act other than in the most clear and efficient manner possible* is to implicate some degree of politeness" (Holtgraves, 2002, p. 41, emphasis added), it may be well worth revisiting how PRPs produce and frame messages and build relationships on behalf of organizations.

Ambient Power: Power on the Periphery

Integral to the development of personal influence is the development of *power*. Power is a multifaceted, intangible concept that is contingent on numerous variables, such as gender, expertise, and status (Holtgraves, 2002). Borrowing from organizational psychology, we draw a distinction between power and influence. Power is a *resource* that a person (PRP) possesses while influence comprises *behaviors* that draw on this resource (Langford & Fitness, 2003). "To gain and enact power, practitioners must exert influence" (Place, 2012, p. 437). Place's statement suggests that power as a resource can only be obtained by specific behaviors that allow practitioners to employ influence. In our view, this exertion of influence can only be studied at the micro level, that is, at the interactional level between people.

Langford and Fitness (2003) list nine *power bases* we can draw upon: legitimate, coercive, reward, referent, expert, information, ecological, network power, and reciprocity. These can be applied to public relations and, more specifically, to our research.

A PRP's seniority and formal authority (position in the organization) will provide *legitimate power*. To be effective, the organization's (or situation's) rules, norms, policies, and procedures must support this power base. We saw examples of this type of power in the meeting between the PRPs and the client (Chapter 5), where the senior practitioner leads the meeting. We also saw it in the meetings led by the group manager, discussed in Chapter 7, who uses her legitimate power to set the agenda and guide the decisions made.

Coercive power will depend on the PRP's ability and willingness to exert punishment while *reward power* refers to her willingness and ability to reward others. While we found no substantial evidence of these types of power being enacted in PRP-PRP relationships or in PRP-client relationships, we did find evidence in the PRP-journalist relationships where punishment was willingly meted out by refusing to cooperate, flooding journalists with information, or delaying information (see Chapters 2, 3, and 6). It would seem therefore that the PRP-journalist relational structure allows for these types of power to be enacted, suggesting that coercive and reward power are implicitly sanctioned. While the extent to which this power is enacted may potentially be mitigated by *referent power*, which relies on "liking, friendship, and loyalty" (Langford & Fitness, 2003, p. 286), we did not find any significant evidence of this. This does not mean that the latter type of power does not exist, but rather, that they are not commonly enacted in the public relations practice we observed.

A PRP may hold *expert power* if she has access to "scarce knowledge, skills, and abilities" (Langford & Fitness, 2003, p. 286) that others need. This type of power was evident in various interactions and relationships, such as the PRP-client interaction (Chapter 5) where the client relied on the expertise of the PRPs, and more subtly in the interactions that explicated the organization-public relationships (see Chapter 7) where the group manager highlighted the risk the dissident resident's group posed and where she set a strategic direction.

In Chapter 4, we also identified *interactional expertise*, that is, "expertise in the *language* of a specialism in the absence of expertise in its *practice*" (Collins & Evans, 2007, p. 28, original emphasis). This type of expertise requires a mastery of discipline-specific language by interacting with communities of practice who have *contributory expertise*, that is, tacit practical knowledge and skills that contribute to their discipline (Collins & Evans, 2007). By that logic, a practitioner must not only practice the discipline but use the accompanying language to be recognized as an expert and therefore wield expert power. In Chapter 4, we speculated that a lack of interactional public relations expertise may have resulted in tensions between two colleagues.

We found in our research that expert power in PRP-PRP relationships was sometimes downplayed, and instead, a more subtle power play was enacted—one we linked to politeness and face saving. This subtle, low-key power, we labeled *ambient power* (see Chapter 4). Using an urban design perspective, we followed Allen (2006) who described ambient power as being on the periphery, low-key and yet ever-present. It lies in the experience of the person who is subjected to it, using *seduction* rather than *force* to influence the other's actions or perceptions. In Chapter 4's first critical incident, we showed how this seduction is enacted through a process of *exclusion* and *inclusion* in a manner that could be described as a "dance of power." It is "felt before it is understood" (Allen, 2006, p. 244) and can, therefore be described as a *peripheral awareness of power*. We believe this power to be of particular relevance to the model of personal influence, and to fit with Place's (2012) assertion that traditional definitions of power do not cover other (feminist) ways of meaning-making of power in public relations. In our summation and in accordance with a feminist view of power (Place, 2012), this power is embedded in relationships and can be as effective, if not more so, than other forms of power such as a legitimate and expert power.

In Chapters 3 and 6, we saw examples of *information power*. This type of power is dependent on the extent to which individuals "control the amount and content of the information that flows throughout an organization" (Langford & Fitness, 2003, p. 286) or, in both examples, between the organization and the journalists. In Chapter 3, information to which the journalist was legally entitled was withheld, frustrating the potential of public discussion and public scrutiny of the organization's activities (possibly to preserve the reputation of the organization). Asserting this type of power, therefore, had consequences reaching beyond the organization.

In Chapter 6, the PRP carefully managed the information shared with the journalist during a telephone conversation in an attempt to prevent the information being published in the media. While wanting to preserve his relationship with the journalist, he also wanted to protect his client. This control of information explicitly demonstrates that information power is integral to the personal influence model.

Equally, through the analysis of interactions we found evidence that public relations work involved the use of *ecological power*, where they (the PRPs) "control the physical and cultural environment and are, as a result, able to shape others' cognitions, behaviors, and emotions" (Langford & Fitness, 2003, p. 286). In the critical incidents discussed in Chapter 7, the PRPs' ecological power was demonstrated in the act of planning and producing messages, as well as deciding the agenda for a meeting with dissident residents. We can, therefore, argue ecological power to be fundamental to public relations work and would argue that it is an indirect outcome of enacting personal influence, thereby moving beyond immediate interpersonal relationships and communication to ripple out to the organization and, ultimately the publics or society.

Of particular interest is *network power*, that is, the PRP's connection to other powerful people. Langford and Fitness (2003) stated that managers who have a strong network and relationships can "streamline decision-making, avert possible conflict, and consolidate various forms of power of all those in the network" (p. 286). Being connected to others with power is a key principle of the excellence theory which stipulates that it is crucial for practitioners to be part of the dominant coalition, or the most powerful people in the organization, in order to be able to practice excellent public relations (White & Dozier, 1992). As O'Neil (2003) pointed out, "public relations practitioners must prove their value and worth by establishing quality relationships with members of the dominant coalition" (p. 153). However, exactly *how* practitioners in actual practice construe power and influence may differ. In her study of female practitioners, for example, Place (2012) found that women regarded power to reside in relationships and in empowering herself and others. How they enacted this influence, however, would depend on the (gender and race) socialization systems that framed their understandings, Place wrote.

In Chapter 2, we identified another base of power, namely *reciprocity*, and proposed it to be fundamental to the personal influence model. Langford and Fitness (2003) stated that a person possesses this type of power if "others feel an obligation to return favors or efforts to the individual" (p. 286), and thus the act of reciprocating is dependent on tacit agreement that the other will return the favor (Adler et al., 2007). It is, Adler et al. (2007) stated, a strategy of *seeking compliance* and therefore of influence.

Suffice it to say that power and influence are important for PRPs to "get things done." As we saw in Chapter 5, for example, the senior practitioner employed strategies of influence to force a decision so they could continue the task and achieve an effective outcome for the client, and in Chapter 6, the PRP managed to persuade the journalist to accept the limited information presented to her. However, more research is required into exactly how power is enacted and how influence is used in, for example, impression management and relationship maintenance.

Ambient Awareness: Connecting through Social Media

In Chapter 3, we discussed ambient awareness and reasoned that this relatively recent phenomenon should also be part of the personal influence model. We proposed that connecting with others through social media and social networking sites recognizes the other's *social presence* in that space.

Discussing the use of mobile phones for connecting socially and creating a *virtual (social) presence*, Mentor (2015, p. 673) described *social connectedness* as, a concept used by social theorists and psychologists to explain the occurrence, value, quantity, and regularity of exchanges we have with people in our social network of family, friends, and acquaintances.

Being socially connected through social media and social networking sites allows PRPs to receive updates and news without necessarily communicating directly with the other. This results in a phenomenon called "ambient awareness."

Ambient awareness can best be described as an awareness that we develop of the world and those around us through accessing social media and being exposed to others' messages and communication (Ince, 2016; Leonardi, 2015). It is a social awareness on the periphery, generated through browsing posts and receiving updates.

Leonardi (2015) believed that ambient awareness contributes to knowledge about "who knows who" and "who knows what" by observing other people's communication and networks, and consequently linked ambient awareness to the emerging theory of communication visibility, that is, being visible through communication. Levordashka and Utz (2016) linked ambient awareness to the theory of electronic propinquity, which suggests that a sense of closeness develops faster when people are experienced with a specific medium. This means that PRPs who are well-acquainted with internet technologies are better at creating and maintaining ambient awareness, and consequently better equipped to develop and use social media and social networking sites to develop relationships.

Observing other's communication and networks does not only allow us to make judgments about that person but results in a *sense of familiarity* with people we may not know very well or do not have regular contact with, signaling their potential *approachability* (Levordashka & Utz, 2016). For PRPs, being approachable and able to identify friendly "others" are important as they will aid in building relationships and connections with information peers (see Chapter 2). As we discussed in Chapter 3, managing impressions on social media is, therefore, an important aspect of developing personal influence.

Sites of Relational Enactment

In this book, we refer to *sites of relational enactment* and meaning-making. The term *sites* can best be understood as "locations" or "spaces" in the most abstract sense. These sites do not need to be physical but can be intangible and virtual. In Chapter 4, for example, we expanded on the idea of sites of relational enactment, by identifying relationships and relationship communication as sites of meaning–making and occupational culture. Referring to Sias (2009) who identified peer–to–peer conversations as key locations for the creation and management of meaning, we proposed that it is in these conversations that meaning about public relations practice is created. Identifying and interrogating *sites* in public relations allows us therefore to deepen our understanding of public relations work, how it is understood, constructed, and enacted.

Social Media

In Chapter 3, we proposed that all relationships are mediated in some way, and using Scollon's (1998, 2001) idea of mediatedness, we proposed that social networking sites and the use of social media can be seen as spaces or sites of relational enactment. If we were to add to this Allen's (2006) idea of spaces as the "space" that surrounds us or the *context of interaction* (Chapter 4), then we can potentially see these spaces as intangible places where power is low key and often on the periphery but nevertheless present. While power is enacted through interacting and communicating with others, it is also present in the *design* of social media and social networking sites. For example, in Chapter 3, we discussed impression management on social networking sites as being "scripted for us" through the design of these areas. While we are able to communicate widely and easily, *how* we present ourselves is influenced by their design and the rules that have been pre-established for us. This idea is akin to how Allen (2006) described the power embedded in urban design. It follows then that social media and social networking sites are not egalitarian spaces where democracy reigns, but rather that potential disparities are embedded in their design. This holds implications for public relations as relationship-building and the idea that social media (in the most colloquial understanding) is an environment where two-way symmetrical communication or dialogue can flourish.

Meetings

In Chapter 5, we identified PRP-client meetings as vital sites of "doing power" (Holmes & Stubbe, 2015, p. 58), and we contended that these meetings are an important (and often overlooked) part of public relations practice. It is in these meetings with clients, in the interactions with their peers (see Chapter 4) and with journalists (see Chapter 6) where relationships and power are constructed, advanced and preserved.

Meetings are not only sites of meaning-making, power enactment, and decision-making, but are also sites of potential moral disengagement, that is, legitimizing an action or decision (by the organization) that could potentially be detrimental by reframing it (White, Bandura, & Bero, 2009). Earlier, we discussed message production and planning as traditional functions of public relations work (see, for example, Tench et al., 2013). *How* these messages are framed during the production phase can potentially morally engage or disengage the interlocutor from the issue, and therefore contain an ethical component.

In their research, White et al. (2009) identified eight mechanisms for moral disengagement: moral justification, euphemistic labeling, advantageous comparison, displacement of responsibility, diffusion of responsibility, disparaging the critics or victims, attributing blame and denying or minimizing the consequences of actions. They analyzed 365 internal documents of industries that are known to produce harmful products (tobacco, lead, vinyl chloride and silicosis-producing industries), and concluded that minimizing, distorting and denying consequences were the most common mechanisms used (35.6%), followed by moral justification (19.7%), disparaging critics or victims (11.3%), euphemistic labeling (10.6%), attribution of blame (10%), advantageous comparison (8.4%), and displacing responsibility (4.4%). PRPs, they said, mainly engaged in denying or minimizing consequences (White et al., 2009). They pointed out, however, that it is not an organization or an individual that makes a morally right or wrong decision, but rather, *collectively* the members obscure their personal accountability by "diffusion and displacement of responsibility" (p. 42). They added,

> People do not operate as autonomous moral agents, impervious to the social forces operating within the corporate system in which they are enmeshed…The different players in the corporate system have to neutralize the moral implications of their role in their organization's products and practices. In doing so, they provide exonerations for each other.
>
> (White et al., 2009, p. 43)

Seen in this light, meetings are not only sites of meaning-creation, agenda-setting and relationship-building (see Chapter 5) and the enactment of power (Holmes & Stubbe, 2015; Sias, 2009), but are also spaces where exonerations for organizational decisions are provided and moral implications are potentially minimized. It is for this reason that Tilley (2009) suggested that PRPs explicitly discuss ethics at all stages of the planning and production process—among themselves and with their clients—to ensure that ethical standards are maintained.

The Nature of Relationships

The Trouble with Organization-Public Relationships

Our research took us to the micro level of interaction and relationship-building. Specifically, these interactions were between individuals in face-to-face settings (Chapter 4) or through mediated communication (Chapters 3 and 6), they included formal meetings with clients (Chapter 5) and internal discussions around the organization's approach to producing messages for its publics (Chapter 7). In Chapter 7, we encountered what can best be described as meta-meetings: meetings about a meeting with a dissident residents' group (a public). In these meetings, we witnessed meaning about the organization-public relationship being constructed.

In exploring all these relationships and the meanings attached to them, we concluded that interpersonal relationships are tangible and discernible. We also concluded that the exact nature or *closeness* may be more difficult to ascertain at first glance. For example, we cannot instantly tell whether two colleagues are merely *information peers* or *special peers* (Kram & Isabella, 1985), nor can we directly observe their network of relationships (other than those published on social networking sites, such as LinkedIn) or the power they hold in that network.

Relationships between an organization and its publics we found to be more intangible and difficult to observe. Rather, these relationships, we would argue, manifest themselves in the organization's *reputation,* and relationships are managed for the potential *risk* they pose to that reputation. This itself brings into question whether we can compare "organization-public" relationships with interpersonal relationships, and whether it was, and is, appropriate to assume the two types of relationships to be similar.

Based on our observations, we found the actual (real) connections and relationships to be formed between PRPs *on behalf* of the organization, and not between the "organization" and publics themselves. It would, therefore, be useful to turn towards organizational theory and communication to explore the relationship between the organization and its publics. This is, of course, the crux of the debate in scholarship: organizations are not individuals, and therefore cannot form relationships in the same way that individuals form them. Yet, public relations scholarship has not substantially addressed this issue and more work is needed to explicate this relationship and set it apart from interpersonal relationships.

Based on the symbolic interactionism theory (Rehberg Sedo, 2013), we propose that PRPs and those with whom they interact interpersonally co-construct the relationship and its relational structure and content. Therefore, parties act towards the relationship in terms of the *meaning* it holds for them. Meaning is produced from the interaction and how it is interpreted. The result may be a relationship that is *distant*, rather than close, in line with Waymer's (2013) suggestion that in non-voluntary relationships (where parties have no choice but to be in that relationship) it is appropriate for parties to distance themselves. Distancing is therefore not a sign that the relationship is on the verge of being terminated (Ledingham, 2015), but rather can be regarded as a natural and normal phase in the relationship with an organization or its representatives.

No Two Relationships Are the Same

The term "relationship" is used in a way that assumes that all understand—and agree on—its meaning, but as a handful of scholars such as Doan and Bilowol (2014) and Zaharna (2015) have highlighted, "relationships" and "relationship-building" or "maintenance" are not understood in the same way across all cultures, and indeed, as we discussed in Chapter 2, each relationship is unique with its own relational structure, interactional rules, and roles. Norms of politeness in society provide guidance in how we should interact in order not to diminish the other's standing. It is disputable, however, whether these norms transfer to the organization-public relationship. Is politeness of concern when activists address issues of social (in)justice or socially (ir)responsible behavior on the part of the organization? Should the representatives of the organization remain polite and attempt to save the face of those who are challenging them? More research is needed to explore these issues and the relevance of interpersonal communication theory for public relations work on behalf of the organization.

As Watkins (2017) stated, "most public relations research is conducted in the context of organizations" (p. 164). Using the reputation and social media interaction of professional athletes, that is, *people* instead of organizations, she examined the influence of dialogic principles on interaction and enactment on Twitter. She concluded that while "social media provides a unique tool for engaging audiences in relationship building activities, including the capability to respond directly to and interact with the public," useful, one-way information also contributed to relationship building (Watkins, 2017, p. 170). Thus, relationship-building is more complex than has been acknowledged thus far in public relations scholarship and two-way symmetrical communication may not be the key requirement for relationship-building.

Conclusion

Effective public relations training and education should include a component on interpersonal communication where new entrants are taught how to develop authentic relationships. To be effective PRPs, they need to appreciate the impact their behavior has on developing influence, maintaining relationships, and decision-making processes. Besides learning how to produce messages and plan strategic communication on behalf of the organization, they must develop a critical understanding of human interaction, meaning-making and the broader societal implications of their work.

As scholars, we must continue to identify and study various types of relationships in face-to-face and mediated situations. In doing so, we can borrow, and learn, from speech communication, sociolinguistics studies, and social psychology to understand the interaction and meaning-making processes better. Importantly, more studies are required that explore the relationships between PRPs, how these are formed, how they construct an understanding of their occupation and how this affects what is practiced.

Studies that involve relationships, meaning-making and message production should go beyond self-reporting through surveys and questionnaires; we should continue to explore innovative research practices so we can study public relations practice *as is* in order to philosophize how it *should be* if we intend to continue developing theoretical insights that bring us closer to praxis.

References

Adler, R. B., Rosenfeld, L. B., & Proctor, R. F. (2007). *Interplay. The process of interpersonal communication* (10th ed.). Oxford: Oxford University Press.

Allen, J. (2006). Ambient power: Berlin's Potsdamer Platz and the seductive logic of public spaces. *Urban Studies, 43*(2), 441–455. doi:10.1080/004209 80500416982.

Bowen, S. A. (2013). Symmetry. In R. L. Heath (Ed.), *Encyclopedia of public relations* (2nd ed., pp. 903–905). Thousand Oaks, CA: Sage Publications.

Browning, N. (2015). The ethics of two-way symmetry and the dilemmas of dialogic Kantianism. *Journal of Media Ethics, 30*(3), 3–18. doi: 10.1080/08900523.2014.985295.

Collins, H., & Evans, R. (2007). *Rethinking expertise*. Chicago, IL: University of Chicago Press.

Culbertson, H. M. (1989/2016). Breadth of perspective, an important concept for public relations. In J. E. Grunig & L. A. Grunig (Eds.), *Public relations research annual* (Vol. 1, pp. 3–26). New York: Routledge.

Doan, M., & Bilowol, J. (2014). Vietnamese public relations practitioners: Perceptions of an emerging field. *Public Relations Review, 40*(3), 483–491. doi:10.1016/j.pubrev.2014.02.022.

Doorley, J., & Garcia, H. F. (2015). Ethics and communication. In J. Doorley & H. F. Garcia (Eds.), *Reputation management: The key to successful public relations and corporate communication* (3rd ed., pp. 45–91). London: Routledge.

Doorley, J., Garcia, H. F., & Hauser, J. (2015). Media relations. In J. Doorley & H. F. Garcia (Eds.), *Reputation management: The key to successful public relations and corporate communication* (3rd ed., pp. 92–125). London: Routledge.

Falconi, T. (2011). *Personal influence model*. Institute for Public Relations. Retrieved from www.instituteforpr.org/personal-influence-model/.

García, C. (2014). Clientelism and guanxi: Southern European and Chinese public relations in comparative perspective. *Public Relations Review, 40*(5), 798–806. doi:10.1016/j.pubrev.2014.06.001.

Goffman, E. (1967). *Interaction ritual: Essays in face-to-face behavior.* New Brunswick and London: Transaction Publishers.

Grunig, L. A., Grunig, J. E., & Dozier, D. M. (2002). *Excellent public relations and effective organizations. A study of communication management in three countries.* New York: Routledge.

Grunig, J. E., Grunig, L. A., Sriramesh, K., Huang, Y.-H., & Lyra, A. (1995). Models of public relations in an international setting. *Journal of Public Relations Research, 7*(3), 163–186.

Grunig, J. E., & Hunt, T. T. (1984). *Managing public relations.* New York: Holt, Rinehart and Winston.

Halff, G., & Gregory, A. (2014). Toward an historically informed Asian model of public relations. *Public Relations Review, 40*(3), 397–407. doi:10.1016/j.pubrev.2014.02.028.

Hargie, O. (2017). *Skilled interpersonal communication: Research, theory and practice* (6th ed.). London: Routledge.

Heath, R. L. (2013). Mutually beneficial relationships. In R. L. Heath (Ed.), *Encyclopedia of public relations* (2nd ed., pp. 587–589). Thousand Oaks, CA: Sage Publications.

Holmes, J., & Stubbe, M. (2015). *Power and politeness in the workplace: A Sociolinguistic analysis of talk at work.* Abingdon: Routledge.

Holtgraves, T. M. (2002). *Language as social action. Social psychology and language use.* Mahwah, NJ: Lawrence Erlbaum Associates.

Holtzhausen, D. R., Peterson, B. K., & Tindall, N. T. J. (2003). Exploding the myth of the symmetrical/asymmetrical dichotomoy: Public relations models in the new South Africa. *Journal of Public Relations Research, 15*(4), 305–341. doi:10.1207/s1532754xjprr1504_02.

Huang, Y.-H. C., & Zhang, Y. (2015). Revisiting organization-public relationship research for the past decade. In E.-J. Ki, J.-N. Kim, & J. A. Ledingham (Eds.), *Public relations as relationship management: A relational approach to the study and practice of public relations* (2nd ed., pp. 3–27). London: Routledge.

Ince, D. (2016, July 11). *Ambient awareness.* Retrieved 20 December 2016, from Oxford Reference, www.oxfordreference.com.ezproxy.aut.ac.nz/view/10.1093/acref/9780191744150.001.0001/acref-9780191744150-e-4440?.

Jo, S., & Kim, Y. (2004). Media or personal relations? Exploring media relations dimensions in South Korea. *Journalism & Mass Communication Quarterly, 81*(2), 292–306. doi:10.1177/107769900408100205.

Kent, M. L., & Taylor, M. (2002). Toward a dialogic theory of public relations. *Public Relations Review, 28*(1), 21–37. doi:10.1016/s0363-8111(02)00108-x.

Kiambi, D. M., & Nadler, M. K. (2012). Public relations in Kenya: An exploration of models and cultural influences. *Public Relations Review, 38*, 505–507. doi:10.1016/j.pubrev.2012.01.007.

Kram, K. E., & Isabella, L. A. (1985). Mentoring alternatives: The role of peer relationships in career development. *Academy of Management Journal, 28*(1), 110–132. doi:10.2307/256064.

Langford, P., & Fitness, J. (2003). Leadership, power, and influence. In M. O'Driscoll, P. Taylor, & T. Kalliath (Eds.), *Organisational psychology in Australia and New Zealand* (pp. 279–301). Melbourne, Australia: Oxford University Publishers.

Ledingham, J. A. (2013). Relationship managing theory. In R. L. Heath (Ed.), *Encyclopedia of public relations* (2nd ed., pp. 781–783). Thousand Oaks, CA: Sage Publications.

Ledingham, J. A. (2015). Managing relationship management. In E.-J. Ki, J.-N. Kim, & J. A. Ledingham (Eds.), *Public relations as relationship management: A relational approach to the study and practice of public relations* (2nd ed., pp. 46–60). London: Routledge.

Leonardi, P. M. (2015). Ambient awareness and knowledge acquisition: Using social media to learn "who knows what" and "who knows whom". *MIS Quarterly, 39*(4), 747–762.

L'Etang, J. (2008). *Public relations: Concepts, practice and critique.* London: Sage Publications.

Levordashka, A., & Utz, S. (2016). Ambient awareness: From random noise to digital closeness in online social networks. *Computers in Human Behavior, 60,* 147–154. doi:10.1016/j.chb.2016.02.037.

Macnamara, J. (2012). The global shadow of functionalism and excellence theory: An analysis of Australasian PR. *Public Relations Inquiry, 1*(3), 367–402. doi:10.1177/2046147x12448581.

Mentor, D. (2015). Mobile phone use enhances social connectedness. *Encyclopedia of Mobile Phone Behavior,* 673–693. doi:10.4018/978-1-4666-8239-9.ch056.

Mersham, G., Theunissen, P., & Peart, J. (2009). The nature of public relations. In G. Mersham, P. Theunissen, & J. Peart (Eds.), *Public relations and communication management: An Aotearoa/New Zealand perspective* (pp. 1–18). North Shore, New Zealand: Pearson Education Australia.

O'Neil, J. (2003). An analysis of the relationships among structure, influence, and gender: Helping to build a feminist theory of public relations. *Journal of Public Relations Research, 15*(2), 151–179. doi:10.1207/s1532754xjprr1502_3.

Place, K. R. (2012). Power-control or empowerment? How women public relations practitioners make meaning of power. *Journal of Public Relations Research, 24*(5), 435–450. doi:10.1080/1062726x.2012.723278.

Plowman, K. D. (2013). Systems theory. In R. L. Heath (Ed.), *Encyclopedia of public relations* (2nd ed., pp. 905–908). Thousand Oaks, CA: Sage Publications.

Rehberg Sedo, D. (2013). Symbolic interactionism theory. In R. L. Heath (Ed.), *Encyclopedia of public relations* (2nd ed., pp. 901–903). Thousand Oaks, CA: Sage Publications.

Samovar, L. A., Porter, R. E., & McDaniel, E. R. (2007). *Communication between cultures* (6th ed.) Belmont, CA: Thomson Higher Education.

Schnurr, S. (2013). *Exploring professional communication: Language in action.* New York: Routledge.

Schriner, M. (2008). *The public role model in public relations: An integrated approach to understanding personal influence in the public arena.* Institute for public relations. Retrieved from www.instituteforpr.org/wp-content/uploads/Maureen_Schriner.pdf.

Scollon, R. (1998). *Mediated discourse as social interaction: A study of news discourse.* London: Longman.

Scollon, R. (2001). *Mediated discourse: The nexus of practice.* New York: Routledge.

Sias, P. M. (2009). *Organizing relationships: Traditional and emerging perspectives on workplace relationships.* Los Angeles, CA: Sage Publications.

Smith, R. D. (2013). *Public relations: The basics.* Abingdon: Routledge.

Sriramesh, K. (1996/2009). Power distance and public relations: An ethnographic study of Southern Indian organizations. In H. M. Culbertson & N. Chen (Eds.), *International public relations: A comparative analysis* (pp. 171–190). New York: Lawrence Erlbaum Associates.

Sriramesh, K., & Enxi, L. (2005). *Public relations practices and socio-economic factors: A case study of different organizational types in Shangai.* Presentation,

International Communication Association Conference, New York. Retrieved from www.researchgate.net/publication/285895205.

Sriramesh, K., Rhee, Y., & Sung, M. (2013). Aligning public relations with the demands of globalization: Conceptual foundations for a theory of global public relations. In K. Sriramesh, A. Zerfaß, & J.-N. Kim (Eds.), *Public relations and communication management. Current trends and emerging topics* (pp. 108–125). New York: Routledge.

Stoker, K. (2014). Paradox in public relations: Why managing relating makes more sense than managing relationships. *Journal of Public Relations Research*. doi:10.1080/1062726X.2014.908723.

Taylor, M. (2004). Exploring public relations in Croatia through relational communication and media richness theories. *Public Relations Review*, *30*(2), 145–160. doi:10.1016/j.pubrev.2003.09.003.

Tench, R., Zerfaß, A., Verhoeven, P., Verčič, D., Moreno, A., & Okay, A. (2013). *Communication management competencies for European practitioners*. Leeds: Leeds Metropolitan University. Retrieved from www.ecopsi.org.uk.

Theunissen, P. (2015). The quantum entanglement of dialogue and persuasion in social media: Introducing the Per–Di Principle. *Atlantic Journal of Communication*, *23*(1), 5–18. doi:10.1080/15456870.2015.972405.

Theunissen, P., & Wan Noordin, W. N. (2012). Revisiting the concept "dialogue" in public relations. *Public Relations Review*, *38*(1), 5–13. doi:10.1016/j.pubrev.2011.09.006.

Tilley, E. (2009). Ethics and public relations. In G. Mersham, P. Theunissen, & J. Peart (Eds.), *Public relations and communication management: An Aotearoa/New Zealand perspective* (pp. 204–216). North Shore, New Zealand: Pearson Education Australia.

Valentini, C. (2010). Personalised networks of influence in public relations. *Journal of Communication Management*, *14*(2), 153–166. doi:10.1108/13632541011034600.

Wakefield, R. I. (2013). Personal influence and pre-industrial United States: An early relationship model that needs resurgence in U.S. Public relations. *Public Relations Review*, *39*(2), 131–138. doi:10.1016/j.pubrev.2013.02.008.

Watkins, B. A. (2017). Experimenting with dialogue on Twitter: An examination of the influence of the dialogic principles on enactment, interaction, and attitude. *Public Relations Review*, *43*(1), 163–171. doi:10.1016/j.pubrev.2016.07.002.

Waymer, D. (2013). Democracy and government public relations: Expanding the scope of "relationship" in public relations research. *Public Relations Review*, *39*(4), 320–331. doi:10.1016/j.pubrev.2013.07.015.

White, J., Bandura, A., & Bero, L. A. (2009). Moral disengagement in the corporate world. *Accountability in Research*, *16*(1), 41–74. doi:10.1080/08989620802689847.

White, J., & Dozier, D. M. (1992). Public relation and management decision making. In J. E. Grunig (Ed.), *Excellence in public relations and communication management* (pp. 91–108). New York: Routledge.

Zaharna, R. S. (2015). Beyond the individualism-collectivism divide to relationalism: Explicating cultural assumptions in the concept of "relationships." *Communication Theory*, *26*(2), 190–211. doi:10.1111/comt.12058.

Appendix 1

Transcription symbols used

(0.4)	The number in the brackets indicates intervals between talk
(.)	A dot enclosed in a bracket indicates a pause too short to measure
=	There is no discernible interval between one speaker finishing and another starting
.	A closing intonation or stopping fall in tone
:	The speaker has stretched the preceding sound or letter. The more colons the more extension there is to the sound
,	Indicates slight upward continuing intonation such as when someone recites a list
[]	Square brackets show where talk overlaps
>talk<	Right and left carats ("more than" and "less than" symbols) indicate that the talk between the symbols was speeded up or slowed down relative to surrounding talk
?	Rising intonation
¿	Rising intonation is weaker than above
°Word°	Words spoken between the degree symbols are softer than those before or after
hh	A speaker's out-breath
.hh	A dot before the 'h' shows a speaker's in-breath
-	A hyphen indicates an abrupt cut off of sound
Word	Underlining indicate the speaker's emphasis
WORD	Shows words spoken are louder than surrounding talk
()	The words within a single bracket are the translator's best guess.
(())	The words within double brackets indicate a description or comment from the transcriber
↑↓	A mid turn sharp rise or fall in intonation

For more information about transcription see the transcription module on Emanuel Schegloff's website www.sscnet.ucla.edu/soc/faculty/schegloff/

Index

For Product Safety Concerns and Information please contact our EU
representative GPSR@taylorandfrancis.com
Taylor & Francis Verlag GmbH, Kaufingerstraße 24, 80331 München, Germany

www.ingramcontent.com/pod-product-compliance
Ingram Content Group UK Ltd.
Pitfield, Milton Keynes, MK11 3LW, UK
UKHW020941180425
457613UK00019B/492